"Many books and articles have been written about Juan Quezada and the potters of Mata Ortiz. Now author Charmayne Samuelson has written an important book that tells the story of anthropologist Spencer MacCallum, who was the first to recognize Juan Quezada's potential as a world-class artist; and who helped the Mata Ortiz potters create arguably the most important ceramic art movement in the second half of the 20th century."

Walter Parks, *The Miracle of Mata Ortiz*

"This is a wonderfully written and truly entertaining book! It is full of many interesting nuggets about Spencer never before published. I really appreciate the exciting stories in it and highly recommend it to anyone interested in the fascinating life of Spencer and the story of Mata Ortiz pottery. Congratulations to author Charmayne Samuelson on a great job well done."

Ron Bridgemon, *The Magnetism of Mata Ortiz*

Spencer MacCallum
Memories – Mystique – Mata Ortiz

Spencer MacCallum

Memories – Mystique – Mata Ortiz

The authorized historical biography of anthropologist Spencer MacCallum

Charmayne Samuelson

Wood Duck Publishers
http://woodduckpublishers.com

Wood Duck Publishers
www.woodduckpubishers.com

DEDICATION AND THANKS

I dedicate this book to my loving husband, a truly joyful soul who happens to be in my life by my sheer luck and exceptionally good karma. His unending support guides me, strengthens me, and uplifts me.

Thank you to the amazing Spencer MacCallum who shared his fascinating personal life story and family photos and arranged for our access to view the "first Deming pots" in the Museum of Man (now the Museum of Us) in San Diego; and to his wife, Emi MacCallum, who supported the efforts to get this story published.

Special thanks and deep appreciation go to the staunch supporters of the potters and of Spencer, Juan, and the Mata Ortiz pottery itself, especially Walter Parks, Dr. Richard O'Connor, and Ron and Sue Bridgemon who also encouraged my efforts to publish this book.

Many thanks go to Juan Quezada who sat for two interviews with me. He was an astute, intuitive man with eyes that cut through to the truth. He told me many things, and one of the most important was this:

"I just want to say, as I have many times, that Spencer is the most honest person I've ever met in my entire life."

Juan Quezada, 2006,
interview with the author,
Charmayne Samuelson

Table of Contents

List of Figures

Introduction

This work is part memoir, part autobiography, and part authorized biography of Spencer MacCallum, meaning it flows as a fascinating story as told by the man himself who lived the life behind it. Spencer chose me to write this book among perhaps many scholars or otherwise well-known authors who would have jumped at this chance, and I am honored that he did.

He liked my style of writing and thought it could best tell the story of his ancestors and of his life, starting at birth. We both seemed grounded in reality, while living in the imagination where creativity blossomed and soared within us. On one hand, he viewed this book as another "project" amongst many he tended to, and on the other hand, he became animated and joyful when telling how his life happened. Over time, I learned that this was classic Spencer.

I met Spencer when my husband, Jon, and I were traveling with Geronimo Educational Travel Studies, based in Douglas, Arizona, leading pottery expeditions to Mata Ortiz, Mexico.

We became friends with Spencer who spoke to our tour groups about how he discovered Juan Quezada and Mata Ortiz pottery. *His story should be published in a complete biography*, I thought, and after mentioning it to Spencer, he said, "*You* do it!" He knew by that time I had been writing and publishing, so he was eager to see what I could do with his story. And I was fascinated by Spencer, and wanted to find out what made him tick. I sensed that touching greatness is what I did when I first met Spencer.

He was totally unassuming, unaffected by material desires other than necessities; aware of, but unruffled by the maddening hoof beat of mankind across the landscape, and absolutely trusting in the Universe to provide what he needed when he needed it. His mission in life had never been to acquire possessions. If it had been, he could have many times over been an extremely wealthy man, instead of experiencing periods of monetary hardship. Nor was his goal that of fame. Even though the role he played earned him deep appreciation, acknowledgment, and stellar regional celebrity status, as well as a certain amount of worldwide renown, it did not place him so high up on a pedestal that he was unavailable.

His greatness included an uncanny ability to discover raw talent, as when he found the Mexican farmer and cowboy, Juan Quezada, eking out a pittance of extra income from making crude pottery. Spencer somehow knew what lay beneath. This amazing story, revealed in this book, exemplifies what made Spencer tick.

When Spencer and Juan struck a deal in which Spencer would support Juan's work—if he would agree to make his "best" pottery—Spencer was very excited about this new talent. To share with the world what a farmer-potter living in a remote village in Mexico could do artistically was exciting! He eventually became the vehicle to promote not only Juan but other artists as they joined this enterprise.

Countless words have already been written about Spencer—tales retold many times of how and when he discovered three replica prehistoric pots in a junk store in Deming, New Mexico, that led him to further discover Juan Quezada, who evolved into the master Mata Ortiz potter. And now, in this biography, we discover a curious ancestry that motivated him to be a discoverer.

An interesting question might be: would the amazing explosion of Mata Ortiz potters' success have happened if Spencer had not made the trek into Mexico to find the single potter of three pots he bought in a junk store in Deming, New Mexico in 1976?

It can safely be argued that no, it would not have happened. In fact, it likely would have been impossible unless Spencer had gone looking for, and discovered, the mystery potter, Juan, and consequently other wonderful artists of the Mata Ortiz area. And, I will go a step further and say that it would be wildly unreasonable to think any fame or fortune of such magnitude would have or could have occurred without Spencer's role in promoting Juan Quezada, and then other potters.

Spencer was Princeton-educated and had degrees in anthropology and art history, and he was, indeed, a scholar. He published many scholarly articles about Juan and Mata Ortiz. Most of them can be found at the Museum of Us, San Diego, California, or online.

This was how Spencer operated—by documentation.

He documented everything, as he was taught to do in the world of science and anthropology.

I interviewed both Spencer and Juan Quezada in their first-ever interview together. Photos of this interview are included in this book. Over the years, the trio of Juan Quezada, his wife Guille, and Spencer MacCallum would tell the story over and over of that fateful day in 1976 when they first met Spencer. They lived it; they knew the truth of the matter. As Juan told everyone, he considered Spencer to be someone of great integrity and mentioned many times his respect and admiration for him. When I interviewed Juan and other potters, there was always a true sense of wonderment that from nowhere, out of the blue, a stranger appeared in their village and decided to fund Juan's work and later, other potters.

As told in stories within this book, you will read how the pre-teen Spencer started off as a young explorer, discovering ancient beads in Mexico, then in college an unknown priceless art collection in one of the buildings at Princeton University, and later when he recognized Juan Quezada as a possible world talent.

Still, he seemed unfazed by the material world and even less so by others who value things above the worth of the human soul. He seemed to be willing to serve the needs of others. He liked the idea of discovering raw talent and helping it evolve into something classy and beautiful. He enjoyed helping others dare to achieve and to be guided up to the mountaintop to stand alongside those that were already there.

His own voice recounting his memories, as well as his feelings about them, and how this or that happened when and where is distinct; and the mystique of Spencer himself brings it all to life as never before. We signed an exclusive agreement that gave me all copyrights to the book. He liked the book and always encouraged me. For that I am grateful. But interestingly, neither he nor I were in a desperate hurry to make it happen. But we both knew it would be published, one of these days.

As an accomplished writer himself, he certainly knew in advance the untold hours it would take to put this story into book form, literally extracting his life from taped interviews which had to be laboriously transcribed into something readable, and then polished into final form. The initial interviews and subsequent meetings happened between 2006 and 2017 at my home in Arizona, during which a copious amount of material was gathered. As Spencer reviewed the drafts, he would return a marked-up copy of the manuscript with edits in his own handwriting.

I was able to complete the manuscript in July 2023. By then my friend Spencer had passed—and much had changed in all of our lives.

In 2019 Spencer was the victim of an accident in which he was hit by a car and literally run over by a distracted driver not watching a crosswalk between the gas pumps and a convenience store in Deming, New Mexico. He had nine broken ribs and punctured internal organs. Born on December 21, 1931, we lost Spencer on December 17, 2020, when he was just four days shy of 89 years old. Two years later, also in December, we lost Juan, who was born on May 6, 1940, and passed on December 1, 2022, at 82 years.

Spencer's story became much larger to include not only Juan Quezada and their mesmerizing relationship, but also hundreds of Mata Ortiz potters, collectors, the players who bought and sold, the discoverers, and the discovered.

As you read Spencer's truth, you will also read the story of how Juan Quezada developed his own methods and style of pottery making. Studying prehistoric potsherds and associating with many potters in the area who were already making pottery, such as Manuel Olivas and others who had grouped together to make pottery for the tourist trade, Juan experimented and came up with his own unique ways to make his pottery, as did each of the potters eventually. Spencer would talk at length about Manuel Olivas and other potters who were experimenting and crafting new techniques, as did Juan. And now, the reader of this story will enter into what I call "Spencer's truth of Spencer's story."

Spencer created this story for himself, and directed and lived it, and I think his admiring public will find here his true spirit.

His childhood, his upbringing, his fascinating ancestry, and his immediate family – and then the adventures that led him to Mata Ortiz—all of it made this man vulnerable, human, and sad, and at the same time smart, mystical, and happy. All of the things that make a person and his memory live on forever.

It makes for a really wonderful story and in fact, here it is, from start to finish:

Spencer MacCallum
Memories – Mystique – Mata Ortiz

"It has always been amazing to me how the very smallest of decisions can change your life forever."

Spencer MacCallum

Chapter One

Spencer's Ancestors; His Parents' Marriage; His
Father the Architect; The Great Depression;
World War II and His Father in England;
Whisked Away to Mexico

When Spencer MacCallum arrived to speak about the Mata Ortiz pottery to a visiting tour group in Nuevo Casas Grandes, Mexico, he would often wear his Scottish tartan tie and tam.

In a matter of seconds, the audience would be drawn to this man wearing a complexity of green and blue plaid that demanded attention.

The lines of the fabric extended into his life; they crosscut his discovery of Juan Quezada and Mata Ortiz pottery and intersected with his lofty ideas of advancing human consciousness through new ideas of social organization.

The memories, tales, and animation stirred around inside him, not in a neat and tidy package, but in a mesmerizing bundle of life and vitality. Outside, the honking horns of old Mexico were quickly blotted out by an adventure into another time and space. Often raising his hand in the air to catch hold of a related "butterfly idea," as he described it, his listeners soon discovered that Spencer Mac-Callum was an anthropologist, a social scientist, and a discoverer of rare and precious things and people.

He was also a caring person with an unending trust in the universe, a scholar of the past who determinedly saw hope for the future, and a man who did not dwell too often on his own personal story.

He skillfully played the various roles he had been given and shared the public persona of Spencer Mac-Callum with the world. The private one he left for us to discover ourselves.

He was a small man in his mid-70s when he was giving lectures to Mata Ortiz tourists visiting to buy pottery.

Spencer was mild-mannered and slightly hunched from osteoporosis, but his movements were spirited, his blue eyes astute, and his ears tuned to the concerto of memories resonating in his head.

There was something even more endearing about him: a sense that he was still mystified as to the catalyst role he played in discovering Juan Quezada and Mata Ortiz when he went looking for an unknown potter in Mexico so long ago, and of the resulting and enormous impact of that quest. In time, many in the village were lifted out of poverty, and a farmer-cowboy-potter was propelled from obscurity onto the world stage of famous artists.

Spencer's memories seemed folded inside his mind like a tortilla wrapped around a delicate filling.

The audience would sit spellbound as one by one the layers were rolled back, exposing for mental consumption the idealistic visions of his mother, the social ideas of

Figure 1. *Spencer catches a "butterfly idea" as he speaks to a tour group at the Hotel Hacienda in Nuevo Casas Grandes, Mexico, circa 2006 Courtesy of the Jon Samuelson Collection*

both his grandfathers, the glamour and romance of his childhood in Mexico when he was taken there to live by his mother. The revelations of his joys and occasional heart-

3

breaks of discovering a man, Juan Quezada, who would become a master potter on the world stage, would come later.

Behind the mirth of his merry eyes was a seriousness of deep concern for the world and for humanity, and for the many exciting avenues by which people could traverse this vast sphere called Earth and inch by inch make a difference for those who would follow. As he began his story in the Hotel Hacienda ballroom packed with tourists, he would rub the soft tartan cloth of the tie in his fingers.

The MacCallum clan tartan cloth of green and blue plaid seemed to give Spencer natural ease in front of his audience. He wore his tartan cloth well. It softened him, just as it did when the tartan cloth was made into a shawl and worn by his mother on her wedding day, and finally, on her deathbed.

It speaks its own language, the MacCallum tartan. Listening, his audience wondered about it, and his clan, and questioned him, and probed him. This seemed to please him.

It momentarily took the attention away from himself, just for a little while, and as he perhaps intended. Spencer would tell just enough to tantalize and beguile. As he spoke, it was soon evident that his subject matter was irrelevant. It was the man himself that intrigued his listeners, and it was unmistakable that his audience loved him.

But during private interviews, he granted access to a more secret and remote part of himself.

He slowly opened his mind to youthful memories full of mischief and adventure.

With a charming trust, he laid out these nuggets to be picked over, ever so gently, with trust.

Others, like the stories he told of his ancestors who were so resolute in coming to America, laid a backdrop of meaningful, yet conflicted, memories of his family, and especially those of his mother.

Figure 2. Lucile Heath MacCallum, wrapped in the MacCallum tartan, on honeymoon in Scotland with Ian Crawford MacCallum, 1928
Courtesy of the Spencer MacCallum Collection

She was full of ideas as to how the world might progress after World War II. She had a vision of the future influenced by Latin America—and was intent on exposing her children to the Latin American language and culture in Mexico at an early age so they might be prepared to contribute to the new world order—the postwar world.

On Spencer's paternal side, there was the clan tradition that the MacCallums were once kings of all Scotland. In support of this family heredity is the fact that the family arms are the same as those of Scotland but with colors reversed. The MacCallum coat of arms incorporates a St. Andrews Cross of blue on a white background, the reverse of the Scottish national flag which is a St. Andrew's Cross of white on a field of blue. The St. Andrews Cross on the MacCallum coat of arms is in the shape of an "X," called a saltire. It is said that the apostle, St. Andrew, was crucified on an X-shaped cross.

Of course, St. Columba, the MacCallum clan's founder, came from Ireland to Scotland in the sixth century when all of Scotland was but a small foothold on the coast.

And just the name of the country summons up images of misty mountains and a Gaelic green countryside, and enchanting whispers from the soft sea breeze, alas, the blue and the green, just like the MacCallum clan tartan.

The more one learned about the MacCallum tartan and his ancestors, the more there was a growing sense of the mystical forces at work in Spencer's life.

In the same mischievous manner as the Scottish fairies, there was a slight grin and a little twinkle in Spencer's eye, and a knowing. As he spoke to the tour group, and if there was a question about his tartan and tam, he would describe his family history with his regal voice, reminding the audience of his kingly ancestors.

Spencer's was an impressive ancestry, and it was soon revealed that this grand legacy inspired him as an eloquent speaker, a writer, a brilliant thinker, and a finder of great things. He represented his family well and told their story with reverent respect. The family tartan and coat of arms were brought to this country by Grandfather John MacCallum, a stone mason whose final examination in

Scotland to achieve journeyman status was to shape a cube of stone into a perfect sphere with a mallet and a chisel. He was successful, and as was the custom of the day, he traveled to the eastern seaboard of America for work, returning in the winters to Scotland.

The MacCallum ancestors had settled in the town of Lochgilphead, meaning head of Gilp Lake, situated in the county of Argyllshire. The family members were traditionally herring fishermen and stone masons. Lochgilphead became a planned town around 1790.

Argyllshire is on the western side of Scotland. Immigrants from Ireland settled in this area in the Sixth Century. They were known as the "Scotti," and the area became known as Scotland. The rich history and ruined castles spawned seaside holiday resort towns, including Lochgilphead. Argyllshire's coastline is rugged and rocky and was supposedly a perfect hiding place for the Knights Templar and their treasure when they fled France in 1307, this legend continually luring tourists from around the world then and now. [1]

The mystic green landscape strewn with henges, stone circles, burial chambers, and peculiar standing stones, all add a mystique to Scotland of ancient days and nights. North of Lochgilphead is the most important collection of historic sites on mainland Scotland.

Kilmartin Glen has 350 ancient monuments, of which 150 are prehistoric, some dating back five thousand years. Of particular note is the ancient fortress of the Scots at Dunadd.

The village of Kilmartin with its Museum of Ancient Culture sits at the heart of this amazing landscape. [2] Today, Lochgilphead is not only a tourist destination but also an important town as a political and commercial center in western Scotland.

The MacCallums were Scottish Presbyterian and over the years there have been various versions of the prefix used in the family. The letters "Mc" are used in either Irish or Scottish names, but "Mac" usually indicates a Scottish name. It is said that when the Scots came to America, they especially did not want to be confused with the potato-famine Irish, so they took great pains to spell their name with the prefix "Mac." Whatever form is used, it is generally agreed that all are abbreviations that mean "son or follower of." [3]

"The name MacCallum means specifically a follower of St. Columba, who was one of the first to settle Scotland from Ireland in the 6th century," Spencer explained. [4]

From this Gaelic land, Grandfather John MacCallum immigrated with his family in 1901 or 1902 to Baltimore. Not because he wanted to leave Scotland but because in an altercation with the laird of a Scottish manor, the laird ended up in a vat of mortar!

Any way you lay it out, a fight with a rich landowner was bad news for John MacCallum.

It's not known whether the laird fell backward into the mortar, or was pushed, but as there was scant sense of humor about this kind of thing in old Scotland. MacCallum hastily fled to America, and then later returned for his wife and eight children to take them over.

In a foreshadowing of events of both Spencer's paternal and maternal families, his Grandfather Mac became quite active in the labor movement in Baltimore. It became a family trait. Hard workers and hard drinkers that the men of the stone were, he one day took to the job site a flask of whiskey for himself and the men, where they were constructing a new jail building.

As they worked and drank, the foreman approached, and Grandfather Mac quickly hid the bottle in the only available place. He laid it on top of the last stone he had set, mortared it over, and placed another stone on top. Brilliant! Thinking the foreman would soon go his way, it would be easy enough to expeditiously remove one or two stones. But the foreman lingered on.

The work certainly could not stop with the foreman looming over their heads, so up the wall went, stone by stone, higher and higher, until it would be impossible to remove the flask of whiskey! Presumably, the whiskey bottle has lain inches from the hands of prisoners for all these many years.

Spencer's father, Ian Crawford MacCallum, known as both Crawford and Ian throughout life (Ian in this book to distinguish from Spencer's brother, Crawford), was conceived on the way to America, and although he was the ninth and last child (born in 1902) to John and Margaret MacCallum, he was the only one to be born in America.

Following Scottish custom, he went to work at the steel mill in Baltimore at an early age so that his sisters could get an education and make good marriages.

By studying with his siblings long into the night he was able to obtain an education quite good enough to pass the entrance exam at the University of Pennsylvania where he excelled and received a degree in architecture.

This was a monumental achievement for him.

He was then hired by the prestigious architectural concern of Warren and Wetmore in New York City, a large firm with over two hundred architects. Noted for the design of the Grand Central Terminal (1903–13, with Reed and Stem), they also designed some of the very earliest skyscrapers in New York City, including the Heckscher Building (1920–21) and the Aeolian Building (1925–27), both on Fifth Avenue, as well as the New York Central Building (1927–29) on Park Avenue north of Grand Central.

They were the premier architects for many railroad lines, and for several hotels such as the old Belmont, the Ambassador, the Ritz Carlton, the Commodore, the Vanderbilt, and the Biltmore in New York and more. [(5)]

Ian rolled right along with their blueprint of success. He was superior in ornamental architecture and lettering. MacCallum helped to design the exterior ornaments of the Grand Central Terminal in New York City and intertwined into the ornate Flemish designs his and Lucile's initials, which were still there as late as the mid-2000s.

Warren and Wetmore Architects also designed the Helmsley Building at 230 Park Ave., Manhattan. According to Spencer, Ian MacCallum did something that was outlandish for the day—he decorated the elevators in Chinese red, as described in an excerpt from the website untappedcities.com: "In the gilded elevators, the Chinese motif has symbols of industry, foliage and classical imagery, and feels like an art installation, painted in Chinese red and framed by gilded wooden molding." [(6)]

Spencer recalled that once while he was in New York City in the 1950s he went into the office tower to see if the famous red elevators were still intact. He was pleasantly surprised they were, marveling that what had seemed so outlandish in his father's time appeared so conservative to Spencer.

World travelers have noted the elevators. Years later in Mata Ortiz, Mexico, Spencer was visiting with a group of tourists, and they began to talk about collecting.

He asked one of the women what she collected.

"Well, I collect elevators," she replied.

The group laughed, and Spencer asked, "How in the world do you do that?" She responded that, of course, she did not mean it literally, but that she collected photographs, information, and the history of elevators.

Spencer told the story of his father designing those elevators. She was astonished. "Those are the very first elevator photographs I ever took!" she exclaimed.

Spencer was equally amazed that this coincidence, or maybe it wasn't, happened "right in Mata Ortiz."

Because of Ian MacCallum's expertise in ornamental architecture and lettering, he was sent by the firm as the lead architect across the seas to Louvain, Belgium. He was the chief of the architect team delegated to restore the library which had been destroyed in World War I.

This was a beloved project to Mr. Whitney Warren, and it is said that Mr. Warren took more pride in his firm having designed the reconstructed library than in any other project. After what has been called The German Fury in Belgium in which many buildings were destroyed, Cardinal Mercier of Louvain had a vision to restore the library. It had been housed in the University halls in the Naamsestraat and was destroyed in 1914.

Cardinal Mercier was extremely popular and even to this day, a poster of the beloved Cardinal known as *Le Cardinal Mercier Protege La Belgique*, "Cardinal Mercier protects Belgium," by the artist D. Charles Fouqueray, can be bought from antique dealers. The Cardinal appealed to the world, and especially to American school children to send in their nickels and dimes, and in 1920 even the Knights of Columbus made a gift of $35,000 to the Cardinal Mercier Fund for the restoration of Louvain University and its magnificent library in Belgium.

When the Cardinal had raised enough money, he engaged the firm of Warren and Wetmore to design the library. Ian enjoyed his role as chief architect on site.

This impressive building was designed in the Flemish Renaissance style and constructed between 1921 and 1928. The library occupies a full city block fronting the town square and has a colonnade around all four sides.

On the four-sided capital at the top of each of the many columns, MacCallum inscribed the names of the American schools that had donated money, without ever once repeating the style of lettering. He had traveled throughout Europe to discover the various styles of lettering that would be appropriate for this building.

When the time came to dedicate the building in 1928, there was an international controversy. Warren and Cardinal Mercier wanted an inscription to be placed on the building pedestals which read: "Diruta Teutonica Furore Dono Americano Restituta," or "Destroyed by Teuton fury; replaced by American gift."

It seemed that the Belgium of the day had two opposing elements, the French and Flemish, and they were generally polarized on most issues. It was controversial whether to put up this slogan.

It became a real topic in the world press. So heated was the issue that the pedestals were carved in secret and were to be delivered to the square to be installed under the eyes of the armed guards. One day a group of townspeople ran to find MacCallum, explaining that someone was putting up *uncarved* pedestals on the building. When they went to the site, the laborers claimed they were following orders. A flurry of cables was sent back and forth across the Atlantic in an attempt to stop the uncarved pedestals from going up.

It occurred to MacCallum that the bells in the tower might create a needed diversion. The populace then exploded onto the square, effectively halting the activity for the moment; however, the plain balusters were finally installed.

On dedication day, the government grounded all air flights so that there might not be interference.

But one pilot did manage to fly low over the ceremonies, just in time to drown out the words of the speaker during the dedication. He also dropped thousands of leaflets with the above motto on them. The pilot was arrested, but the next day the general population proclaimed him a hero. Spencer discovered that his father wrote down all of these events and they were published in the Journal of the American Institute of Architects. [7] [8]

In 1928, while working on this project, Ian's fiancé Lucile Heath traveled to Belgium. He took a few days off and the two of them went to his ancestral home of Scotland to marry, and then honeymooned in Europe.

A year later, and just at the beginning of what might have been Ian's illustrious career, the Great Depression happened.

Warren and Wetmore, so proud and dignified before the dark days of gloom, now had to lay off employees. MacCallum, to his credit, was one of the last to go.

By early 1929 Ian MacCallum's family had grown to include his and Lucile's first child, Crawford John MacCallum.

Family members' recollections about those days were depressing not only for the country but for his father as well.

Spencer recalled the general assessment of his father during these times. "It just ruined his state of mind. Everything collapsed. To the family, it seems that Ian never psychologically got over it. It was as if a bomb had fallen on his dream of working in a large and prestigious architectural firm."

The Great Depression dealt a crushing economic and emotional blow not only to the MacCallums but to the entire country. Dashed hopes, business failures, riches to ruins—the mood was hard to overcome.

With chaos erupting around them, a family member suggested he move his family from New York City to Winchester, Virginia.

It was a good economic move. Carving out his own niche, Ian opened a small architectural office designing residential homes. He somewhat recuperated and his creative nature resurfaced.

"He was something of a poet," Spencer recalled, "and he liked to compose chronograms. It's a very esoteric art form."

It's a bit of verse, containing within it a date that an event occurred, or a building was built. From New World Encyclopedia, *A chronogram is a sentence or inscription in which specific letters, interpreted as numerals, stand for a particular date when rearranged.* [9]

Spencer explained it thus, "How to get the date is to take every letter in your verse that serves in the Roman numeral system, i.e., the I's, the V's, the M's, the L's, etc. Add the sum of all of those letters and that will give you the date you want. But you have to have just the right number to get the date. My father wrote chronograms for each house he designed."

One of Spencer's favorites was, "Friendly chatter, bottle platter, the saints above, no ill can matter," the letters totaling the date of 1959. "This would be extremely difficult," Spencer noted, "as you actually start with the date and then go back and figure out the words, and the verse has to make sense to boot!"

The next dozen years were spent building his architecture practice in Winchester, Virginia. By now the MacCallum family included two children, Crawford and his younger brother Spencer.

Spencer liked to say he was bought and paid for.

After his father and mother moved to Winchester with their first son, Crawford, Lucile was desperate for another child.

The family and the nation were still reeling from the shock of the Great Depression and there was no money for such a notion.

It was the midst of the depression and times were tough all around.

Just before their move, Lucile's father, Spencer Heath (known as Popdaddy by family and friends) came to visit. One day he happened upon his daughter crying, and she explained that they could not afford a new baby. He went out of the room and returned with a check for one thousand dollars.

It would be normal to look at this circumstance as simply an act of a generous father wishing to make his daughter happy, but the ensuing years will show that this event laid the groundwork for a deep and extremely significant soul connection between grandfather and grandson Spencer.

Although their relationship did not fully develop until much later when Spencer was in college, these two souls were inevitably tied together thereafter.

In Winchester, Ian, Lucile, and their children Crawford and Spencer lived in what they called the "The Big Old House."

"It was a magnificent house," reflected Spencer, "and was set high and back off the tree-shaded street." The house was noted for its 1830s architecture. Although it was a wonderful house, and that helped soothe the wounds of his father, it was not a comfortable house. The age of the house made it difficult to heat.

"But inside, oh, there was a grand staircase," Spencer smiled, "and majestic columns in the front of the house. The house really was architecturally brilliant, and my father loved it."

Lucile went to work in those days as well, opening the first licensed nursery school in the state of Virginia. Spencer remembered children running around the yard, an old wood stove in the kitchen where everyone gathered, a white picket wooden fence, rabbit hutches, and the gardener who used the word "ain't" all the time, the word becoming one of Spencer's favorites, to his parent's consternation.

Spencer had beautiful golden curls. His mother had taught him to say, when asked where he got those curls, "The angels gave them to me."

But one day he was down by the fence and some older boys came along, taunting him with, "Hello, little girl, what's your name?"

16

Figure 3. Crawford and Spencer inside The Big Old House, Winchester, Virginia, circa 1935
Courtesy of the Spencer MacCallum Collection

Figure 4. *Crawford and Spencer outside*
The Big Old House, circa 1933
Courtesy of the Spencer MacCallum Collection

Spencer was mortified and went to his older brother Crawford, whom he had nicknamed Crawfish by then, who told him to respond, "Go lay an egg." He saved up that answer and just as you would with a real egg, was ready to hurl it at the bullies, but they never taunted him with that again. He laughed that for the rest of his life he was ready to use it, but an opportunity never appeared! Spencer's family lived in the big old house until he was around six years old.

Things were looking up and Lucile was ready to establish the family's social standing in Winchester. Her grandfather, Popdaddy's father, had been educated in England and had come from a wealthy family. He had married and had children, then his first wife died. He remarried and had a son, Spencer Heath (Popdaddy). But Popdaddy and his children, mainly Lucile, felt this second Heath family was never really quite accepted.

Therefore, Lucile wanted to establish the family's social standing to the height she felt it should be.

In Winchester, the Episcopalian church was *the* most prestigious church to attend, had the wealthiest members, and was directly across the street from the big old house, so the family had become Episcopalians. Lucile blended into the ladies' groups and clubs, or wherever she saw an opportunity to establish her family as leaders in the community.

She was keen on knowing what to do, when to do it, and where to make her presence felt, especially by participating in charity events.

She flourished in church society and felt that she was elevating the family's social status not only in the church but in the larger community where they lived.

As for Spencer, he did not like attending the interminable Sunday sermons. "The minister was Parson Nelson, and he was ultra-conservative. He was dark, angry at God, and he always wore black, and the choir, too!"

Figure 5. *Lucile MacCallum with a friend (identity unknown) participating in a charity fashion show, Leasburg, Virginia, 1962 Courtesy of the Spencer MacCallum Collection*

But in time Spencer and the kids came to love Parson Nelson, mainly because he had a good heart. "We kids would often bury any dead animals we found, and one day we put a poor, dead pigeon in a cigar box and took it Parson Nelson's house. We asked him if he would do a service and he didn't hesitate one second, performing a memorable burial service, and taking it all very seriously."

One day Parson Nelson died, and everyone was mortally sad, until a new minister arrived on the scene and ordered new vestments for the choir. Out went the old black ones and in came new red ones! Out with the sadness and in with mortification! It was terribly shocking to the congregation, so much so they were incensed! However, the new minister was eventually as much loved as Parson Nelson, so the congregation finally accepted his ways. The red vestments, and he, stayed in the church. Spencer's cousin, Irvan Thomas O'Connell, Jr., also lived in Winchester and was the same age as Spencer's older brother, Crawfish. Spencer loved nicknames and therefore also crowned his cousin, Irvan, with a funny one—Corpy. It seems he was the bossy type at summer camp. Spencer gave him Napoleon's nickname "The Little Corporal," then shortened it to Corpy.

Spencer, Crawfish, and Corpy tried to get into mischief as much as they possibly could.

Not too far from where they lived was a long metal structure with both storage and carport spaces.

Agile kids could play in the rafters and swing from the ceiling from one space to another. They made a makeshift clubhouse in the rafters with cardboard boxes they found at home or behind stores. They placed on the door of their inner sanctum a bird skull on a stick—the totem and protector of the clan! One day Spencer was sick and confined to home in bed.

Crawfish and Corpy rushed into his room with a fantastic tale—that a pie company had rented one of the garage compartments and was storing little cellophane-wrapped minipies in one of the storage areas, and no lock on the door! Whoa, what a discovery for hungry little kids! Spencer got well fast and before long they were feasting on the delicious apple, cherry and other assorted mini-pies. Still naïve, they failed to clean up their evidence and threw the wrappers all over the storage area.

In the next few days, they managed to raid the pie containers several times and planned to rendezvous the next day for yet another feast.

As Spencer rounded the corner of the alley, there were men walking all around outside the storage areas. He reasoned that if he turned and ran, he'd be suspect for sure; so, he nonchalantly walked right by the men. "That was the wrong decision," Spencer laughed. "One of the men called out to me, 'Hey kid! You've been in these pies, haven't you? And where are the others?'"

Spencer denied it all.

But the man was soon marching him out onto the street. About that time Corpy and Crawfish spied Spencer and ran for cover.

The next thing Spencer knew the parents were meeting at Corpy's house. In fact, there was a wide swath of thieves in the neighborhood!

By now, it was discovered that the three boys were not the only kids who had discovered this treasure trove of sweets. Turns out most of the neighborhood kids were taking advantage of the goodies. In the end, the parents paid for the pies, but as Spencer put it, "It was sheer stupidity to park those pies under the noses of all the neighborhood kids."

Spencer's youthful days in Winchester were carefree. The family moved temporarily to an apartment for a little more than two years while his father designed and built a new house for the family.

Eventually, the new house was ready, and it was considered a masterpiece by his father, who was known as *the* architect Ian MacCallum. He had become highly respected in the area and had established and was growing his clientele by this time. The family moved into their beautiful new home, and 1939 rolled into 1940.

Spencer and Crawfish brought in the New Year and new decade by laying out dominoes in the form of 1940 on the living room floor of their new house. That was a good memory. However, the siblings were typical in most ways brothers can be, and according to Spencer, there were times that their relationship as brothers, along with the normal sibling rivalry, was difficult to understand. It seemed that they had a deep love and affection for each other when they were not doing their best to be mortal enemies as kids sometimes do.

Over time, the years would tell their complex story again and again. As a child, Spencer found that he enjoyed nature, being alone, and collecting nature samples more than spending time with other kids.

He developed an interest in flowers and animals, becoming friends with a naturalist who took him on long hikes in the beauty of the outdoors.

He was encouraged to make a wildflower garden by transplanting large varieties of flowers in his garden, and

Figure 6. *The house that Ian built,*
Winchester, Virginia, circa 1940
Courtesy of the Spencer MacCallum Collection

he was simply amazed at the birds and butterflies that were attracted to it. Through this friendship, he nurtured a growing love for all living things, and started a bird nest collection.

In his youthful days, he was picked on by the bullies, hating recess in elementary and junior high school, and trying to hide against the fence in a corner of the playground to make himself invisible. "I had a streak of fear in my psychological makeup, which made me a good target for the bullies. I was very vulnerable." But one day he found that he could run faster and better than anyone in the school. He discovered he could run home through the woods and close the windows and doors in the house before the bullies could get there. Later, he put this boosted self-confidence to work and lettered in track all four years at Phillips Academy Andover, a prep school in Andover north of Boston.

He loved cats and dogs, too, recalling the find of a halfdead cat in an alley trashcan. Lucile treated its eyes, and they nursed it back to health, naming it Melissa. "It had more personality than any cat I've ever seen since." But the pet that meant the most to him was a dog named Rascal.

Rascal actually belonged to another family in the town, but he clung to Spencer and followed him everywhere, so much so that the family eventually gave the dog to Spencer. He went with Spencer to school each and every day, waiting patiently on the hillside for his master to get out of class. Spencer kept an eye on him all day long out the schoolhouse window.

Rascal was entirely devoted to Spencer, and protective. One day Spencer was home in bed sick and his best friend positioned himself as a guard at the foot of the bed, not allowing other family members to approach. With mutual loyalty and dedication, the two were inseparable until they were literally forced to part, an event that brought tears to Spencer's eyes throughout his entire life.

When this tragic event happened, everything in Spencer's orbit spun out of control.

It would never be the same again.

Chapter Two

***The Mexico Years; Discoveries and Adventures;
The Beads; Lucie and Ian's Divorce***

Another worldwide disruption would once again change Spencer's family forever. World War II literally exploded on Earth, and when the United States entered the war, Spencer's father, Ian, was sent to England.

Lucile was now on her own again with her husband overseas, and thinking beyond the two wars that had impacted the entire globe made Lucile realize that her children would need a more sophisticated education, one that included travel. Her rationale for travel to Mexico, she told everyone, was that exposure to another culture and language would enhance her children's chances of success in the future—as all people would need to understand and adjust to the new world order after the war.

Lucile had always desired to expose her children to a foreign culture while they were still young, but could not do so up to this point, so she made the bold decision to take the children to Mexico. Spencer was now ten years old and Crawford was twelve. It was also agreed that their cousin Corpy would later join the family for this adventurous journey to Mexico.

Much later both Spencer and his brother, Crawford, understood that Lucile also had her own personal motivations that drove her south of the border. But the fact that she did at least understand the *potential* role her children might one day play on the world stage was, and is today, impressive.

No one at that point could have foreseen the eventual impact Spencer would make on so many lives both in Mexico and the United States. It is uncanny that his mother had the foresight and intuitive perception to think it was highly possible that her children would someday make a difference in the world, especially if exposed at a young age to Mexico's culture.

Spencer's mother intuited the global connections which would occur after the war. "Clearly the United States would dominate the relationship with Latin America, which included Mexico, Central, and South America," she had told the boys. There was certainly not much understanding of Latin culture and language in the United States at that time.

Lucile, herself, did not understand the Latin language or culture and didn't know anyone who did, but against all odds, she was determined to set out on this journey.

It was 1942. The war had taken hold.

Lucile MacCallum and everyone "at home" wanted to contribute to the war effort and help the allies to a rapid victory.

She felt there must be a better way to pitch in than knitting with the ladies on Thursday evenings.

According to Spencer, there was a lot of media speculation about how things would look after the war.

"Before the war, America had traded almost exclusively with Europe. It was contemplated that a new hemispheric unity would prevail and that after the war, trade and cultural relations between America, Latin America, and other countries would increase." Juxtaposed to later becoming an adventurous visionary, Lucile seemed to have been overshadowed and perhaps weakened for much of her life by her Victorian father, as well as her complicated husband.

In retrospect, it seemed that she sought for herself some magical potion of happiness in the distant and romantic land of Mexico. Was escapism the motivation behind that Mexico adventure? Or was it truly the idea of giving her sons various cultural experiences? Or was it a convoluted combination of both? Perhaps it was the notion of having complete freedom from the two men she felt dominated her: her husband and her father.

Whatever it was, the stars were aligned; it was suddenly time to pull off the great escape from the old and the great escape to the new.

Lucile rented out their house, the tenants agreeing that they would take care of Rascal. All the necessary arrangements were made, and the family was ready to depart. The pet had been introduced to the new family and Spencer tried to positively reassure him. "But he knew the game was up and that I was going away," Spencer lamented. As they pulled away in their car, Rascal broke free and chased the car block after block after block.

Lucy sped up until finally, the car outdistanced him, and the family sadly left him behind.

Spencer was looking out the back window of the car with his breaking heart, feeling powerless to avert this disaster. He should never have agreed to it, he reflected. Even though he knew he could not have done anything about it, this experience stayed with him throughout his life. It taught him a great lesson: never leave anyone, or anything, that you love. Each night throughout their adventures in Mexico Spencer would gaze and wish upon a star, wishing that his best friend was happy.

Spencer was not told for a very long time what happened to his dog. After the family left their home for Mexico, Rascal's heart was also broken. "He never got over it either," Spencer said with sadness, "and he refused to eat, howled constantly, and was totally inconsolable. No matter what was tried, he was slowly dying of starvation. Finally, he had to be put down. He had literally starved himself to death."

Even after Spencer grew up, he never forgot his pal. He replayed that scene in his mind many times over the years. Oh, how he wished that he had been older and able to insist that Rascal travel with them to Mexico.

The heartbreak of losing him was only the first of many boulders that tumbled out of control down a very slippery slope. The years during and following the war took an enormous toll on the family.

The trio had left Virginia in a 1939 Chevrolet. It had two horns: a country horn and a city horn, and it was a smash hit in Mexico. [10]

Their gasoline rations barely delivered them across the country to the border at Laredo – and it was a time for firsts – cotton fields and a flat tire among them.

And their adventures were just beginning.

In Sequin, Texas, as their first flat tire was being repaired, Lucile remembered that someone back home had told her to be sure to rotate the tires, so she thought she'd help the gas station mechanic by loosening the nuts and bolts on the three other tires.

She did such a great job that when the mechanic returned with the repaired tire and leaned on the car, all the wheels fell to the ground.

She was duly chastised and resolved in the future to leave the fine art of auto mechanics well enough alone.

Lucile thereafter paid little attention to the tires. About a year later, they were driving down a steep slope near Pico de Orizaba on the way to Vera Cruz. "One of the tires blew out," Spencer remembered. "Luckily, Lucile was able to stop the car and we were safe, but it could be seen that the tires had traveled that last of many miles on canvas. The rubber had worn perilously thin." As they continued exploring Mexico, and whatever her complex motivations had been, she clung to and further romanticized the idea of "doing her part" to help the war effort.

In her mind, Lucile would return to America with two young men who would be furnished with some smattering of understanding to help usher in this new age of global understanding. This would be her contribution not to the war effort, but to the post-war world. She clung to this unusual idea!

The early years in Mexico were financed with meager funds. Even though Popdaddy was reasonably wealthy, and from time to time helped the family with special needs, he did not support his adult children with the basic daily necessities.

He had a stern view of how folks handled finances.

That was the responsibility of their spouses. Besides, he had loaned Ian a sum of money during the Great Depression, which still had not been paid back. It was a continuing reminder and source of humiliation and broken pride for Ian.

To further complicate what seemed to be a dark depression, Ian had been assigned an extraordinary duty. His mission in London was highly specialized and was one that quickly turned sour for him. He knew and loved European architecture as few people did. Ornate architecture had been part of his genius, his calling, and his passion. After his work on the magnificent Louvain library in the post-World War I years, he now regrettably witnessed and grasped during World War II the horrid bombing destruction of many magnificent buildings as no one else could have. Unfortunately, and because he was an architect, he was assigned to study aerial photos using stereoscopic equipment before and after every air raid to assess the damage. As a true lover and expert of fine European architecture, he was forced to watch it destroyed before his very eyes. [11]

Unknown to Spencer and his brother, his father had also embarked on what became a prelude to divorce while overseas. An ocean and the haunting past and the damning present now physically separated him from the family. He began to emotionally distance himself from his family. There was no longer a family "at home" awaiting his return—they were traveling around down in Mexico, and strangers were living in his house.

Behind his desire to divorce was Ian's affair with another woman, but Lucile did not know about it and might have surmised that Ian was still despondent over the depression and his stymied career. It was much more complicated than could be seen by anyone.

The losses of the previous years and this war had left an indelible mark on this man and what once had been a promising career. While Ian's life was undergoing hellish turmoil, so was Lucile's. She was dependent on her husband in London to send money for her and the children. But soon after he went overseas, Ian began a relentless push for divorce. Lucile was adamantly against it. The breakdown in their marriage was ramping up, with these two people now continents apart in mind and body.

At any rate, she relied on him for their income. There was once a delay in funds, and even though Spencer thought that his father may have withheld these funds for the family on purpose, as well as love for his wife, another perspective comes from Crawford. "In my memory, there was one time only, a two-week delay in funds, and Lucile told us it was a postal service snafu. We had all the bananas we could eat and were never really hungry."

Crawford also summed up his opinion about his parent's relationship like this. "I never blamed Ian for having an affair during the blitz in London. He was living on potatoes and whale blubber and walked out of a building one night which blew up before he reached the corner, and then later returned to the states a skinny caricature of himself. Rather, I blamed Lucile for not agreeing to a divorce so he could marry the woman who loved him as Lucile never had." What can be said as true is that no one ever really knows the dynamics between two partners in life.

Even though at times the trio lived day by day, and Lucie had an errant husband she did not understand, she always declared that those years in Mexico were the best years of her life. She was not only on a mission to expose

32

her children to the cultures of Mexico, but she was also free at last from the constraints of her father and his strict morality.

Prior to the war and the Mexico excursion, Spencer remembers that his mother had been sick quite a bit, had many quarrels with her husband, and felt intimidated by her father. It seems to Spencer that Lucile was much more her real self in Mexico. In fact, she reinvented herself while there. She dyed her brunette hair blonde and started a new life, as "Lucie."

Lucile before Mexico, Lucie during and after Mexico. The combination of Ian's activities in Europe and Lucie's adventures in Mexico did later bear fruit, but by then it was sour, poisonous, and unpalatable.

Of critical importance, however, to Spencer's development were the two and half years the little band of adventurers freely roamed the Mexican country, where to his impressionable mind they met the most fascinating people— anthropologists, artists, and archaeologists—and had fabulous adventures that none of them forgot.

They lived in Mexico City for a while, then resided in Taxco, where they were fortunate to live several months with the family of architect and anthropologist, Baron Alexander von Wuthenau, who was researching early peoples in Mexico. He and other scholars of the time suggested that there were a variety of ethnic or racial types present in Mexico and Central America in prehistoric times. Wuthenau authored *"Unexpected Faces in Ancient America"* and *"The Art of Terracotta Pottery of Pre-Columbian Central and South America."*

Baron Alexander von Wuthenau was from Germany and was a cousin of the British royal family. He taught art history at Mexico City College in the 1940s and assisted the Mexican government in the restoration of its colonial art treasures. [12]

The Baron had arrived in Mexico on the heels of Nazi wrath. He did not agree with Hitler's policies and had just enough time to escape to Mexico before the war broke out.

The Baron successfully restored the Archbishop's Palace in Taxco, also known as the Casa Humboldt House where the great scientist Alexander von Humboldt had stayed on his trek from South America to North America in the 19th century. Humboldt had spent extensive time in the Americas providing invaluable geographic information.

Figure 7. The reinvented "real" Lucie with new blonde hair and new friends, Mexico, circa 1943. Lucile before Mexico – Lucie during and after Mexico. Courtesy of the Spencer MacCallum Collection

But because the Baron was German, the government froze his assets. The family operated an inn of sorts in their home for extra income. Spencer recalls that the little MacCallum band celebrated Christmas with the Baron and his family in the traditional German way with a feast of lavish food, drink, gifts, songs, and caroling.

Although they were leading a life of adventure, Lucie tried to make sure they had balance in their lives. She taught at the American school in Mexico City, and this allowed her children to attend the school. During that time, Spencer would venture out to an adobe quarry at Tlatilco outside of Mexico City. "It was an enormous pit. With long steel rods, the workers would force the clay to tumble down into the pit where workers at the bottom would make adobe bricks." Spencer related.

Tlatilco was a pre-Columbian site in the Valley of Mexico situated near the modern-day town of the same name. The culture that spawned Tlatilco was one of the first to arise in the Valley, on the shores of Lake Texcoco. Between the years 1500 B.C. and 500 B.C. Tlatilco flourished.

Spencer was introduced to the quarry by Wolfgang Paalen, an Austrian-Mexican painter and influential art theorist during the war years. He befriended Lucie and the children. He was particularly interested in a certain type of pottery that was sometimes uncovered at the quarry. Paalen felt that this pottery was very similar to Northwest Coast Indian Art. He told Spencer that if he ever found any pieces, he would buy them from him.

An older student at his school, Jessie, continually pestered Spencer to take him along to the quarry. Spencer did not much want to do that, but he finally gave in. On the day they went to the quarry, the boy wandered off on his own and Spencer was hanging around some of the workers digging clay to make adobe bricks. "Suddenly, as if they had broken open an anthill, I saw that the hole in which they were digging was producing some small, round, clay pellets." The men paid no attention to them. But Spencer asked them to let him examine the hole. He rubbed one of the pellets and saw immediately that the small objects they were casually throwing aside were highly polished blue jade beads about the size of a thumbnail, from a necklace from the formative era between 600-200 BC.

"I figured that this was an ancient burial," Spencer smiled. "Although I was only eleven years old, I understood the importance of excavation under controlled conditions. How to get the men to stop their work and wait for the archaeologists to excavate this burial?" He tried to stall the men, but they paid no attention to this little kid and would not stop. The museum had already spent many months excavating here and had not found anything of value such as this.

Spencer did the only thing he could think to do. He asked the men if he could pay them for the *canicas*, marbles. They agreed on the price of two "marbles" for pesos equivalent at that time to a penny. They would slow their shoveling and allow Spencer to go through the clay with his hands and pick out the marbles. By now, Jessie had joined in.

They retrieved more than eight hundred beads, as well as several pieces of beautiful pottery in the form of squashes with elongated necks, and some light green jade beads. Spencer lamented, "It would have been fascinating to excavate the burial properly, but then we were rushed by the workers to gather up all this treasure and leave. We went back the next morning to see if we could get more beads, but the workmen had finished their work and covered over the site."

By now, another of the family's good friends was the anthropologist and cartographer Pedro Armillas. [13] A refugee of the Spanish Civil War, along with other injured soldiers, he had been saved by the Quakers and taken from one of the hospitals in an attempt to save his life.

Spencer noted that he was very well respected and was often cited as an authority on the beads Spencer had found. "He stated that to his knowledge, and at that time, that was the largest cache of jade ever found in the valley of Mexico, and the largest jade necklace ever found in the New World."

Spencer reflected that it was a shame that this burial had been opened in this manner. He had always had misgivings about it, but as a child, there was not much he could have done at the time.

The beads that Spencer found then later traveled on a circuitous route after leaving his hands, with a few returning at another time. In a long, complex, and heartbreaking story, especially for a young kid, many of the beads left his possession and did not return. He did not know their fate.

However, he did manage to hang on to some, and at one point Lucie asked for a few to make into a necklace. "I remember staying up all night, the entire night, looking through these beads to select not the best, but the twelve poorest beads to give to my mother." In an ironic act of karma years later when Lucie died, Spencer inherited her jewelry, including the jade bead necklace. "The very worst beads of the whole bunch came back home to me—the poorest of the beads which I had so greedily selected for my mother."

Spencer laughed, "There's a moral to this story somewhere, but I hate to dwell on it."

Many years later, Spencer could not meet a mortgage payment on the family farm, Roadsend Garden, because he had speculated in gold on margin. He learned the hard way about margin speculations.

He needed five thousand dollars to make this payment, so he took some of the beads to a dealer in New York City who had been recommended by a friend. He was paid the exact amount needed for the mortgage and in the end, it was ironic that some of these beads "saved the farm."

While in Mexico, the MacCallums lived for a time in Guadalajara and then in Chapala and Ajijic on Lake Chapala south of the metropolitan area. With 405 square miles of surface area, Lake Chapala is the largest natural lake in Mexico, and the third largest in Latin America. [14] It's about fifty miles long from east to west with a maximum north south width of about 12.5 miles. Despite its size, Lake Chapala is quite shallow, with an average depth of only slightly over thirteen feet.

The family adventures around Lake Chapala were full of not only archaeological surprises, but also rather ordinary times spent with friends, relaxing and enjoying the culture of Mexico—such as enjoying the delicate whitefish taken from the lake. Vendors filleted then lightly fried the fish, then served them with *limón*, lime. Folks arrived from miles around in the early mornings as the local fisherman were pulling in their nets, brimming with huge batches of fish.

In Ajijic, there was a natural grassy area around the lake. An old burro had been put out to pasture there to spend his last days. Spencer and he became fast friends, and he would spend hours picking up rocks so that Mr. Burro could have a nice grassy area on which to laze about. Lake Chapala is where Spencer's fiery interest in archaeology continued to ignite.

While walking along the edge of the water, he looked for pieces of obsidian blades that had been made into prehistoric knives, and sometimes found entire arrowheads. All in all, those days seemed magical to Spencer.

While Spencer was developing this scientific bent, his mother and Crawfish also developed a natural curiosity about everything in Mexico, and together, the trio began to have a true immersion experience. Corpy joined them later in 1943 so that his own mother, Lucile's sister, Beatrice, was free to join the Women's Army Corp (WACS) and do her own part for the war effort. Thus, it was time, Lucie decided, for the children to get back to a school routine again. She enrolled them in a private school in Guadalajara. During this time, they split up and lived with different families, and Lucie explained that in this way they would achieve a more rounded experience.

Whether this reason or economics was her motivation, it mattered little to the kids. It was all an adventure to them.

Spencer remembered it as carefree life.

When the group visited Oaxaca, the local archaeologist appointed young Spencer as his apprentice. Spencer went with him every morning to the Monte Albán Archaeological Ruins, a large pre-Columbian archaeological site in the Santa Cruz Xoxocotlán Municipality in the southern Mexican state of Oaxaca.

The site was built by the Zapotecs as a ceremonial city as far back as 500 B.C. and was inhabited until about 850 A.D. It was an important center of commerce and government. Spencer never forgot that he celebrated his twelfth birthday in a previously unopened tomb in those ruins. His mentor allowed him the honor of opening that tomb entirely by himself, with Spencer wearing a pith helmet, short pants and all.

Later, while living on Lake Chapala, Spencer, his brother, and Corpy went to public school. It was quite a different experience from the private school they had attended.

It seems that the little Mexican kids wanted to know some English words for *groserias*, so Spencer would call out different food items, such as tomato, bread, and potato. Spencer didn't catch on to what they were up to until about a week later when he and his mother were walking down the street. These little kids started calling out "tomato," and "potato," and would collapse into fits of laughter. Turns out, they thought Spencer had been teaching them dirty English words, because that is what they had asked for with the Spanish word *groseria*—rude, vulgar, or swear words.

At one point, the little family was living at Teotihuacan. Noted archaeologist César A. Sáenz became a good friend to Spencer.

He was a researcher at the Instituto Nacional de Antropología e Historia and was just beginning what became a distinguished career as an archaeological researcher. He published many papers and books on his findings and left an important legacy in the archaeological investigations of Mexico. [15]

He and his sister had a guest room in their house by the museum. Sáenz told Spencer that he could stay there any time he wanted, so Spencer would travel out to the museum on Fridays after classes at the American School. Spencer spent a lot of time around the ruins and had a passion for visiting the local farmers around them. Not to buy farm products, but instead, at each little hut, he would inquire if they had ever found in their fields *"monoitos,"* little clay monkeys.

One day a woman said to him that although she did not have *monoitos*, she did have something of interest! She disappeared into a room and then brought out a chunk of adobe with a fresco painting on one side, depicting a hand with droplets of water dripping from the fingers.

As any good archaeologist would certainly make a drawing of this artifact on the spot, Spencer asked her for paper and she handed him a sheet from her daughter's school notebook, along with a stub of a pencil. He drew the amazing fresco. When Spencer returned to the museum, he showed it to Dr. Sáenz, who speculated it looked like Tlaloc, the god of rain.

The next week when he arrived on Friday, four very important adults—Dr. Sáenz and three other men— greeted Spencer. They had come from Mexico City just to meet Spencer, and one was the Director of the National Museum of Mexico. They asked him to take them to where he found this fresco.

As it turned out, two years previous a similar chunk of fresco had turned up for sale at a gallery in San Diego,

California and they could not repatriate it. From its style they knew that it had come from Teotihuacan. It had caused much scandal at the time. The best they could do was to try to locate the temple from where it had come, but they had not been able to locate it. Now, Spencer, with the curiosity of a true archaeologist, had found the exact clue they needed! An important feature story ran in the Mexico City newspaper the next day with this headline:

Norte Americano Niño Con Alma de Anticuario…
or
North American boy with the soul of an antiquarian…has made this discovery!

The authorities eventually located and restored the temple. By then, Spencer's interest in Mexico was unquenchable!

"Lucie allowed us to have some extraordinary adventures in Mexico. After we had been in Mexico for a couple of years my brother, Corpy, and I decided we were plenty "street smart" enough to take on the world. We had learned enough Spanish at this point to get by."

Their Spanish classes were by virtue of immersion. The very first sentence Spencer learned was at the breakfast table.

His brother and mother had decided that he would not be allowed food unless he could ask for it in Spanish. The sentence was, *Paseme el pan tostado, por favor,* or "Pass me the toasted bread, please."

All the members of the little MacCallum band learned Spanish in the two and half years they lived in Mexico. "By now I was twelve, and my brother and cousin were each fourteen. We wanted an adventure, so we figured out how we could travel to Mérida without flying directly there from Mexico City or taking a ship. We pressed Lucie to let us take this trip alone.

Mérida, Yucatán was and is an economic and social center of southeast Mexico, and today is a tourist destination of first class. It is known as the White City for its clean streets, houses and people, and it is an obligatory starting and finishing point for those visiting the State of Yucatan. Mérida depicts much of the splendor of Colonial Mexico. The Spanish conqueror Francisco de Montejo founded Mérida in 1542 on the site of a former Mayan city he destroyed.

Lucie trusted the judgment of their friend Pedro, so depending on if he agreed to it, she would let them go. Surprisingly, he said, "Yes!" The boys were elated. Lucie and Pedro sternly instructed them that they must stay together at all times. But Spencer and his brother shared a normal sibling rivalry relationship, so after they departed on their journey, and as soon as they could, the trio split up. Spencer and cousin Corpy went ahead, and brother Crawfish followed two days behind.

It was a trip that included a bus ride to Vera Cruz, an Isthmus of Tehuantepec train to the Pacific Coast, another bus ride to Cristobal in the mountains in Chiapas, and a transport plane ride carrying chicle products, used in those years to manufacture chewing gum. They flew over jagged and turbulent mountains and Spencer and Corpy finally landed at Villahermosa. Traveling on the train along the flat strip of land of the isthmus, Spencer remembers "We were racing through the night. Corpy and I discovered how we could step from one car to the other," he said.

Figure 8*. Crawford and Spencer, circa 1944*
Courtesy of the Spencer MacCallum Collection

"Oh, it was dangerous, but to us, it was great fun."
The two boys were befriended by Mexican traveling sales-
men. "They taught us how to play twenty-one and gave us

balloons to entertain ourselves. We were having a great time blowing up these balloons, but we couldn't figure out why it was so uproariously funny to everyone on the train. As it turned out, they were not balloons, but condoms!"

From Villahermosa, the two took a riverboat launch loaded with a cargo of oranges, barrels of oil, and sacks of rice and were allowed to eat as many oranges as they wanted. In the hull below were passengers—several traveling Mexican families.

Spencer and Corpy were considered unusual and "distinguished" guests of the riverboat. There was one cabin for the skipper, and he gave it to them. The boys spent some time playing Honeymoon Bridge with silver coins that Pedro had advised them to take on the trip. On top of the boat, the crew spent a lot of time playing twenty-one.

Corpy considered if he was good enough to play with them. Should they risk using their silver pesos to beat the crew? After all, Spencer was impressed because Corpy regularly beat *him*. So Corpy went for it.

On the riverboat for five days, Corpy managed to break even! What did Spencer do to pass the time? There was a mother and her three young daughters traveling on the boat. Occasionally they asked to use the boys' cabin for personal grooming. The crew started to tease the boys and the young ladies and decided that one of the young ladies, Maria, and Spencer would have to get together.

It became the height of jokes and teasing and urging. Unbeknownst to the boys, the ladies were not a family, and the brothers were oblivious that the women were a madam and two of her "girls."

Spencer declined, but never forgot that experience.

Finally, they landed at Tenosique on the Usumacinta River, very near the Guatemalan border. There, Spencer and Corpy were to await the arrival of Crawford. While waiting, they met and befriended a mysterious American man in his twenties. Every time Corpy would try to get his picture, the mystery man would turn away. One day the man left on a chicle plane. As his two young friends were seeing him off, and as the prop was revving up, the man leaned out and pointed to Corpy, "Let me see your camera." He then removed a piece of cardboard he had secretly placed behind the lens. "'I don't want you to not get *any* pictures after this.'" He grinned at the boys and flew off into the clouds, never to be seen again.

As they waited for Crawford, they amused themselves trying to pick off *pinolillos*, "tiny bugs that itched like fire," they had picked up on the paddleboat. Crawford finally showed up on the paddleboat Carmen. They all agreed they now wanted to visit the ruins of Palenque. Backtracking on the paddleboat to Emiliano Zapata that evening, they learned that two trucks would be headed in the direction of Palenque shortly. They hitched a ride on one of them, which was more like the remains of what had once been a truck. The glass in the windows was gone, the seats were bare springs, and every so often the truck would spit fire and smoke. The driver would stop, tinker under the hood, and before long the little caravan would take off again.

Finally arriving at a sawmill camp in the middle of the night, they needed a place to sleep.

The best spot in the camp was on top of a table. With one blanket among them, they managed to get in the middle and stay warm in the cool night air.

From the sawmill camp, the boys hiked half the morning to the village of Palenque. By this time, Spencer had been steeped in archaeology, absorbing everything about it. At this tender age of twelve, and thanks to Lucie's encouragement and the patronage of the archaeological community in Mexico, the young lad felt he had found his calling in life.

The trio raced on horseback up to the marvelous prehistoric ruins, with Spencer in the lead.

The boys strolled and gawked in wonder. Then something magical happened to Spencer: he found a burned jade bead on the ground. But how could this be possible? Already versed in Palenque's history, Spencer knew that jade had not previously been found at these ruins. This was the late 1940s and Palenque at that time was still somewhat remote and did not yet have the thousands of tourists tromping over the city. Artifacts could still be discovered in the soil.

Spencer excitedly put the bead in his pocket to deliver this treasure back to his "colleagues" at the National Museum in Mexico City. There, Spencer had found another mentor, the Director of the Museum. Spencer had been allowed free entry to the Museum and the Director's door was always open to the eager young archaeologist. He was anxious to share his "find."

However, by the time the trio arrived back, Spencer had lost the bead, and as he quipped later, who would have believed him? Spencer noted that many years later archaeologists did indeed find a large cache of jade in a tomb there. In 1954 Alberto Ruiz Lhuillier initiated exploration and consolidation work at one of the temples, clearing its supporting substructure. During excavation, a tomb looted in ancient times was discovered that contained twenty-five jade beads. To Spencer, nothing ever quite rivaled the fact that his was the first discovery of jade at Palenque.

He lamented, "I have always treasured that moment, even if no one else knew about it."

The trio soon decided to get back to Tenosique in order to continue their journey. Why not go by horseback? They hired a guide, along with some questionable horses and gear. It took two days and one night. There was a path that originally had been cleared for a railway, but it was not too overgrown, and the group made their way with caution. As night fell, they came upon a family of Indians and stayed with them. The Indians had wonderful long, string hammocks, which they let the boys sleep in. All through the night, the boys heard jungle lions roaring; only later did they learn they had been hearing howler monkeys, not lions. Around the fire, the Indians saw that the boys were still having problems with the *pinolillos*. They showed them how to press beeswax onto the little bugs and the wax would pull the bugs out of their skin. It was a wonderful relief!

The second evening they camped along the Usumacinta River. The guide and the horses turned back while the boys searched for a way to cross the river. They took off their shoes and made their way down the river path. The cool dirt felt good to their feet. In the semi-darkness, there were inky blobs of blackness on the path, which were as big as a grown man's hands.

They sounded like "thud," "thud," in the night. The boys hopped over them.

They were horrified to discover that the big black blobs they had so casually hopped over were tarantulas.

They reached a little thatched hut by the river and some people offered to take them across the river. Once across the river, the boys met a group of men that had been hunting. Spencer had been very interested in taxidermy and looked with relish at a baby alligator, which had been shot and slung across a man's shoulder. He gave it to Spencer!

It was now Christmas Eve, and Spencer spent part of the night skinning the alligator with a rusty single razor blade by the light of a wax candle. The next day the hunters sold him an ocelot skin, rolled up in a newspaper and still heavy with fat. In Mérida, Spencer had both the alligator and the ocelot professionally tanned. He had the alligator for quite a long time afterward.

The boys finally did reach Tenosique and from there they traveled to Campeche and finally to Mérida via train. The train had a big bulbous smokestack and a cowcatcher on the front. It had been brought down from the United States. There were three classes: a seedy passenger car, a second-class boxcar with a long wooden bench on either side, and an open boxcar for the third class. The first class was right behind the engine, which the boys figured would be the best compartment. That was a mistake as it was right behind the engine and the cinders blew all over them. Along the way, Mayan Indians would run up to meet the train offering tamales wrapped in banana leaves—delicious and steaming hot.

The trio had planned to meet Lucie on Christmas Eve in Mérida, but they were a week late and had previously wired her twice so she could modify her plans. But she did not receive the telegrams. In a panic, she herself sent out telegrams to each train stop inquiring if anyone had seen these three gringo kids. She was frantic and had already begun to grieve that she had lost the boys.

But when they finally showed up in Mérida, Lucie was overjoyed, even though they had been a month without proper baths, their skin was streaked with red marks from scratching the relentless *pinolillos*, and their clothes were ripped, worn out, and covered in dirt and cinders.

The first thing Lucie did was get the boys cleaned up. She then confessed that after they had set out on their adventure, she had a growing fear that it was a mistake to let them go. However, she had calmed herself, refusing to be scared. She told herself, "Lucie, you can be as scared as you want to, but never let your fears guide what you let the boys do in life." She knew that her fears would have a negative impact on the boys' future. Having once-in-a-lifetime adventures, and being the adventuresome soul that she herself was, she could not stand in their way. She told them that to not have gone on this marvelous adventure would have been far worse.

During the Mexico sojourn, Lucie accepted money only from her husband, trying to maintain her independence as long as possible.

Along with the small income Ian sent, she also worked when possible.

As the little band traveled around, sometimes with people they had met, they would settle in what seemed to be safe places and where she could obtain work as a salesperson in gift shops, or in restaurants, or teaching in schools.

With all the friends they made, they could then travel with other people until arriving at the next place they wanted to live. Spencer felt their lives were magical.

Two things motivated them to move around like this: Spencer's intense interest in archaeology and Lucie's desire to broaden their education.

Spencer's growing scientific bent also gave them a mission.

Lucie sought out the archaeological community and made sure the family lived in proximity to these scientists. As for Lucie, she was enjoying a newfound freedom from her father and her husband in the colorful nightlife of Mexico. Spencer remembered, "When she became a blonde she basically and psychologically changed her identity. She loved to nightclub with her friends. She became the "real" Lucie." Born in 1903 she was in her early 40's during their travels in Mexico and felt invincible. At the time, she seemed to be having "the time of her life" as were the boys, but there was a dark wind on the horizon that was headed their way.

Soon, it was time for the little band of adventurers to head back to the United States. It was disappointing to everyone on different levels. The two and half years in Mexico changed all of them, as if they had been reborn. The contrast between cold and stern Winchester, Virginia to the warm, humid softness of Mexico suddenly could not be bridged.

Lucie returned to Winchester with the family, only to face an extremely nasty divorce brewing out of control. As a result, there soon developed a personal challenge for Spencer, a devastating and embarrassing case of stuttering that morphed into a very serious situation.

In later years, Spencer asked his mother why, with the divorce looming and a sometimes-strict father waiting, had they returned to the United States at all. Her answer surprised him. Her main reason for returning was she did not want her boys to be under the influence of the *machismo* culture prevalent in Mexico at the time.

She was concerned with the impact this male chauvinism might have on them.

Lucie concluded, however, that even though there were some negative cultural influences, they were few amongst many positive influences.

As her sons were approaching puberty and young manhood, she could see that they could be very impressionable.

Lucie was also concerned about another negative influence. At that time in Mexico, it seemed that all the little kids copied each other's papers and tests. Fresh from Mexico and back in the Winchester, Virginia classroom, Spencer asked the girl next to him to move her arm so he could see her paper. She was very shocked at this, and turning to him, spoke in a loud voice, "Why Spencer Mac-Callum!" in such a way that Spencer has not forgotten it to this day.

Spencer was inherently shy, and now that he was back at home the family disharmony started to play a negative role in his life. He began to carry a stone in his pocket so that when he met someone he was nervous about, he could maintain his composure by pressing hard on the stone rolling through his fingers. Spencer began to feel detached and shut out from his peer group, although he remembers that a friend insisted it was Spencer who isolated himself.

He felt different, and was different, from his peer group. He had lived two magical years in a foreign country, had special friendships with noted scholars, and he had grown up in a way that would not have been possible in Winchester.

In contrast, his family was now being torn apart by a distant father and an anguished mother—a recipe for suffering under a very negative situation in his life.

It was difficult to balance his emotions.

In retrospect, Mexico was magical. Virginia was devastating. The people down south were warm, charming, playful, and inviting. The folks in the northeast were cold and judgmental. Spencer had felt love, and respect even though he was a youngster, everywhere they went in Mexico. Back in the northeast, he felt sullen, traumatized, and suddenly, for the first time in his life, totally alone.

He escaped the next summer to the farm of Mr. Stadden Cooper near Mountain Falls, Virginia, a little place in the mountains west of Winchester. Though not Spencer's uncle, he was called Uncle by Spencer, who found that comforting amidst the family turmoil of divorce.

The farm had no electricity, and everything was done in an old-fashioned way. To Spencer, it was a curious youth's most wonderful summer, and more importantly a refuge away from the drama taking place at home.

He learned how to trim the wicks of kerosene lamps, how to milk Blackie the cow, and how to pitch in with the hard work of bringing in the hay. He named a newborn calf after Sarah, a girl he was goofy in love with, and always remembered.

Always lucky in unearthing treasure, he found rare arrowheads, most of which had been long exhausted in the Virginia area. One of his chores was to chop wood for the kitchen stove and he was fortunate to find an intact arrowhead embedded in a log he split open.

In this day-to-day world of farming, and although he didn't care for it, he was taught how to chop off the heads of the chickens roaming freely in the yard. He said he never forgot it, although he wished he could.

Uncle Stadden's place of Americana sheltered Spencer at this critical time in his life.

There were so many nurturing things to do. Spencer could feel the coolness and inhale the musty smell of the cellar.

With its hard-packed earthen floor, the shelves around the room were stacked high with cans and jars of home-cooked goods from pork chops to delicious treats like peach butter. And there was a springhouse with water running through it where a crock of milk was kept in it to keep it cool. He attended church one mile down the road with Uncle Stadden, who read from the Bible every day before breakfast. No one was allowed to touch one bite of food until he had finished reading.

Spencer would run barefoot up the sandy road and through the woods every day to the mailbox. It felt so good on his feet, he recalled—and then on Saturdays, they would go to the market in Winchester and take their eggs and homemade cakes. Spencer would work at the family grave plot on the farm, thinning out the overgrown honeysuckle. When Sunday came around, he wanted to do that instead of going to church. He pleaded with Uncle Stadden, but Uncle Stadden was adamant, "No sir! To church we will go."

"That way of life is gone now," Spencer mused.

But the relationships he developed with the land and with Uncle Stadden during that period of his life helped Spencer to cope with the anguish brewing at home.

During their time in Mexico, and for whatever personal reasons that may never be entirely known, Spencer's father had begun a relationship with a woman he met in London. From the onset of the Great Depression forward, his parents' marriage had been on rocky ground and Ian and Lucie fought quite a bit. The stress of the depression years, the war, Ian living in London, and Lucie off with the children in Mexico, all set the stage for a permanent breakup. Evidently, Ian's London affair lasted through the war years and not beyond. Still, he did not reveal his fling to Lucie while he was in England, even though he had begun to seek a divorce while overseas. Returning to the states, he did not again live with Lucie and the children, and he relentlessly pursued a divorce. He wanted out, and regardless of the true nature of their relationship, it certainly cannot be known now. Although divorce was the end goal for Ian, Lucie resisted the inevitable as long as she could.

Anger and words flew between the two, and Lucie became suicidal. According to Spencer, those were very "bleak and black times," and it was during this time that he developed an incapacitating stutter.

Eventually the inevitable happened and the MacCallums officially parted. The bickering during the divorce proceedings and the years after were exceedingly difficult times for Lucie and her sons. She had kept a detailed account of their adventures in letters to her husband over in London. Tragically, these were lost when Ian burned them sometime during their divorce proceedings.

Popdaddy had married for the second time to Ada Lee, and during this time her niece and namesake, Ada Lynes, had traveled over from London for a lengthy visit.

Popdaddy divorced Ada Lee in 1938 and afterwards wanted to spend more time in New York City. To do so, he hired his ex-wife's niece to manage a property for him. Known as Roadsend Gardens, it was a nursery enterprise of ornamental evergreens. As fate would have it, Ian (Spencer's father) met and began a relationship with Ada Lynes, eventually marrying her.

According to Spencer, his father had maintained a civil relationship with Popdaddy after his divorce from Lucie, although Spencer's brother, Crawfish, did not remember it as friendly. Ian eventually moved to the eastern shore of Maryland, continuing in semiretirement his architectural practice by restoring colonial-era homes.

Neither Spencer nor his brother Crawford enjoyed a warm relationship with their father after their parents divorced, and to Spencer, it seemed that his father's second wife, Ada Lynes, discouraged active family ties with his two sons. During this time, Lucie was unstable and felt humiliated that Ian had remarried soon after their divorce.

Spencer and Crawfish did not have much contact with their father. In fact, when their father died years later, it is Spencer's memory that Ada Lynes did not notify them, but that the news came from a family friend. Unceremoniously, and regardless of what they felt was this irresponsibility by Ada, the two sons showed up at their father's funeral.

In retrospect, and no matter the perceived wrongs, Spencer missed out on getting to know his father who had been a brilliant architect and a unique person of high intelligence. "It was obvious he had impeccable taste in the arts," Spencer lamented. To Spencer, this family drama of sadness haunted him for the rest of his life.

Lucie, Spencer, and Crawfish all experienced happiness, joy, and freedom for those two and half years in Mexico. It was difficult to face the harsh realities of the family break-up when they returned.

Even so, for the little band of wanderers off on a lark in a foreign country, that touch of joy ever remained with them, even though it was extremely difficult to replicate again. Spencer reflected that perhaps his father and mother were just simply mismatched. Still, he felt extreme sadness that he did not know his father well.

Spencer felt that he and Crawfish, descended from the MacCallums and the Heaths, had ancestry that fortified them with intelligence, aptitude, inquiry, and a love for the adventure of it all. And the fortitude and stamina to meet and conquer all challenges in life, and to keep moving forward.

Their lives from that point forward have proved that out.

Chapter Three

The Heaths; Popdaddy, Larger than Life

Spencer Heath, known as Popdaddy, and his ancestors were engaging figures in the family. His parents and grandparents had moved their family to northern Virginia before the Civil War. The land they farmed on Wolf Trap Creek was known as a "run" where wolves were actually trapped.

When the Civil War erupted in 1861, the fighting drew perilously close to the Virginia farmhouse.

Bullets ricocheted throughout the structure and narrowly missed family members hunkered down inside. The family made a quick decision and abruptly evacuated to Washington.

Granma Payne, Popdaddy's maternal grandmother, was lovingly known as a strong woman, a humanitarian, and a doctor. She could not sit by and do nothing when her fellow man needed help during the war.

She specialized in homeopathy and was arguably another of Spencer's family ancestors who exhibited greatness of vision despite obvious disadvantages against her, for not everyone in those days accepted homeopathy as a legitimate branch of medicine. Homeopathy stimulates the body to heal itself and was introduced in the United States in 1825.

Figure 9. Granma Payne was awarded a pension for her heroic work, photo circa 1860
Courtesy of the Spencer MacCallum Collection

Evidently, several European-educated doctors supported the practice and many schools popped up.

Opening this path of medicine to many people, the doctors were able to help thousands of patients who might not have been able to secure medical help.

During the middle of the 1800s, and against all odds at the time, women were allowed to enter these medical schools. [16]

The American Medical Association was founded in 1847 and by 1849 had already established a board to investigate what they represented to be "quack medicine."

According to Spencer, some folks at that time, including Granma Payne, viewed the AMA as using a long arm to eliminate competition, such as this branch of medicine. As such, Granma Payne was not allowed to practice in a hospital.

Not to be thwarted, she opened a private "hospital" in her home. She was allowed to take in only one sort of patient: those from the "dead rooms" of the hospitals where Civil War soldiers were left to die after all attempts to save them had been exhausted. Space was needed for those who might have a better chance of survival, so it seemed there could be no harm in allowing Granma Payne to take these men into her home.

The patients were sure to die anyway before too many hours or days passed. However, to the astonishment of the medical community, Granma Payne miraculously cured hundreds of soldiers at her home hospital. Part of her success may have been due to the fact that she demanded cleanliness in her hospital, as opposed to other facilities. She was one of the hundreds of women who came to the need of the sick and injured during the strife of the country.

Years later, a petition was made to Congress to recognize Granma Payne.

According to Spencer, many testimonial letters from patients and their families poured into Congress to validate her self-sacrificing efforts to save lives. [17]

After the war ended, the family returned to what remained of the family farm in Virginia.

The house had been used as horse stables by the Union troops, and after having served its usefulness, the troops burned it to the ground.

Before the family had hastily escaped to Washington, they had relied upon a long-time trusted servant to hide the family silver. In an ironic situation reminiscent of Spencer's paternal Grandfather MacCallum's hidden whiskey in a jailhouse brick wall, the family had instructed the servant to hide the silver in a stone wall on the farm. Upon returning to the land, the servant was not to be found and was presumed dead; however, there were miles and miles of stone walls on the farm.

It was labor-intensive and costly to tear down the wall to find the silver. It had been overwhelming just to rebuild their home.

But the storm gods intervened and about fifteen years later a tremendous storm sent crashes of electric energy down on the farm.

A bolt of lightning broke open a section of the stone wall, exposing the silver, blackened by age, and wrapped in wool socks that fell apart at the touch; but nonetheless, it was the family silver recovered. Six serving spoons and six teaspoons remained for years in Spencer MacCallum's possession.

It was three hundred years later that this land was bought by patroness Catherine Filene Shouse and was renamed Wolftrap Farm, in Vienna, Virginia. She then donated 100 acres of land to create the Wolftrap National Park for the performing arts. Their website today proclaims they are the only national park dedicated to presenting performing arts. [18]

Popdaddy grew up on that farm in Virginia. Born in Vienna, Virginia in 1876, he exhibited a strong bent for engineering at an early age. He would make waterwheels in the middle of the farm streams. He would tear apart and rebuild just about anything. His own grandfather always challenged him by saying, "Just supposin'. Just supposin' you *had* to do it?"

Popdaddy had a personal epiphany at an early age, and in his mind, he reasoned that it was not necessity that inspired man's greatest inventions, but beauty.

He expounded and followed this philosophy all through his life. A famous quote of his day was taken from a poem written by Ellen Sturgis Hooper (1812-1848). "I slept, and dreamed that life was Beauty. I woke, and found that life was Duty." He turned it around and often quoted, "I dreamed that life was duty, and woke and found that life was Beauty." At the age of 9, Heath was writing graduate-level essays that would rival that of any graduate student.

Music is sound falling in regular successive waves upon the ear, producing in the amateur an elevated feeling of calm serenity. Wonderful effects are produced by the power of music. There is music in nature, the strains of sweet melodies from birds, the roar of the ocean's surf, the murmuring of rippling brooks, and the low whistle of the evening breeze which touches the chords of our immortal souls, reverberating with beautiful music.

One day when he was around twelve years old, his mother left the house to run an errand. Concerned at leaving her innovative son home alone with a brand-new sewing machine that had just been delivered to the house, she cautioned her son, "Don't you touch this machine while I am gone." The second she disappeared around the corner he completely dismantled the entire machine bit by bit, meticulously laying out each part on the living room floor.

He then began to reassemble it. Just as he heard his mother's wagon returning from her errand, there was still yet a single spring that would not slide into place. But a miraculous "unseen third hand" appeared, and just at the last second before his mother walked through the door the spring found its rightful place in the sewing machine. He always claimed that his mother never knew of this fantastic engineering sleight of hand. Not surprisingly, Heath eventually obtained an engineering degree.

Alvin Lowi, who was an engineer and a friend of Heath's, wrote much about him. "Heath completed his technical training at the Corcoran Scientific School in Washington, D.C., then went to Chicago where he embarked on a career in electrical and mechanical engineering. In 1898 he married Johanna Maria Holm, suffragist and life-long friend of Susan B. Anthony. The couple made their home in Washington, D.C. where Heath worked for the Navy Department designing coaling stations around the world, and at the same time attended National University Law School at night. He eventually received his LL.M. (previously used as the current equivalent to a Master degree) and LL.B. (previously used as the current equivalent to a doctorate degree) and became a patent lawyer."

Popdaddy later built a home, Roadsend Gardens, in Elkridge, Maryland, where he experimented with horticulture and ornamental evergreens, and where he began writing. One of Popdaddy's important works was completed in

Figure 10. *Popdaddy sitting for a promotional sculpture circa 1945*
Courtesy of the Spencer MacCallum Collection

1946 and later published in 1957. The title, *Citadel, Market and Altar*, by Spencer Heath, is a work that addresses the major functions of a viable society. [19]

He also wrote about various social issues involving land ownership and societal issues and published works about land arguments, esthetics, creativity, and articles on aeronautical engineering, and creativity, some of which appeared in technical journals, and he became a notable figure in intellectual circles, even having his bust modeled for a display to promote his propeller company. These are the details, the facts. It is from grandson Spencer that we get a sense of Popdaddy's human nature. We learn that it was

Popdaddy who later had the most profound impact on his grandson, Spencer. Popdaddy was fascinating to his grandson, and sometimes amused Spencer with stories of his life. He told him that when he got his very first job in Chicago in the 1890s, he decided to celebrate. He took himself out to the best restaurant located within the best hotel of the day and ordered the most expensive item on the menu, even dessert. Splurging on whatever he wanted, he spent the grand sum of a quarter!

Popdaddy was smart and could see that world events were changing. McKinley had been inaugurated US President the year before in 1897 and Teddy Roosevelt was appointed as the Assistant U.S. Secretary of the Navy.

Roosevelt became a powerful figure in the McKinley administration. Part of Roosevelt's initiative was to establish America as a world power and one way to do so was to build a global Navy that could protect United States trade interests, all of which required worldwide coaling stations. Coaling Stations were necessary in the late 19th century so that steamships that burned coal could refuel en route.

The need for coaling stations was one of the reasons the U.S. annexed several islands during and after the Spanish American War, specifically Hawaii, Guam, and the Philippines. [20]

Heath wanted to be in a position to make money in war profits and was especially keen on whatever the Navy was doing.

He had graduated at the top of his class and had by this time become a patent attorney, capitalizing on his knowledge of engineering and his experience working for the government. His client list included Christopher Lake and his son, Simon, inventors of the even-keel-submerging submarine. Popdaddy soon became the Lake's partner and together they remained aware of what the Navy was up to.

Simon Lake, especially, was already deep into designing submarines. Inspired by Jules Verne's *Twenty Thousand Leagues Under the Sea*, Simon Lake designed and submitted plans to the Navy in 1892. In 1894 he built his first experimental submarine, the Argonaut, Jr., which was successfully demonstrated at Atlantic Highlands, New Jersey by Sandy Hook. [21] The success led to the formation of the Lake Submarine Company of New Jersey in 1895, which built the Argonaut. In 1898 it was the first submarine to operate successfully in the open sea. It subsequently drew a congratulatory telegram from Jules Verne himself.

While my book *Twenty Thousand Leagues Under the Sea* is entirely a work of imagination, my conviction is that all I wrote in it will come to pass.

A thousand-mile voyage in the Baltimore submarine boat (The Argonaut) is evidence of this. This conspicuous success of submarine navigation in the United States will push on underwater navigation all over the world. If such a successful test had come a few months earlier it might have played a great part in the Spanish American War. The next great war may be largely a contest between submarine boats.

Submarine navigation is now ahead of aerial navigation and will advance much faster from now on. Before the United States gains her full development, she is likely to have mighty navies not only on the bosom of the Atlantic and Pacific but in the upper air and beneath the water's surface.

Jules Verne

Behind the scenes, and according to Popdaddy as told to Spencer, the Lakes were trying to compete for the government contracts and asked Heath to gain the attention of the Washington bureaucrats. When unsuccessful, the Lakes approached various governments in Europe, as did other shipbuilders of the time. Popdaddy told Spencer that the Lakes were unashamedly wined and dined by the German government but were finally informed that Germany could not use their invention. However, the Germans simply took the Lakes' ideas and developed their own even-keel submarine, which, according to Heath, almost cost the allies World War I. This was the first of many incidents forecasting a long adversarial relationship between Heath and the American government's war department.

In 1908 Emile Berliner, who had already made a couple of fortunes developing a receiver for the telephone, as well as the flat disc phonograph record, became a client. He thought he could make a third fortune helping design and develop a helicopter.

In partnership with Heath, they developed a propeller for the uplift of the machine, the Paragon Propeller. Today, there is a display at the Smithsonian Museum of a collection of propellers designed and manufactured by Heath, along with Heath's and Berliner's early models of their helicopter propellers. [22]

Heath was by this time hooked on aerodynamics, and he bought a building in Baltimore and constructed a plant.

When Heath set up his business in Baltimore, it was a seafaring town and they, of course, knew all about ship propellers, but not aircraft propellers. He went around to establish credit at the hardware and lumber stores. But when it was discovered that he was making airship propellers, not sea ship propellers, his credit was instantly cut off. What a fool that Heath was!

As it turned out, he never needed that credit because things took off fast.

Prior to World War I, Heath produced the first mass machine-produced propellers, and soon established research, development and manufacturing facilities for various aeronautical specialties.

His company, American Propeller and Mfg. Co., supplied more than three-quarters of the propellers used by the Allied governments in World War I.

Heath's mind worked with an uncanny ability. He could design machinery in his mind, and then would run tests at different RPMs to discover the strengths and weaknesses of his invention. He would put his idea right into production. He was far ahead of his time and even after America entered the war, he was so self-confident in his inventions that he maintained and continued an open-door policy at his propeller plant to anyone who came to visit.

He was once asked, "Doesn't your competition come in and inspect the plant in order to follow what you are doing?" His reply was keen and amusing. "Yes, they do follow me. That's what keeps them behind me, where they belong."

Though there was not much American military interest in air flight before the war, there was a notable customer of Heath's who was interested: King Vajiravudh, then King of Siam, was a great experimenter of air flight. He was Heath's principal customer before World War I, and soon, because the King of Siam was such a good customer, Heath gave up his practice as a patent lawyer. He enjoyed the King's company and intelligence.

The King of Siam was astute. Having been educated in England, he understood the importance of bringing Thailand into the technology of the day.

King Vajiravudh was born in Bangkok on January 1, 1881. Following the death of his elder half-brother in 1895, he was appointed Crown Prince. In England, he developed a great love for literature. He devised a system of transliteration of Thai into English and translated the many works of Shakespeare into Thai.

On July 11, 1917, Siam declared war on the Central Powers, thus entering the conflict on the side of the Allies. In June of the following year, an Expeditionary Force of twelve hundred Thai men, including an aviation contingent numbering about three hundred and forty, was sent to France, the only Asian soldiers to take part in the war on the Allied side.

Thai pilots flew only a few operational missions toward the end of the fighting. Then more than 100 Thai officers were sent to flying schools at Istres and Avord air bases in France, of whom ninety-five qualified as military pilots and received advanced training in observation.

The King needed a lot of propellers.

As World War I loomed, the government suddenly took notice of Heath's propellers and air flight in general. Franklin Delano Roosevelt was Assistant Secretary of the Navy from 1913 to 1920. He introduced cost-plus invoicing to military suppliers, but Heath was against this new method, reasoning that this stymied competition. This further darkened Heath's relationship with the government.

Figure 11. Popdaddy and the Paragon Propellers story,
Santa Ana, California, spring 1961
Courtesy of the Spencer MacCallum Collection

He could see that the government of that time, and he, did not see eye to eye. Not only that, but when the United States entered the war, furniture manufacturers of the day had large inventories of unwanted mahogany on hand.

They couldn't sell their furniture and thought that a good place to use mahogany was in airplane propellers. Heath fought the idea, knowing that mahogany was not strong enough material to withstand the aerodynamics of flight, and he would demonstrate this fact by snapping planks of Mahogany wood in the bureaucratic faces.

He pleaded for natural Maryland oak, which, he explained, was as strong as steel itself.

In a 1920 promotional pamphlet of the American Propeller Company, the properties of oak were stated as the material of choice for the Paragon propellers.

Still, Heath and the war department continued an antagonist relationship. He once discovered a fatal flaw in a set of government specs for a new propeller design, causing the propellers to break apart in flight at the cost of many lives. When he advised the government that he could not make the propellers according to their specs, they threatened, "You'll make them or be shot!" It was wartime. Disobeying the government had serious consequences. Heath made the propellers under the watchful eyes of the government inspectors.

The night before the propellers were to be shipped, crates of them sat on the loading dock. In the dark of night, he and a helper went down to the waterfront and with crowbars, hammers, and nails, pried open the crates. For days, Heath had been guarding his own secret weapon:

a rubber stamp he had made in anticipation of this night. He stamped each and every propeller with the words, "Made under protest. Condemned by the manufacturer." He then resealed the crates. Heath had fulfilled his obligation in making the propellers and in shipping them. According to Heath, he was able to track the propellers to a government storage facility somewhere in Texas. As far as he could determine, the propellers were never used. Their final fate is unknown.

Whether or not these propellers have been destroyed by now or still exist in the vast hinterland of government waste is uncertain.

Still in existence, however, are the thousands of documents and artifacts related to Popdaddy's propeller business.

Evan Davies, director and founder of the Institute of Historical Survey Foundation, Las Cruces, New Mexico (IHSF), and Spencer had a long friendship, and when the time came for Spencer and his wife, Emi, to move to Mexico, Spencer asked Evan to take Popdaddy's historical documents and artifacts pertaining to the propellers.

In the years following, Evan and his staff began what is now more than a ten-year project to classify and store this treasure chest of information.

The IHSF serves as a major resource for educational researchers with vast, diverse historical collections. "From historical documents to archival photographs, images and sound recordings, the mission is to acquire, conserve and share historical artifacts for education, research and production." [23]

Also included in this treasure trove are small propellers made into clocks, which Popdaddy made for friends and family. During this time, the propeller business was a family business. Living in Baltimore, Maryland, home to the propeller business, Heath's wife Marie worked at the propeller plant as the bookkeeper. Marie Holm Heath, along with her childhood friend Susan B. Anthony, had been very active in the women's movement around the turn of the century. Marie had been a secretary to a U.S. Admiral and was well-known in the movement before she married Heath. The MacCallum family has books inscribed by Susan B. Anthony passed down to them from his grandfather.

Heath the engineer, patent attorney, inventor, and businessman had now become widely known to business associates as Popdaddy—a smart man with good ideas who was clever about money. He began to perceive worrisome signs in the economy. Fortunately, Popdaddy sold his propeller business and his patents to Bendix Aviation only a few weeks before the stock market crash of 1929, then worked for them for two years as an engineer.

Figure 12. Small propeller clock that Popdaddy made as gifts
Photo © Courtesy of Institute of Historical Survey Foundation

But Bendix did not need or want the name Paragon so it became a lasting legacy, not only to his grandson Spencer, but to his great-grandchildren as well. A new Paragon company emerged. The Chairman and CEO was Taber MacCallum, son of Spencer's brother, Crawfish. Taber honored his great-grandfather, William Spencer Heath, by using this name.

Taber MacCallum co-founded an aerospace company, Paragon Space Development Corporation, and he and his wife, Jane Poynter, were two of the team of eight scientists who lived for two years in the first sealed biosphere.

Taber is known to have the facility to visualize a mechanical piece of machinery and its entire structure and operating systems in his mind, exactly like Popdaddy. In his family life, Popdaddy and Grandmother Marie Holm were married for twenty years and had three daughters. Like the family of Susan B. Anthony, Popdaddy came from a Quaker and Unitarian background. He and his family attended the Unitarian Church in Baltimore, which could likely be the place where the two young women, Susan B Anthony and Marie Holm Heath, became friends.

Popdaddy doted on his three daughters, often buying them presents and dolls. He took the three daughters to a department store to pick out a doll. Lucile chose a doll in the image of the Kaiser's baby. The baby was known to have a deformity in the face and, true to likeness, so did the doll. [24]

When The Kaiser found out about these dolls, he was outraged at this insult, rudeness, and invasion of the family's privacy. He had all the dolls collected in order to destroy them. However, one shipment of these dolls had made it to the United States and Lucile had picked out one of them! As Popdaddy moved on with his life, he and Marie eventually divorced. Heath then married Ada Lee who had moved from Britain to Baltimore and worked as a cashier in a local restaurant. That marriage ended in 1938. He had no other children and did not marry again. She was the aunt of Ada Lynes, who later married Ian MacCallum, Spencer's father.

Figure 13. Lucile and the Kaiser Doll, circa 1909
Courtesy of the Spencer MacCallum Collection

The property that Heath had purchased after the war was a hundred acres in Elkridge, South of Baltimore. Heath created Roadsend Gardens as an evergreen nursery to furnish the nursery stock.

It was an enchanting place, but before he could get the project off the ground, a utility easement for giant poles had been created by eminent domain.

But it was not long before Heath's dream began to turn into a nightmare.

According to Spencer, "The land was going to be host to giant steel poles and powerlines marching across the landscape. It ruined the dream for my grandfather."

Still, Heath continued to grow ornamental evergreens as a commercial nursery until after World War II.

After retirement, he began to spend more and more time at his apartment in New York City, developing his ideas about social organization. Interested in "everything," Heath studied math, science, philosophy, and horticulture, as well as his professions of engineering and law.

He often remarked that the difference between a horticulturist and a farmer was that one made his living in the country and spent it in the city and the other made his living in the city and spent it in the country. Intrigued by science and fascinated by society, Heath wanted to meld the two into a successful model for humanity, to develop a science of society.

Of course, there were already the social sciences, but Heath wanted to depart from that description and form his own studies of "socionomy."

Popdaddy told Spencer that he had been awakened on the philosophical level by socialism in the late 1890s. Describing those early years, Heath admitted that for about six months he had been "a flaming socialist," but quickly discerned with his engineering mind that the model of socialism offered at that time could not work. He continued to look for a social model of equality that would.

Heath discovered the Henry George movement, which was very strong on free trade.

Though Heath had been attracted to Georgism, he himself was not in favor of taxes of any sort and became at odds with the followers of Henry George. He was very disappointed in the group.

Georgists wanted to rid the world of the big, bad wolf. Heath was trying to understand it.

Around 1938 he traveled to England and was considered as a possible candidate to head up the international Georgist movement. This never took place, though around the same time he bequeathed in his will a sum of money to the Georgist movement with a stipulation that the money not be used in an adversarial position against landlords. Spencer laughed that this was Popdaddy's sense of humor. The prior forced utility easement on his Roadsend Gardens had a deep impact on Popdaddy's thoughts about social reorganization. He felt that more legislation meant less freedom for the people.

Popdaddy was very involved in these social issues when, at the same time, he appeared larger than life in Spencer's world, and much later, Spencer took up the call of Popdaddy.

As a young adult, Spencer was experiencing traumatic emotional problems in his life while attending Princeton. By that time the stuttering brought on by his parent's divorce had become a major speech impediment, and he was a loner. As a heavy rock with just enough weight is placed on a teetertotter to unbalance it, Spencer found himself under the heavy load of serious depression.

His literature class had been studying Franz Kafka's novel, *The Trial*. Schools of thought consider Kafka's work surreal and even ridiculous, while others try to determine a deeper meaning in the writings.

The argument of the book in allegorical terms was that man does not deserve to live as a human being until he has actually gone through the act of cutting his throat.

Spencer had been wrestling with this idea. What did it mean? Kafka's character had a dream in which he was expected to slit his own throat, but because he did not have the courage to do so, it was done for him, and so he died "like a dog."

Spencer could not see a way out of the dilemma as Kafka had put it. Worse, here was Spencer, a loner at Princeton, with low self-esteem and a suffering stutterer, all of which retarded his ability to be a part of and communicate with the world. And he was hearing that he was "guilty" just because he existed as a human.

In retrospect, Spencer knew that he had taken the book far too literally—and seriously; however, this book, on top of his personal problems, sank him into a deep depression.

Then came one of the major turning points in his life. Popdaddy, in his 80's at the time, paid him a surprise visit. The grand old man sat in Spencer's Yucatan string hammock drawn across Spencer's dorm room. Popdaddy was a large man in stature and in presence.

He was well-educated, a philosopher and thinker, and wealthy. He was an author, an inventor, a public speaker, and a shaker and a mover in New York City.

Figure 14. *The handsome young man, Spencer MacCallum, at Andover, 1950*
Courtesy of the Spencer MacCallum Collection

Heath really did seem larger than life to Spencer. He moved within intellectual circles of wealth and influence and had an aura of power about him.

Although Spencer's mother Lucie had felt dominated by him, Spencer now felt in awe of him.

They talked all night until the morning light broke through the window curtains. Heath was a life raft to the young man who was adrift in a fog of confusion. Spencer began to see light for the first time in a very long time, as Popdaddy could explain complex things in simplistic ways. It was Popdaddy who became the single most influential person in his grandson's life, especially after rescuing him when, as a college sophomore, he had become dangerously depressed.

Popdaddy imbued the essence of the stalwart Heaths and steadfastly stood on the bridge between the paternal side of the ancestors and his descendants.

Greatly influenced by Popdaddy, and grateful for bringing him up out of the vortex of despair, Spencer found he had a new, self-described mission in life—one of finding and bringing to light Popdaddy's writings, teachings, and philosophies. Although it could be said that Spencer accomplished this by using the vehicle of ideas, just as did Popdaddy, Spencer also became a vehicle himself.

He was able to touch greatness wherever he found it, and with a keen spark just in the right place enlighten it with life and vitality and purpose—and those whom he discovered knew they had just been touched by the greatness of Spencer himself.

Spencer believed that he was the only person in the family who took a serious interest in the work of his visionary grandfather. It seems that grandfather and grandson were destined to have a strong alliance, although Grandfather Heath's regular quip about buying and paying for Spencer did become a standing joke for the family. Grandfather Heath later would proudly state, "It was the best investment I ever made."

With the dawn came the light of understanding. Popdaddy could seemingly explain anything to his namesake.

Spencer finally understood that Kafka's character had felt an emotional burden of the human dilemma extending back to the beginning of the human race, for the sins against the human race. That it was only when one could cut through the entanglements of the mind that one could see the truth. To progress toward truth, a person had to diminish everything else, including the ego.

Before Popdaddy arrived that night, Spencer had had it in his mind that Kafka proposed this throat-cutting be taken literally.

However, Popdaddy advised Spencer to always look at things in context. The history of the human race is fraught with great achievements, as well as appalling atrocities. Looking within, man carries a heavy burden for humanity, but this is also a strong motivation for people to serve and uplift mankind in whatever way possible.

This night with Popdaddy was astounding to Spencer. He heard incredible thoughts and ideas not expressed by anyone else, including his teachers at Princeton. Spencer realized that Popdaddy was someone he could learn from, someone he could listen to. Popdaddy had solved Spencer's predicament and became his emancipator. He fascinated Spencer, and grandfather and grandson became close. But

Spencer's incapacitating stutter became a challenge for his new savior. His stutter had begun as a phobic fear of words. "You can see them coming, and you know you're not going to be able to say that word. My throat would be raw from trying to form a word. I was very immature, and I think I also used the stuttering as a crutch to avoid social situations."

Popdaddy found a clinic that could help. Asking Spencer if he would care to take a year out of Princeton, he arranged for him to use his New York apartment in Greenwich Village, which was walking distance from the speech therapy school, at that time known as the National Hospital for Speech Disorders. Spencer settled into the new surroundings. He had the incentive to cure himself and worked hard at speech therapy. Having met a girl the previous year at Andover, he set a goal to be able to visit her and her family the next summer in the Midwest without stuttering.

He accomplished that goal, but even in adulthood when he was under stress, the stutter would come back.

"That's a flag that I'm under stress. I have to change my immediate environment to prevent it from happening." That year spent at Greenwich Village became a time of maturing, changing, and growing, and emancipation from his debilitating stuttering.

When he returned to Princeton after a year of speech therapy, Spencer began to shine.

Chapter Four

Princeton; More Treasures
Discovered; Popdaddy the Savior;
Summer Adventures
During College

Spencer attended prep school from 1946-1950 at the Phillips Academy, also known as Andover. It was a boys' school until 1973 when it became a coeducational independent boarding high school, located about twenty miles north of Boston.

At the beginning of his Andover years, he had been interested in the archaeology program, but his interest soon waned. "In comparison, the archaeology of New England had little of the rich art that characterized that of Mesoamerica. I was beginning to feel that archaeology was more Lucie's thing and not my thing." It was a natural rebellion, of sorts. As a rite of passage, he wanted to distance himself from the childhood circumstances of fulfilling Lucie's ambitions for him. Although later he would come back to the arena of his first love when he studied anthropology. Archaeology, which is focused more on the study of material remains was where he began, but his heart was leaning toward anthropology, which focused on the social and cultural aspects of prehistoric and historic peoples.

Spencer felt he wanted to branch out and learn something new. When he returned to Princeton, he spent a lot of time looking through the Princeton catalog and happened upon one area of study he had not previously considered: Art History. Later there would come the time when he would be required to write a thesis. As he was searching for a topic, he was told by a professor that at the Guyot Hall Museum of Natural History was a treasure awaiting to be newly discovered, as it had been ignored for years. He made fast tracks to the building and made a discovery that was there for the taking.

According to Spencer, in the basement was a display gathering dust of Northwest Coast Indian art. It was a fine collection and as it turned out, it really had been "lost." Scholars knew the collection existed, but it seems that no one knew where it had been "stored." The Reverend Sheldon Jackson had gathered the collection, and after his death, his estate had donated a large part of his collection to the Presbyterian Seminary in Princeton, New Jersey, and the remaining collection to the Sheldon Jackson Museum in Sitka, Alaska.

A Presbyterian missionary, he had served as General Agent for Education in Alaska in the 1890s and in that capacity had made annual trips to Alaska, traveling extensively throughout the region. He took collecting seriously, acquiring nearly five thousand items during his travels.

While others were also collecting in Alaska and sending their items to noted museums, universities, and societies around the world, Dr. Jackson was the only one who collected pieces for an Alaskan museum. The Sheldon

Jackson Museum was founded in 1887 to house the collection, and is in Sitka, Alaska. [25]

This museum's collection today is noted for its breadth. Among its best-known pieces are totems, Eskimo masks, Tlingit, Eskimo, Aleut and Athabaskan baskets, and traditional clothing noted for its beautiful ornamentation and fine sewing.

The Reverend Jackson had first traveled to Alaska in 1877 to continue his missionary work with Alaskan Native peoples. While there he founded several schools and work training centers. He was concerned that native cultures would disappear, so he collected artifacts from the various Native peoples in Alaska.

According to Spencer, at that time these artifacts were considered curios or artifacts, not art. At some point, Guyot Hall, where they were to be displayed, was to be remodeled, and someone had put the collection in the basement out of the way. It was never returned to Guyot Hall, and over time the collection was forgotten. For Spencer, it was exciting to rediscover this rare collection, an event reminiscent of the Mexico days when he was discovering rare jade beads and other ancient artifacts. He decided to pursue this theme as his thesis. This was just what he needed at the time, an exciting archaeological find, even if in a museum!

Majoring in Art History, with his personal focus on Native American art, Spencer learned a great deal about ceramics, as well as other material artifacts. He further expanded this interest when he moved to Washington State to attend the University's Northwest Coast Indians program.

All of which helped his ensuing career.

The professor in the Department of Art & Archaeology at Guyot Hall gave Spencer complete access to the collection. Spencer cleaned it, painted the display cases, and organized the collection. He understood that it was unusual for a New World thesis to be allowed by the art history department because, up to that time, most had been about European histories. The professor went to bat for Spencer and fought to get permission for him to write his thesis on this subject.

Early in his final Spring semester Spencer went to New York, fifty miles away on the train, and stayed at his Grandfather's Greenwich Village apartment located at 11 Waverly Place to work on his thesis. Each day he would go to the New York Public Library and stay there until they kicked him out at night.

At the library, he became totally absorbed in the Northwest Coast Indians. This study helped to educate Spencer on the similarities of many tribes in the United States and Mexico. Some might even say this was part of Spencer's destiny – by understanding the anthropological and archaeological connections, Spencer was able to identify great artistic talent when he saw it.

When he returned to Princeton, he had missed the entire first half of the semester and almost failed for flagrant neglect. One of his courses was in Anglo-Saxon literature and the class was currently studying *Beowulf*, one of the oldest surviving epic poems in what is identifiable as an early form of the English language.

Spencer had some fast explaining to do about his absence to the professor, so thinking on his feet, he explained that from his research of the Northwest Coast Indians, he had learned how to understand the extreme boasting of *Beowulf*, and the difference between public and private boasting. He had concluded that *Beowulf*, like Native Americans, boasted for the sake of their public image.

Throughout *Beowulf*, boasting is presented as a key component of one's reputation, a valid way to assert one's position in a hierarchy determined by deeds of valor.

Beowulf's boasting increases his honor and raises the level of expectations for both those around him and the reader. The gods were with him. Remarkably, the professor gave him the benefit of the doubt. Spencer escaped with barely passing grades.

But it was all worth it as Spencer's collection was considered a great success. Later, in 1961, Erna Gunther displayed it at the Seattle World's Fair. Gunther was an anthropologist, and chairman, of the University of Washington for six decades. [26]

Gunther (1896-1982) was called upon to organize the indigenous art exhibit, having served as director of the Washington State Burke Museum for thirty-one years. This exhibition was one of many that she planned and prepared.

Gunther was perhaps most widely known for mounting exhibits of Northwest Coast arts and cultivating a public appreciation for the aesthetics of these cultures. She visited museums and art collections throughout the world and asked them to lend some of their pieces for an exhibition. Spencer's collection was one of those, and he was proud that the Princeton Art Museum is today noted for two exceptional collections. One was a collection formed by his friend, Gillett G. Griffin, in the 1960s of Olmec ceramics and jades, and the other distinguished collection is the one Spencer found under years of dust.

Spencer's collection was on exhibit from January 22 through March 2, 1969, titled Art of the Northwest Coast, along with the Illustrated Catalogue of Exhibit written by Spencer.

Continuing his journey as a discoverer, Spencer recalls another significant find. "I had heard that a Florida gentleman in his 90s had several exceptional collections I might be interested in. I went to see him, primarily to view a rare art collection of remarkable 19th-century Haida argillite carvings. Argillite is a sedentary rock used by the indigenous people for carvings. It became a very popular art form and is often inlaid with other stones. The Haida have occupied the archipelago off of Canada's northern Pacific coast for at least the past eight thousand years, according to archaeological evidence. I was astounded by the beauty and artistry of this collection.

"He also had priceless pieces of paper handwritten in the 1830s by Colonel Benjamin Reynolds. He was a U.S. agent for the Chickasaw Indians, and together with a delegation from their people traveled west of Arkansas to explore and select a new and permanent residence for them. Reynolds was instrumental in arranging the Treaty of Pontotoc of 1832." [27]

Colonel Reynolds had made a similar expedition the previous year and for his second expedition, his superiors instructed him to take a second group of Chickasaws on this journey. The journal of his first year was known. "But this, the second journal, had been lost," said Spencer. "I held it in my hands in Florida and was just in awe. In the journal, the Colonel recounted the difficult time he had in trying to protect the Indians. The settlers considered them sub-human and the good Colonel did the best he could to feed and clothe them and protect them from the locals.

You had to admire him for what he was up against in that day and time," Spencer reflected.

Also in the man's collection were two editions of the *Cherokee Phoenix* newspaper, in both Cherokee and English. The Cherokee script had been developed by the Cherokee Chief Sequoyah around 1928. Spencer admired Sequoyah, and later when he met Juan Quezada, Spencer saw a close parallel between the two men's accomplishments in teaching themselves their skills.

In anthropology, Sequoyah's accomplishment is considered to be an intellectual high watermark in human history. He was an intellectual, but totally unlettered. Sequoyah was impressed that the traders and others could communicate thoughts with marks on paper and decided it could be done with the Cherokee language. Sequoyah was living with his wife in a log home on their farm and had all his notes there, but it was taking a very long time for him to write the Cherokee language. His wife was doing all the work on the farm. According to legend, the situation took a toll on his family life, and she burned the house, and his precious papers, to the ground.

Spencer said, "But Sequoyah persisted, and indeed, not long after the fire he succeeded. In a relatively short time, most of the Cherokee became literate. Sequoyah assumed he could create an entire written language, and he did." [28]

Spencer bought the entire collection, paying him ten thousand dollars for it.

The man was shocked at the good price. Having only about another six months to live, and tremendous medical expenses to pay, he had been happy to sell it. Spencer later sold the Reynolds journal and the Sequoyah papers to the Princeton University Library and Spencer reflected, "It was as much pleasure placing something well as it was in finding it."

During his college years, Popdaddy continued to have a beneficial influence on Spencer. He was the mentor, and his grandson the student. As Spencer moved out of his clumsy shyness and stuttering, he began to emerge as a man who was eager to learn what the world had to offer.

Popdaddy began to expound to Spencer the ideas of a practical society without a governmental structure as we know it. Spencer thought it was strange. It was certainly foreign to everything he had been taught. But his grandfather, who was a success in law, engineering, manufacturing, and business, as well as Spencer's savior and mentor, was passionate about these new ideas. Popdaddy had been working on a book about them, *Citadel, Market and Altar,* and had not found a publisher. Soon Spencer made a commitment to Popdaddy that when he graduated from Princeton, he would help him self-publish the book and they did.

Spencer said he was very slow to mature through prep school and college and did not like to think what his life would have been without his grandfather. To Spencer, it was obvious that they were meant to be together in this lifetime.

Spencer and Popdaddy would attend Sunday services at the Unitarian Church in New York City. Popdaddy and the minister were friends and would often discuss philosophy, or what they would call "Trinitarianism." Heath would expound on science and felt that events had three measurable aspects: mass, motion, and time. He would compare these to the three aspects of the trinity: substance, power, and eternity. In Popdaddy's mind, they exactly corresponded with each other, and he thought that many spiritual leaders on the planet had intuited this "fact." So it was that Popdaddy moved through life, seeking, wondering out loud, and thinking through the problems of society. This carried through and impacted Spencer's way of thinking also.

Popdaddy's main area of interest was creativity, which he equated with spirituality in the form of inspiration.

Heath had seen at an early age that sensitivity to beauty was a prime catalyst to stimulate creativity.

Combining his thoughts on these two categories, Heath authored and spoke on "The Spiritual Life of Free Men," seeing Jesus as a forerunner and leader in the science of society, teaching humans the principles of how to behave toward each other and live properly with one another. Spencer saw the wisdom in this philosophy and tried to implement these principles in his own life, and his life's work later on.

Heath and Spencer both seemed to posit that when mankind was inspired by beauty, there was less need for policing, rules and government as we know it because man's actions were spurred by a higher place of consciousness. However, when there was no inspiration but only the rote routine of life, man became desperate, depressed, unimaginative, and dull. Heath wanted to help liberate the higher, creative artist within every man. This message, and goal, was deeply instilled within Spencer.

Spencer did promote these ideas and wrote that the great significance of this universal principle was how it manifested in society. His research had shown that while this is a universal principle all over the world, many cultures have adopted a negative form of the principle. Spencer pointed out that simply not harming another person did not help that person.

But if one was actually "doing something" for someone, then a lot of good could come from that activity.

Figure 15. Popdaddy, circa 1960
Courtesy of the Spencer MacCallum Collection

Of utmost importance was how an individual wanted to be treated. Spencer saw that this principle was a basic component of private enterprise. Serving others and having regard for their wishes is how success could be found. One of Spencer's main goals in life had been to bring his grandfather's thoughts into the mainstream discussion on social organization by publishing papers and giving speeches. Because Heath did not circulate in the world of academia, there were no students to follow and pursue his work; but Spencer saw the brilliance of his grandfather's ideas and during his adult life promoted them wherever possible.

Popdaddy once told Spencer that there was only one area in which his grandson would disappoint him and that would be if Spencer did not carry and develop Popdaddy's own ideas further. This could have motivated Spencer to make this his life mission as well.

Another area of focus was the philosophy of science, and Heath felt that this was really his most important area of contribution. At the turn of the century, science had turned to the physics of energy.

Heath explored the physics of action. He felt that science could be greatly simplified by understanding the whole, rather than the part. During his life, Spencer wrote and spoke on these ideas himself.

Spencer's grandfather was a person who loved nothing more than to think. It was his recreation. He would take a problem, like—what is light? He would talk about how light had two properties, not only the speed of light but also self-propagation. These things intrigued him. He loved using his mind. Shortly before he died, he said to his best friend, Al Lowi, and to Spencer, "You're going to have all the fun. But you have to make way for the young shoots to come up."

Spencer noted that Popdaddy had a complex life. He had enough money to travel, but he mused that he could sit in his armchair and travel all over the world in his imagination. He had friends everywhere and spent a lot of time traveling in his big car to several cities as an entertaining houseguest.

"Later on, a friend of the family would come down from Princeton to visit," said Spencer. "He loved to argue any point with Popdaddy. They would sit in the little kitchen around the table. Even if Popdaddy had a cold and wasn't at his best, they would talk all night long. Popdaddy would get so stirred up, he'd be cured by morning!"

Those Princeton years were turning points in Spencer's life: Popdaddy swooping down to rescue him from despair, fixing his stuttering and instilling social and philosophical ideas in the young mind of his grandson. Spencer finding major archaeological collections during those years was instrumental to his psychological makeup. All of this, plus his youthful summer adventures during his college years, helped to set the stage for what followed later, an event that had an impact on thousands of people and the world.

As Spencer finally emerged from his shell, the summers between college semesters for both him and older brother Crawford filled their lives once again with adventure. They had tasted it, lived it, and breathed it as kids; now as young adults, the past few years were behind them, and they could once again enjoy exciting expeditions into life.

It was in their blood, and Lucie's, too.

In a profound moment of understanding, Spencer realized that adventure was not something you did just on vacation, it was a mindset; and this awareness became a pivotal footing of his personality and character. It informed his life going forward.

By this time, Crawford was attending Lawrenceville School, a prep school in Lawrenceville, New Jersey. Come summer, it was time to break out! The brothers were both eager to hit the road.

During the summer break, the family went on an adventure to Santa Fe, New Mexico. Lucie worked in the gift shop at the famous La Fonda Hotel while Spencer and Crawford worked as busboys in the dining room.

Spencer recalls that to strengthen his handhold while handling huge trays of dishes, the busboys would dunk a napkin in water and wrap it around their wrist. That worked pretty well. It was the swinging door that gave Spencer a problem. One day he was walking from the dining room into the kitchen and the swinging door came back at him too fast and hit the tray.

"It was a very prolonged cascade of China falling to the floor. They all broke, of course. I will never forget it. What a memorable evening for everyone in the restaurant!" He thought he would be fired immediately. But the house detective had a shine on his mother, and he went to the cook and convinced him not to fire Spencer.

The two brothers ended the summer on a high note by taking a trip to the Grand Canyon. They made their way down to Albuquerque then headed west and finally arrived at the Grand Canyon. They had planned to hike to the bottom and take the mule train back to the top, but there had been fierce summer storms and the mule trains weren't running. Crawfish wanted to go to the bottom anyway, so they separated. Crawfish hiked all the way down, while Spencer explored the rim.

The brothers had little money and were winging it by literally camping out—Crawfish at the bottom and

Spencer at one of the viewing areas on the rim. They each had a blanket, but even though it was hot at the bottom, Spencer at the rim almost froze because it turned very cold each night. Finally, Spencer crawled under a concrete table in one of the viewing areas. He could hear critters prowling about. It was a very cold and scary night. But the trip was all worth it, many times over, as it was near the end of their vacation, and they soon returned to Santa Fe to reunite with Lucie. She had wanted to make one purchase before they returned to their respective homes—a nice piece of Indian jewelry. Spencer had that bracelet for years and discovered it had a lot of value when she purchased it, and even more as time went by.

As unrelated as this may seem, this became yet another link for Spencer to Mexico. Later, in 1994, Spencer and his wife Emi were living in Pine Hill, New Mexico, close to Zuni. Spencer wanted to find out about this bracelet so one day he carried it to Zuni.

In Zuni he was directed to the Gallup area. There he would find Mickey Vanderwagon.

Mickey was a trader at the Yah-Ta-Hey Trading Post just north of the city. Mickey informed Spencer that the bracelet was indeed very fine workmanship. In fact, it was of the quality he would have in his own private collection. Mickey concluded that two different artists had crafted the bracelet and, amazingly, he knew by looking at the piece of jewelry by whom it was made and in what year it had been made. He knew the silversmith's name and the stone carver's name. At that time, around 1980, Mickey thought it would be worth about two thousand dollars.

Spencer introduced Mickey to the art and story of Mata Ortiz and the men soon became friends. In later years, Mickey traveled with Spencer to Mata Ortiz numerous times to buy pottery. Mickey became interested in helping to establish a silversmith trade in Mata Ortiz and helped to initiate a new jewelry business.

Back in Andover, and during Spencer's second summer, he wanted to go on an adventure in South America. Lucie had taken a job in Colombia, South America for a year, teaching children of American engineers in an oil camp. The plan was for Spencer to work on a boat for his passage. This was not only a necessity—it would be another adventure.

Spencer wrote letters to various steamship companies and most of them rejected his offer. However, one company referred Spencer to the owner of a banana boat. A deal was made, and Spencer traveled on his own from Andover to New Orleans to wait for the boat to head out across the seas.

It was a long ten days, and he stayed at the Catholic Maritime Club, which Spencer remembers was a very clean flophouse for seamen. While there, the older men took him under their wing, as well as to the bars. They introduced him to the ways of the seafaring world while drydocked. They periodically sent him out to check on the whereabouts of the police. Even though the men had fun with Spencer, he remembers that the evening turned serious when the men decided to impress upon him the importance of finishing college, so he would not turn out like them. To Spencer, this was a true example of how strangers can really care about other strangers. It touched him, and he did not forget it.

The boat arrived and the crew unloaded the bananas and got ready to sail. Spencer recalls that working on the boat was extremely difficult. One of his jobs was to hammer rust from the deck to prepare it for painting. During the week-long trip, an older fellow befriended him and taught him how to wash his clothes and look out for himself.

Before they got to Guayaquil, Ecuador, his friend told him that the city was the "pearl of the Pacific," but from Spencer's perspective, it was anything but. His friend was eager to visit the cantinas, which were easy to find by just looking down the dusty streets for a white electric Norge refrigerator sitting outside their doors.

Better than a sign, this advertised that cold drinks were inside. As the sailors approached, the women of the houses sat in the windows and beckoned to them.

Spencer was taken to a cantina and there was a beautiful girl who sat next to him, swinging her leg against him. In his naiveté, Spencer thought she was trying to keep her balance.

His fellow seaman asked Spencer if he wanted to sleep with her. But Spencer at least knew enough to know that venereal disease was rampant, so he declined. After a lot of teasing, the sailors drove him back to the boat and then they returned to the cantina!

By this time, bananas were being loaded by the dock workers all night long by lantern light, but Spencer was now the only seaman on the boat as everyone else was on shore.

He recalls that he must have even disappointed himself by refusing the beautiful senorita.

After Lucie had traveled to Columbia, and before Spencer had departed on the banana boat, there was news of conflict in Columbia. Spencer had assumed that she was not in harm's way. However, when Spencer arrived in

Guayaquil to meet up with Lucie, he was shocked to hear she had been held captive by the rebels!

She told him that when she arrived in Columbia, the country seemed to be at peace. But soon, there occurred the most violent and destructive riot in the country's long history of conflict. On April 9, 1948, Gaitán, a popular presidential candidate, was assassinated at midday in the heart of Bogotá. An angry mob immediately seized and killed the assassin. In the ensuing riot, some two thousand people were killed, and a large portion of downtown Bogotá was destroyed. El Bogotazo, as the episode came to be called, was an expression of mass social frustration and grief by people who felt they had lost the man who represented their only potential link to the decision-making process. [29]

The rebels had captured the oil camp in which Lucie was working and had confined Lucie and the rest of the Americans in one small building, holding them at rifle point!

During that time, a United States plane would fly over the village with mail drops. Spencer had sent a letter with all the New York Times mail clippings about the rebel war, and not knowing that Lucie had been captured, he had naturally assumed she was fine.

The mail miraculously found its way to the captives, including Spencer's letter to Lucie.

It was his letter, along with the newspaper clippings, that informed the captives in the oil camp what was going on outside the building in which they were held.

The rebels had been looking for someone they considered a traitor, whose fate would surely end in immediate execution had he been found. The captives were hiding this person in the rafters of the building where Lucie was captive. At one point, one of the Americans was granted permission to leave. The plane would be waiting for him. Incredibly, the American captive hustled the wanted man into the trunk of the car. As he sped off, everyone was petrified they would be found out.

Somehow, both men got onto that plane and escaped. Finally, the government got control again and things normalized. By the time Spencer arrived in Guayaquil, Ecuador, Lucie and the other captives in Columbia had been freed and Lucie was safe. The world discovered later that the rebels had been stockpiling ammunition and powder and had intended to annihilate the oil camp as a statement to the world.

Lucie left Columbia immediately to meet Spencer in Guayaquil, Ecuador. It had been too much of an adventure even for Lucie!

Safe and sound now, they traveled overland by bus to northern Peru, to Lima, to Machu Picchu, then up to Lake Titicaca, on a steamer across the lake, by train to La Paz, Bolivia, and back by train to Arica, Chile.

Hiring an Indian guide, Spencer and Lucie, along with a friend he had just met, climbed to the top of nineteen- thousand-foot Mount Misti Volcano in Arequipa, Peru. [30]

The climb is known to be very difficult and dangerous. Spencer marveled that he and Lucie could do the hike. Although it was very uncomfortable, Spencer forced himself to take pictures. There was an old iron cross up there and suddenly their Indian guide was doing a ritual. Spencer was feeling the effect of the altitude and could not remember if he was winding the pictures. When he had the film developed, there were three double exposures and two triple exposures. Spencer reflected, "What the mind does to you at that altitude! I only had three pictures that came out."

Later, Lucie and Spencer took a colorful bus ride the entire length of Peru. "It was the most rattletrap bus you ever saw, held together with hangar wire. The Indian people had pigs and chickens and big bundles. We traveled into the most incredible desert country with palm trees and sand dunes, and oh, it was so beautiful. We occasionally stopped and the Indian women would just squat down with their billowing dresses and soon there would be a trickle running down the road."

Spencer laughs as he remembers that emblazoned on the truck side panels were the words, *Rapido y seguro como la luz del dia, meaning r*apid and sure as the light of day.

There were more adventures over the next few summers, such as cruises on a friend's yacht in the east Maine area, and notably a six-week trip to Europe by himself on a bicycle.

"I had once ridden my bicycle from Andover to my home in Virginia alone. I reasoned that if I could manage that, why couldn't I ride my bicycle around Europe? I had planned to take a student sailing ship from Quebec to Rotterdam. I began to hitchhike from Andover up through rural Maine with my bicycle by my side, but no one would stop for me. I ended up taking a taxi for the last two hundred miles in order to get to the ship on time. Using almost all of my funds, I finally arrived in Holland, but on such a strict budget I only had less than two hundred dollars for the entire six weeks I was to be there. I could only afford to stop at a youth hostel once a week. The rest of the time I camped out." Spencer would carve out a place that was dry and comfortable. Most notably, he was able to spend about six weeks in Louvain, Belgium, even having a meal at the university library which his father, Ian, had restored.

"I was overwhelmed by this experience. Memories of my father came flooding back and I could only imagine what a genius he truly had been. I looked at the carvings of the school names on top of the columns around the colonnade. My father's own hands had carved these American school names which had donated money for this project. Remembering that he used a different style of lettering for each one showed my father's great talent. And to me, it showed the caring side of his nature."

As Spencer journeyed on from childhood to manhood, he was beginning to put a perspective on his life and his family members, including his grandfather, father, mother, and ancestors—as well as his brother.

Crawfish was a child prodigy and had achieved one of the highest marks on the entrance exam to Princeton in its history to that date. He was every bit as complex as Spencer and the rest of the family, and all of them had helped to set the stage for young Spencer to step onto it.

The two-edged sword of positive and negative family dynamics impacted all of their lives, then and into the future, for a very long time. In fact, for the rest of their lives.

Chapter Five

Relationships And Delusion

It was around the age of five that Spencer realized a shift to a more competitive relationship with his brother, Crawford, who was two years and seven months older. This persisted well into adulthood for them both.

At first, it was normal sibling rivalry, playing tricks on each other, and roughhousing. Spencer remembered a time when he kept his brother at bay holding him upside down by his hair on the playroom floor; he hung on for dear life out of fear his brother would really hurt him if he let go. Although he was young, he was old enough to sense real danger.

Spencer would run to the kitchen seeking cover behind Lucie. And cover and protection he would get. But Crawford would not do that; he was the silent type and did not seem to express feelings very well. "Crawford took more after my father's side, and I took more after my mother's side. He kept to himself, never letting you know what he was thinking," Spencer said.

Later, as adults, Crawford himself shared with Spencer a memory he had about Lucile. He remembered having feelings of extreme unworthiness and had tried to talk to their mother about it. Her response to him was something like, "Well, Crawford, I can't imagine you feeling that way." Therefore, Crawford reasoned, if she couldn't imagine these feelings, then why bother to explain?

"He never tried again," Spencer said.

In an interview with Crawford, he reflected on the childhood years with their mother. To him, Lucie was always a complex question. "It was incredibly brave of a forty-one-year-old, beautiful young woman to think of going to Mexico with two young boys. There's no way to understand how she could envision doing that, considering how far away it really was. There was no connection. There we were, living in Virginia, and not knowing a soul in Mexico. The war was raging in Europe. She took us out of school and just headed out. Lucie didn't speak Spanish or know anything about cars. Incredible."

Amazing, indeed, as that was an era when there were no cell phones, no google maps, and no instant access to technology, let alone people.

Crawford thought that when Lucie was young, she was charming and lovely and could make social contact and friends with anybody, and in his opinion, Spencer inherited this gift from her.

But along with feelings of insecurity about his mother, and his admitted jealousy of Spencer, Crawford also had a testy relationship with Popdaddy. It was demonstrated at an early age that Popdaddy ruled the kingdom of money in their family. Crawford thought Popdaddy was crusty.

And because he was very wealthy, people would appeal to him to borrow money. There was reason to believe that Lucile had anticipated that Popdaddy would finance their trip.

But he refused to help them during their struggles in Mexico. "You'd have to grovel at his feet to get a nickel out of him," Crawford said. Or perhaps cry for it. "In fact, we all knew that Spencer was born because Lucile was literally crying to have another child, and Popdaddy gave them one thousand dollars to do that.

"He wouldn't give you money for anything unless you begged. My father hated him for this aspect of his personality," Crawford said. This family dynamic played out in a very negative way in Lucile and Ian's marriage as they struggled with finances; sometimes Popdaddy helped them and sometimes he refused.

"So, in Mexico," Crawford continued, "we had to depend solely upon my father sending money from England. At one point the money got held up, and the way I remember it, Lucie told us it was a postal error; but Spencer recalled that it was Ian who delayed it on purpose. We each have a different memory of this situation—whether it was Ian or the mail service that delayed the money."

Memories of issues such as this colored how each son saw their parents—Lucie was mistreated by Ian; Ian was mistreated by Lucie. They were both mistreated by Popdaddy. The complexity of these perceptions stayed with the boys.

Even so, Lucie managed to scrimp enough money together for horseback rides through the nearby town of Ajijic. It was an adventure itself, as the only route for the kids to get there was through the woods on horse, or on foot. Crawford reflected that Lucie made it a point to not worry the boys. "We were really poor and haggled with every hotel—and although I was always embarrassed by it, we somehow felt very prosperous as long as we had our trusty Chevrolet that just kept on running. As did Lucie."

Crawford thought she inherited from Popdaddy the kind of vision that would help her to prepare the boys and her nephew for life after the war, but she was not an easy person, and became more difficult as she aged. "She didn't know how to love. She was not a loving person, but she may have loved Spencer more, being the younger one. This was part of our family story, part of the problem of why Spencer and I had a hard time as brothers. I was very jealous of his relationship with Lucie. Were there grounds for jealousy? I think that Lucie went out of her way to treat us equally – in her mind – but I'm also sure that since I was the firstborn, she was under the influence of the day to not coddle her children, as in earlier days parents let their children "cry it out" and did not attempt to comfort them when they were hungry or tired. This is what happened to me.

"However, by the time Spencer came along, I think she threw those old-fashioned ideas out the window and just did it. Therefore, they had a closer relationship. Spencer and I fought until we were in our forties, and only after Lucie passed did we reconcile a bit."

Spencer recalled that in college the two brothers were often isolated from each other. From Spencer's point of view, "I wanted to be closer to Crawford and that's why I chose Princeton, but I didn't see much of him. Crawford couldn't have his time taken up by a kid brother."

Crawford said that back in the Princeton days when Spencer was struggling and stuttering and felt like he was drowning, it was indeed Popdaddy who showed up at the right moment for Spencer. "My brother and I were not communicating then.

"Actually, that's been a great disappointment in my life, that we didn't connect in those days. However, I was also having some serious problems with depression myself at the time."

But for Spencer, Popdaddy eventually filled many voids in his life, and became a vital link for him. Spencer always thought it must have been part of the grand plan.

Spencer became Popdaddy's captive audience, and the more he listened the more he realized that Popdaddy might have been, in some ways, on the cutting edge of anthropology and other sciences. And to him, it didn't matter that his language wasn't correct or up to date.

Spencer agreed with Crawford of his assessment of Popdaddy. "I understood what Crawford was saying about him, that Popdaddy always had to be right and claimed he understood everything, even when he didn't. I remember Popdaddy sitting on the edge of my bed and reading out loud into the wee hours of the night. Then, it would be really late morning before he'd get up. During these times, I remember I wanted to share with Popdaddy what I had been learning about anthropology, but Popdaddy wanted to tell me about anthropology."

Spencer said the "Popdaddy situation" set up resentment within himself about his brother. He thought that Crawford was always so impatient and intolerant because Popdaddy wanted to get his ideas across to the world at large, and his brother would not even listen.

Crawford was analytical and always the one to find fault in things, as Spencer thought about him, so maybe this inharmony was to be expected. "At any rate, we just didn't get along back then because his job was to shoot down, analyze, find fault; and my job was to build up, explore ideas, and think about possibilities.

"However," Spencer continued, "to somewhat negate Crawford's opinion about Popdaddy, a family friend, physicist and engineer, Alvin Lowi, Jr., who specialized in thermodynamics, speculated that it was unfortunate that Popdaddy spent so much time working through his theories. In fact, Al had shown how discussing physics can be studied in not just one way but in several ways, and to Al this was because in his opinion it really was a matter of semantics. That was confirmation of my confidence in Popdaddy." [31]

As far as Popdaddy's and Spencer's political views were concerned, Crawford noted that Spencer would declare he was not a libertarian, but Crawford maintained that his ideas on the value of a non-government society, and freedom to express oneself without structure, were libertarian in view.

"Spencer was a beautiful writer," Crawford remembered. "He was very clear and articulate. So even though we could not see eye to eye on these ideas he was writing about, it was not that I had a counter proposal either," he laughed.

"My grandfather," Spencer recalls, "was interested in the fundamentals of the philosophy of science. He didn't hesitate to ask scholars to assist him in digging for answers. My brother couldn't support that because, in his view, Popdaddy didn't use the *correct* language."

This did not seem to faze Spencer's view of, or relationship with, Popdaddy.

In fact, if anything, it strengthened it.

Spencer said that Crawford thought in realistic, rational terms, and would comment that "Popdaddy couldn't understand the simplest fundamentals of algebra and physics; and when this led to problems or heated discussions, Popdaddy would say that he understood better than old fogies like Einstein."

These kinds of comments from Popdaddy drove Crawford to distraction, Spencer reflected.

Eventually, the tracks between the brothers widened and veered away from each other. Spencer finally accepted that Crawford and he were just different; and they each continued their own life's journey.

Crawford later went on to Cornell, and then the University of New Mexico, teaching there and receiving his doctorate, then continuing work as a physicist for Sandia Labs in Albuquerque, New Mexico.

As a scientist, Crawford eventually took an intense interest in gamma-ray astronomy using gigantic balloons that would float above most of the atmosphere. "It was the cutting-edge technology of the day," he said. [32]

His science career blossomed.

Spencer fondly recalled that his brother also "had a wonderfully rich career as a witch, and as an elder statesman in the witch community, with regular rituals, drumming all night long, and sweat lodges."

Crawford's dual nature was a topic of speculation between the two of them. Crawford talked about this himself, how it was possible for him to compartmentalize these two selves: one a witch, an artist, and a composer of ritual and theater; and his other self which seems opposite—the scientist, the quantitative person, the person who looks for problems and solutions.

Crawford once told Spencer how wonderful it was that he had made the world better by improving people's lives, and that he had made a difference. "I'm tremendously proud of what he did later in life in Mata Ortiz. I think it was marvelous. He had an exquisite sense of beauty. He could see the beauty in art where others could not.

"I've seen the original pots he found in that junk store. They looked like any other pots to me. But for Spencer to have that unique ability and artistic taste to have recognized them for what they were, and then to go find the artist in Mexico, well, I would never have done that. And Mata Ortiz at that time was at the end of this long, dirt road, at the end of nowhere. Even though later he had a contract with Juan, in the beginning, he made only a verbal, totally non-businesslike arrangement with Juan. That agreement was just incomprehensible. As a consequence, there's now a positive economic impact for the village. It's incredible, and it continues to evolve. But for Spencer to have bought those pots and then to have traveled to Mexico to find who made them is totally idyllic."

Crawford acknowledges, however, that one of the more interesting aspects of Spencer's personality had nothing to do with Juan and Mata Ortiz. "Spencer knew, of course, the discovery of Juan was important, and he understood Mata Ortiz was what he, himself, was most noted for.

"But he had developed by then a mission to disseminate his philosophical works and social projects of Popdaddy.

"Spencer was complex in that way, and although he understood the importance of Mata Ortiz, at times he would rather have talked about social anthropology.

Crawford said, "He truly felt that he could change the world by publishing the ideas and philosophy which came to him from Popdaddy."

Perhaps Spencer also incurred an obligation to Popdaddy, as these ideas eventually became his own.

What is more interesting, however, is that Spencer had a difficult time acknowledging that he had already changed the world. He called Mata Ortiz "a not unwelcome distraction," but he still had the feeling that it was a detour, that he had a further mission in life. In retrospect, it seems that Spencer had a difficult time accepting the wonderful role he had played for so many people.

"So, at any rate," Crawford continued, "Spencer thought there was real value in the communication of ideas, because he thought that's what changes the world. So, as an example, you could say that the Federalist Papers had more value than what Hamilton actually put into action."

Difficult as it was for Spencer to accept his visionary role in Mata Ortiz, at a certain point Spencer realized that he had invested so much money, time, and heart into the project that it would be difficult to extract himself from it.

Crawford told Spencer that when Juan's work became the very best, traders with more money than Spencer would woo him and Spencer would be cut out. That is, indeed, what happened. Spencer could not compete, but he didn't want the pottery project to destroy his friendship with Juan.

Regarding Spencer's relationship with Juan, "Spencer never spoke ill of anyone," Crawford said, "whereas I recognize reality.

"I don't trust many people, unless I know them well.

"Spencer really had faith that people, and the world, would be good to him, and my belief was that they probably would not."

Crawford continued, "Even so, I was envious of how Spencer made friends and talked to people. Although we did not have an intimate connection, I appreciated him."

For people with siblings, perhaps a compliment like this from an older brother or sister is worth more than all the lifetime accomplishments rolled into one.

It's a hallmark, an indication that everyone has finally grown up, perhaps have reconciled some differences, and matured enough to truly appreciate one another in adulthood. It's a precious treasure that can be savored from within.

For Spencer and Crawford, it seemed that it was a long time coming. Much later in life, they did exhibit a healthy respect and admiration for each other and truly valued the time they spent together.

Crawford passed away April 24, 2023.

In other relationships, and as Spencer grew up and matured, and became a man, he explored other relationships: sometimes in painful love, and sometimes in painful delusion.

During the years when Spencer was studying at Princeton and also going for extended stays at Popdaddy's apartment in New York, romance blossomed.

"In 1954, I met Mary. I was living at Popdaddy's apartment in Greenwich Village while attending speech therapy and she lived in the apartment next to ours. I was "taking a break from Princeton" as Popdaddy called it so that I could benefit from the speech therapy. I would watch Mary come and go to the elevators. She worked as a legal secretary."

The two were close in age and she was living next door alone. Spencer was excited about her, and there was no one around to tell them what to do, or not. It felt like romantic freedom, and maybe it was time to make a move.

"When I met Mary, I was scared to death to get emotionally involved as I had already experienced the death of what I called true love when I was a teenager. My first love was a girl named Sarah. She lived in Winchester, Virginia and when we came back from Mexico, I fell head over heels in love with her and never had such a crazy experience as that since."

Spencer said he wanted to do things for her all the time – as a vision of her was constantly in front of his eyes. He saved up every nickel and dime and went to the jewelry store and bought her a very nice silver bracelet. He gave it to her, and all was well until the parents decided it was not appropriate for a thirteen-year-old boy to be giving jewelry to her—but she wanted it, and was also just as smitten as Spencer, so, in the end, the parents gave in to them.

But Spencer was nervous about his big brother moving in on him. He felt that Crawfish was very suave with girls and they seemed to fall all over him. Spencer lacked this smooth touch.

He would watch his brother flirt with Sarah, and he would become jealous. But nothing really came of their romantic notions. Spencer spent some time on a farm that summer and he named a new calf after Sarah. Thinking that she would think it was a great honor, he proudly told Sarah about it. But she was less than impressed.

To further appease her, he gave her two of his most precious jade beads! "And good ones, too," he declared.

Unfortunately, Sarah became ill and died about a year later. Spencer did not retrieve the beads and doesn't know what became of them. He was so stricken by her death he forgot about them for quite a while. "What a wallop that was on me. I was so much in love. I felt that all the popular songs of the day were written just for me.

"So that when I met Mary, and because I had not had a physical relationship with a woman, I had a strong fear of commitment. It was a part of my makeup. I decided I would play it cool, even though I was determined I was going to meet her. How could I do it? I thought of a ploy. I would be at the elevators when she was getting ready to leave. One morning when I heard she was going out her door, I slipped out first to the elevator. As I stood there, she came, and we waited for the elevator. It sometimes takes a long time, doesn't it, for the elevator to come?" Spencer laughed. "Well, I had not pushed the button, but she assumed that I had!"

"So, we had a chance to talk a bit because, you know, the elevator was taking a long time. Finally, she pushed the button. I always felt that was a neat way to meet her. It worked and it was great." This was Greenwich Village in its heyday, and the young couple enjoyed going out and walking around the village.

"That was my first adult relationship, and she was a very fine person. She and I both blossomed in this relationship, and that was really nice to see. I even thought about marriage, but I was emotionally immature at the time. At the time, I wondered if I made a mistake about not getting serious. She was a fine person and would have been a good match for me, but I was scared of marriage, and she wanted to have children. I'm sure she would have been a wonderful mother. So, it looked as if it was not going to happen.

"I remember Mary so well, so fondly, because just as a human being, entirely aside from our great physical relationship, she was just a really good person."

Spencer graduated from Princeton in 1955 with a degree in Art History and furthered his education in anthropology by enrolling as a graduate student at the University of Washington to earn a degree in Social Anthropology.

The university had various degree programs in Native American studies. He graduated with a master's degree in Social Anthropology with a focus on Northwest Coast Indians in 1961.

He would travel coast to coast between Greenwich Village and Seattle, Washington. He was still seeing Mary, but he could not make himself commit to her. The relationship faltered and they each moved on.

It wasn't too long before he met a girl in Washington State.

"Classes and life were going well at the University of Washington and soon I met Tina. She was quite a girl, very refined, intelligent, and sensitive. We did some nude bathing in Lake Washington, Tina and I. She was especially interested in solar mythology. I don't know why or where I had heard that interest in solar mythology was a presage of death.

"I didn't know what to make of that really. Well, it then turned out she had a heart condition. The general consensus of her family was that she was going to be fine, and that this condition was something she could live with. I traveled back home during the summer, and during that time she entered the hospital for another operation. Her father arranged for us to talk by phone."

As Spencer was en route back to Seattle in the Fall, things took a turn for the worse. But once again, Spencer was not prepared for the death of a second love.

"On the day I arrived back at the campus, I immediately went to her house," Spencer said. "I was stunned to learn that she had passed away. The funeral was to be the next morning. That hit me hard. I remember sitting on a green slope on campus looking out over the grassy knolls, and never had my senses been so acute, or the grass so green, or the sky so brilliantly blue. From somewhere I could hear the most beautiful music I had ever heard in my life. I remember sitting there thinking that her death could do either two things to me, strengthen me or weaken me."

He decided to allow it to strengthen him and knew that he wanted to, and would, continue his studies in anthropology of Native Americans.

His studies helped to ground him, and he connected with the studies of various tribes up and down the southwest of the United States, including the Athabascan tribes, the pueblo tribes, and those in Mexico and South America. Now Spencer had his Princeton bachelor's in art history, and the University of Washington Masters in anthropology and later decided to transfer to Chicago to get his doctorate in anthropology.

But a new nemesis appeared.

It was in 1962 that Spencer began to feel unwell, and increasingly had a difficult time doing research and writing for his doctorate. He began to struggle with his health on various levels, physically and with his mental acumen, and was eventually diagnosed. Fate had stepped into the picture in the form of a debilitating disease: hypoglycemia.

This disease manifests as a drop in low blood sugar, also known as glucose. Glucose is derived from food and is a major source of energy in the body. Some categories of food that are considered major sources of glucose are potatoes, rice, vegetables, milk, and fruit.

After consumption, glucose nourishes the cells of the body and insulin helps the cells absorb it in the body. But if the body cannot process enough glucose, it manifests as hypoglycemia. Some of the symptoms of hypoglycemia are fatigue, lack of concentration, hunger, shaking, sweating, headache, blurry vision, and anxiety.

There are times when hypoglycemia can be a threat to life with seizures, and other nervous system damage.

Spencer still struggled with stuttering when he encountered difficult times in his life. Not being able to work on his doctorate was indeed one of those times of stress.

"With the hypoglycemia, stuttering and the stress of trying to earn a doctorate degree, my mind and body went into overload."

In later years, studies have shown a link between stuttering, diabetes, and hypoglycemia. It is not known if Spencer had diabetes, or if knew about these connections. The studies between these connections were not carried out until the early 2000s. However, it seems possible that this dovetail of circumstances was something he could not control at the time.

This situation was delivering to him a double whammy of physical ailments that not only were depressing in themselves, but when he realized that he was being stopped in his tracks, physically and mentally, it took an even further toll.

These health issues deepened down into a depression which prompted Popdaddy to take action on Spencer's behalf at a critical juncture.

Spencer was not able to finish a proposed dissertation on the ethnography of a community, so his hopes of a doctorate degree were not only delayed but finished. Once again, he felt he was sinking and could not properly function.

Not able to attend college to work on his doctorate, not able to work in the world, Popdaddy once again came up with a viable game plan for him.

Chapter Six

The Healing Years, The Lost Years: 1962-1976

Popdaddy established Spencer in an apartment he kept in the community of San Pedro, a neighborhood within the city of Los Angeles, California. "Popdaddy was traveling most of the time, so it was convenient for both of us for me to stay there."

In Spencer's words, "1962 to 1976 were both healing years and lost years. During the lost years due to hypoglycemia, I would suffer terrible headaches, fuzziness, and confusion. I was muddled, and it was difficult to finish any project at all, even though I could plow through it."

Spencer said that he could easily function with regular duties and relationships, even travel, but when anything became too complicated, or technical like writing, or if he had stress, there would be a lot of confusion.

Unfortunately, Popdaddy died in 1963. Spencer then remained in the apartment for a while and continued to write and get some pieces published for both Popdaddy and himself. They had formed a partnership of sorts with Spencer taking on the project of assembling Popdaddy's works, editing them, and organizing his files; then implementing some publishing of both his own and Popdaddy's writings, all of which were focused on social issues or anthropology.

In that timeframe, Spencer did publish in 1971 *Jural Behavior in American Shopping Centers: Initial Views on the Proprietary Community*, and in 1970 his Princeton master's thesis, *The Art of Community*, was published by the Institute for Humane Studies, Inc., Menlo Park, California.

This work can best be described by Spencer's Preface to the thesis:

The concept of proprietary community administration which is pivotal to much of this book was original to my grandfather, Spencer Heath, and was a principal theme of his final and major work, <u>Citadel, Market and Altar</u> (1957).

It has been my privilege to make use of many of the ideas which he expressed in more general and philosophic form.

In my studies in anthropology, I tested and extended some of them specifically to primitive village organization, on the one hand, and to current developments in real estate—contemporary land tenure—on the other.

During periods of social evolution like the present, forms and practices change rapidly.

Specific facts and illustrations soon become out-of-date, as may already be the case in some instances in this book for which the work extends back over a decade.

Essential principles of human association do not change, however, and the reader is invited to give these his attention. By progressively understanding the 'timeless aspect,' our creative command grows.

In a field in which the relevant literature is still so little established as in the social sciences, the amateur with scientific curiosity and sound intuition suffers no great disadvantage.

It is hoped, therefore, that the present work will provide a stimulus to investigative thinking among informed readers outside of the established social sciences no less than within.

Spencer would describe this timeframe as a period of continuing to research and write about social anthropology as well as exploring the wonders of romance and adventure.

After Popdaddy passed, there was less pressure to get Popdaddy's work published in a certain timeframe, and more time to heal from hypoglycemia.

Suddenly, Spencer was somewhat liberated, from school and from family.

He now had a sizable inheritance from Popdaddy, and he wanted to be independent for the first time in his life. As he healed and was able to keep the hypoglycemia and the stuttering under control, he wanted to spread his wings, and go out on his own.

For most of the years that Spencer spent on the west coast he did not see anyone of significance until he met a gift shop owner. She assisted him with choosing a greeting card and soon they were dating and quickly became involved.

"This relationship was quite a story," Spencer said. "She was very attractive!

"She introduced me to an acquaintance of hers who was renting out his very attractive house up in the Hollywood hills. I had been looking for another place and was ready to give up the apartment. The house was close to the famous Hollywood sign. It was a wonderful place to live, and I lived there for at least a couple of years. It was overlooking government land and there were no developments around it at all. The deer would come very close. It was a nice place with complete privacy.

"We spent a lot of time together and had a wonderful physical relationship. I even thought that she should submit her photo to Playboy. She always needed extra income, so why not? I thought she would have been perfect for the part, but she never did pursue it. However, I began to see some strange facets of her personality and I decided to end it."

Spencer said that after he moved on, he had a relationship with Shawna, a married woman, whose marriage was on the rocks. When they became friends, Spencer had been exercising by running at a high school track near where they lived. He encouraged her to do the same. "Eventually she could even do the ropes!"

They became more than friends. The woman and her husband did finally have their marriage annulled by the Mormon Church, even though they had been married in the temple, and temple weddings were supposed to not ever be broken.

Spencer became smitten with her, even finally, and surprisingly, wanting to marry her. He dreamed of building the couple a dream home of adobe with his own hands. They discussed marriage a lot, and he knew that if he married her, he would have to become Mormon. This was no small thing. She had a degree in Mormon theology from Brigham Young University and was very open about her religion. But Spencer knew that he would have to be able to understand the Mormon theology on his own terms, so he needed time.

"She made me laugh as no one had ever made me laugh before or since," Spencer smiled.

One day, Spencer expressed a long-time desire for a unique adventure to hunt unicorns and wanted her to go along with him. This desire to hunt unicorns started in his college days at Princeton. A professor in the biology department was the instructor of a morphology class. "One day he was late for his class and lying across his desk was what appeared to be a unicorn horn. It was obvious to all of the students that it was not artificial. But how could this be? We all knew that unicorns were mythical."

Apparently, the professor used this tactic each year for this lecture. When he finally arrived at the classroom, he got the response from the class he was looking for and began to explain. During the Middle Ages, unicorn horns were at the height of demand and brought their weight in gold. A cup made of a unicorn horn had magical properties and therefore if one drank from it, could not be poisoned.

"No one knew where they came from. They were so valuable that traders kept their sources secret. A writer finally traced them to the northernmost shores of the North Sea where they sometimes washed up on the beaches. Today we know they are not land creatures at all. They are sea mammals, whales. They are narwhals."

Narwhals are strange, beautiful and legendary, all at the same time. When a male narwhal grows into the second year of his life, a phenomenon occurs in which his left tooth begins to grow outward in a spiral shape. It can measure up to ten feet in length over time. This tooth, sometimes called a tusk, grows in a counterclockwise direction. Scientists are not sure of the function of this strange tooth, but it has been conjectured that it could be used in defense, offense, or in courtship. And in obtaining food or used in sonar communication. Legends abounded that this creature was a unicorn, because when sighted that was the first part of the animal sighted. [33]

The Europeans' fantasy came to be known as horse-like creatures. They live around the North Pole, at the top of the world, and are concealed by the Arctic ice. Their population is estimated to be around a hundred thousand, although that number seems to be declining.

Ever since that class, Spencer had wanted to secure a unicorn horn. For years, he had looked for one. One day someone told him that a curiosity shop in Seattle, Washington had one with a broken tip. It was for sale for ten thousand dollars.

About that time, Spencer read a story by a writer in the LA Times about how the Eskimos hunted them and sold the tusks to the Hudson Bay Trading Co. His article was entitled *The Unicorns of the Northern Seas*. The journalist was Chuck Hillinger of the LA Times. [34]

"After I read that article, and finally in the healing zone with health issues, I decided to go hunt one myself. I wanted to corner the world market on unicorns."

Spencer and Shawna were going to make this trip together and be married on the plane, right over the magnetic North Pole. Their symbol would forever after be the compass rose to point to the north. But according to Spencer, the Mormon Bishops stopped it because they did not want her to travel unmarried on the trip, even if they were going to be married once they arrived.

"We decided to marry before we went; however, for other reasons, Shawna kept putting it off."

Over the next several months, Spencer finally realized that they were never going to take that trip together, nor were they ever going to marry. They grew further and further apart, and not really understanding what happened, the two finally parted for good.

Although they didn't marry, this loving and caring relationship got him over the fear of marriage, and for that, he was always grateful. About a year later, Spencer made the trip to Baffin Island. He knew the British manager of the Hong Kong Bank in Los Angeles and decided to establish some real credit. Spencer daydreamed that if he ever wrote a story about this trip, he would open it with, "Spencer went to the bank manager for a signature loan for travel to the North Pole to hunt unicorns with the Eskimos."

And he did. He went to the manager for a signature loan in the amount of ten thousand dollars. Of course, the bank manager had to establish the reason for the loan. He told the bank, "It is for travel to the North Pole to hunt unicorns with the Eskimos."

"I needed the ten thousand dollars because cash would give me much more flexibility when traveling in unknown situations."

The manager seriously considered the request and agreed. "Now that you've granted me this loan," Spencer asked him, "I'm curious as to how you are going to write it up? Are you going to document that the loan is for hunting unicorns at the North Pole?"

His response to Spencer was very British. "Oh, no," the bank manager replied, "we would want to avoid that. I'll put it down as travel and exploration in the Arctic."

"I tried to figure out how to carry this much cash with me on my trip. I thought of a hollow cane, but I was afraid I'd lose it." Finally, Spencer decided to carve out the inside pages of a paperback book for his stack of hundred-dollar bills. He chose a title that would likely hold little interest to strangers. "I thought about The Book of Mormon, but I didn't want to engage in religious conversations. I finally settled on Roget's Thesaurus. I had it sticking casually out of my pocket.

Finally, someone asked me why I was carrying it. I answered very coolly, 'I'm a writer and I enjoy words.'"

Spencer spent a lot of time figuring out what to wear in Alaska. Would there be ice, snow, or mud? He decided to wear everyday shoes and wait to see what people were wearing when he arrived there. His running shoes were worn so badly on the end that his toes were sticking through the holes, but as it turned out, the Eskimos were all wearing running shoes just like his, except they had toes. He was teased about his "air-conditioned" shoes.

By chance, or again, surely it was destiny, Spencer met some divers on the plane who were going up to photograph the Narwhals. They were commissioned to do undersea diving because the Eskimos thought that by this time there would be a lot of Narwhal tusks on the ocean floor. They were all thinking that this could be some big money. In the Arctic, it is common for people to help each other. You could bump on a plane, hitchhike, as it were, as did these divers.

Spencer said he was fascinated by the divers and stayed in touch with them for a while after his trip, but they did not have much luck in photographing the Narwhals.

Later, Spencer became friends with a social worker who was teaching the Eskimos competitive team sports. He mentioned to her his desire to acquire a unicorn horn.

He asked her to ship any she might find to him in Vancouver. Eventually, he was able to acquire one.

Spencer also became friends with Sam, an Eskimo leader, one as close to a traditional leader as Spencer would find. He was Vice President of the Co-op.

Spencer learned a great deal from him. "One night in the barracks Sam came in. He was sort of gimpy and had only one eye. He needed ninety dollars so he could buy some supplies.

He pulled from his jacket a beautiful carving, a necklace he had carved from ivory. On it was portrayed each of the life forms of the arctic. I loved it immediately and wanted to buy it. I proceeded to get out my money and there was silence. Sam began to speak to me in Eskimo and someone translated, saying that Sam was asking me, 'Do you like it?'"

Spencer stopped, suddenly realizing that he had begun his transaction in a very cold, businesslike manner, as is quite often done in the states. "I got the hint and began to backpedal. I came to my senses and began a conversation with Sam."

Turns out, Sam's grandfather had made many trips across the sea over to Greenland when it was frozen. It would take six weeks by dogsled to go over and trade, and he taught some of the Greenlanders to do this kind of carving. He showed Spencer how the carving was made, which lent its own beauty and depth to the necklace. Finally, Spencer felt lucky—and they made a deal for what became another of Spencer's prized possessions.

Spencer traveled around the Arctic, bumping onto planes to see the sights. The pilots at the North Pole knew how to read the stars as compasses. They didn't concern themselves with magnetic compasses, as they did not work there. The pilots often warned new pilots because it might take years for a greenhorn to learn how to read the stars.

A pilot told Spencer a story. "A greenhorn was flying and got lost and was running out of gas. By chance, he picked up a radio contact from another pilot who tried desperately to teach him how to read the stars to find his way home. The radio contact was lost and that was the last the trained pilot thought he would hear about the greenhorn. The greenhorn had strayed twelve hundred miles off course and by chance saw the lights of the airport at Tulle Air Force base in Greenland. He landed safely but as the story goes, would never fly again."

During these years, Spencer continued to work on the papers of Popdaddy. He found great pleasure in using his art history degree and his social anthropology degree in a way to explore Popdaddy's great wealth of writings about social issues.

Spencer was fascinated by how societies developed, from the Northwest Coast Indians to the Native Americans in North America to the Amerindian tribes in Mexico.

Spencer still suffered through various phases of stuttering and hypoglycemia. He learned how to heal himself, with proper medications, so that when the disease was active, he could function properly.

Spencer also became engrossed in yard-saleing, visiting dozens on any given Saturday.

Digging around in other people's junk might yield him a true treasure.

When Spencer spoke about the lost years, he felt he was at times just existing and could not get any projects completed. He often did not feel well, and for periods of time he would not be able to concentrate, nor even really remember those times.

He was able to have a relationship or two, to explore a bit with travel, to go on "digs" to yard sales, and to try to exist as best he could with his health.

Then as he began to heal, he became more active and enjoyed visiting friends. Friends he visited in California became major vehicles in the Mata Ortiz events later. As usual with Spencer, a set of events was put into place that created a "destiny" that cannot be denied.

Chapter Seven

Mata Ortiz And the Magical, Unbelievable and Circuitous Adventure Why Spencer Was in Deming, New Mexico in the First Place

Many years ago in the early 1970s, Spencer found a pot at a yard sale on the Palos Verde peninsula not far from San Pedro, a community within Los Angeles, where he was living.

"I was a yard sale junkie and I found many treasures over the years. I bought the pot for $15 and after researching it, I thought it might be a classic Paquimé pot, around the 14th century, of the Ramos polychrome style," he said.

"It didn't look entirely like the classic Southwest Native American pottery which I had studied," Spencer continued.

"Coincidentally, the style that most influenced Juan Quezada was classic Ramos, the edges of the red areas outlined in black. The Ramos polychrome style consists of red and black painted pottery; thus, the word poly means more than one color. It is characterized by fine line work in black and red.

"The bold red motifs included triangles, circles, and long ribbons, and are often outlined in thin and precisely executed black designs."

There are combinations of thin, parallel, and curvilinear lines around the pottery." [35]

Paquimé pottery comes from the Casas Grandes area in Chihuahua, Mexico. The UNESCO World Heritage Foundation states that "the Paquimé culture dates from 700-1475 AD and reached an apogee in the 14th and 15th centuries."

The archaeological zone of the settlement lies today in what is known as the Casas Grands Municipality. Archaeologists and anthropologists have determined that this civilization played an important role in trade and religious practices between the Puebloan culture of the Southwestern United States, especially into Arizona and New Mexico, and Northern Mexico and well into Mesoamerica.

"However," Spencer continued, "I knew nothing about Paquimé pottery. I continued to research it because there was always the possibility that a piece of contemporary pottery could be distressed to look prehistoric."

With his lifelong interest in archaeology and anthropology and his research into the Northeast Coast Tribes and Native American Tribes in North America and Mexico, Spencer knew the difference between a Southwest pottery piece and a Ramos Polychrome pot.

"There was something unique about it. I found out years later how the pot ended up in a yard sale.

There was a woman from Chihuahua working as a housekeeper for wealthy families on the peninsula and one of the families collected Southwest Indian art.

"The housekeeper had this pottery in her possession and wanted to give the family a meaningful gift, so she presented this pot to them," he said.

"It was an amazing story, really."

"Apparently, the people did not recognize the pot as belonging to any of the pottery styles they collected or as having any value, so one day it ended up at their yard sale." Spencer said the pot sat on his piano for a year.

He would walk by it sometimes several times a day. Authentic or fake, he wasn't sure, but he was intrigued by it. It spoke to him. "So, you see," Spencer reflected, "this is the pot I had at my home and in my life, and it was THIS pot that taught me its language—so that a year later when I walked into Bob's Swap Shop in Deming, New Mexico in 1976 and saw the now famous three pots, I could understand what they were saying.

"They just stood up on their hind legs and shouted at me that they were made by someone who knew who he was."

These three pots are the ones that initiated Spencer's quest for the potter, which led him to their maker, Juan Quezada. In this part of the telling, Spencer referred to the Mexico days with Lucie and the way she spurred him on to study archaeology and anthropology. That was a gift she gave to him. Those experiences continually sparked his thirst for discovery.

He stated that it was Lucie that gave him the gumption to explore and discover and that she would have been exceedingly proud when he and Juan, so many years later, traveled to Mexico City for Juan to receive from President Ernesto Sedillo the Premio Nacional de Los Artes award, Mexico's highest award to a living artist. He thinks that this would have been one of the proudest moments of her life and would have validated her original mission of bringing the two cultures of Latin America and the United States together. "It was only Lucie's vision which inspired me to buy the pot on the piano, and later recognize the similarities of it with the Deming pots." [36]

This original yard-sale-sit-on-the-piano pot was how Spencer recognized similar pots in the junk shop. But how did Spencer come to even be in Bob's Swap Shop in Deming, New Mexico?

During his childhood travels in Mexico, the family had become friends with a young woman, Louisa Downey.

"She and Lucie became great buddies, and we ended up exploring and traveling together for a while."

After the MacCallums returned to the United States, Louisa stayed on in Mexico. It was there that later she met Edward Miller Solomon.

There is no such thing as coincidence. Spencer discovered Juan Quezada because in 1976 he went into that junk store in Deming, New Mexico, and he was in Deming because he had made an investment in a gold mine. He had invested thirty thousand dollars in a gold venture with Edward Miller Solomon and his wife Louisa.

It happened like this.

Solomon's history was fascinating as he played many roles in the course of time, one of which eventually led Spencer to Deming, New Mexico. He was an eyewitness to, and a participant in, history!

As told to Spencer by Solomon, he was born into a very wealthy and prominent Jewish family from South Africa and educated in Europe and in Canada.

He had a degree in animal husbandry from Canada, but as a young man, he had moved to Mexico thinking he could make his own fortune by improving the quality of livestock in Latin America. Along with that would be an improvement in the lives of ranchers in the area.

Solomon said that he had a string of valuable Arabian horses he was breeding in Mexico, and there was a very real possibility that he was going to lose them at some point during the Mexican Revolution, which began in 1910. Panic erupted in Mexico, and worsened as the war went on.

Solomon related that as he was trying to figure out a way to escape with his life and his horses, the lives of those living in Mexico turned desperate and chaotic. He knew a South African man who was working with Pancho Villa during the revolution, and this friend was a close associate of Felipe Ángeles, the confidant and military strategist for Villa. [37]

By the time Villa had defeated Porfirio Diaz, Villa's troops were bedraggled. The opposing army was just south of Mexico City, but Felipe Ángeles urged Villa to give the troops a much-needed reinforcement in body and mind by withdrawing the troops up to the north country in Chihuahua until they could recuperate and take on enemy forces again.

So, Solomon said that at Ángeles urging, Villa agreed to move north. Felipe Ángeles and Solomon's friend were urging Edward to join Villa's forces, all of them figuring that this would be one way that they could not only escape, but also Solomon could travel north and get out of Mexico with his life and his Arabians. In return for safe passage north, he agreed to act as secretary to Pancho Villa and take on the job of delivering Villa's loot robbed from ranches and individuals to various banks in the north for safekeeping.

But Solomon said that Villa would stand on a hill and declare with hatred and vengeance, "I'm going to at-

tack and kill every one of the enemy!" even though Ángeles continued to warn him of the beleaguered status of the
troops.

However, it was to no avail. Solomon said that early
one morning around two a.m., and without his adviser's
forewarning, Villa ordered his crack troops, his personal
dorados, the golden ones, to take a position in front of his
main body of troops. Without prior disclosure to his men,
a shot rang out and the enemy, assuming this was Villa attacking, ordered his forces to advance and attacked Villa's
troops and the people in the city.

This turned into the worst battle of the entire war.

Solomon, Felipe Ángeles, and others witnessed this
slaughter from high on a hill overlooking the plains. In the
gray light of dawn, they saw the most gruesome bloodshed
and butchery they had ever seen. Not only Villa's troops
but the women and children who traveled with the army
were massacred.

Ángeles turned to his companions and said angrily
that Villa had brought this on himself. He did not know of
any military code of honor that they themselves should
follow which required their death in this fiasco. At that
they fled, and so did Villa and others.

They reached El Paso, crossed the river, and escaped. Edward Solomon and Felipe Ángeles eventually became partners in the dairy business together.

Later Edward made regular trips to Chicago to bring
back high-quality dairy stock to El Paso.

He'd ride with the cattle and instruct the engineers
how to start and stop the train slowly so as not to injure
the stock, and he would gift the engineers with money so
they would do as he wished.

Edward developed a reputation as a keen business-man. One day a stranger approached him, enticing him to invest in gold options. He handed him an envelope and they made a deal for Edward to buy options for several thousand shares. A few days later when he returned from a trip, a man met him at the station and asked him if would sell the options, telling Edward that he would give him a huge profit. This seemed suspicious, so he replied that he would check the prices first and would let him know. As it turned out, the price was considerably higher than what the man had just offered.

The price skyrocketed. Edward sold his options immediately, and although the price plummeted after he sold, he was now a wealthy man. He was then known as a very smart man in any kind of business transaction.

Edward spent time back east in many successful business ventures through the years. Eventually, he went to Deming, New Mexico. It was around 1915 and Edward had been told that at Gage, New Mexico, west of Deming, there was a gold mine that had once been owned by William Randolph Hearst. It was reportedly a very rich mine, so rich that when ore came out of the ground, it could be loaded onto a train of burros owned by Mr. Gage and taken straight to Denver without having to process it.

But Hearst had abandoned the mine after underground water flooded it, and the mine had changed hands. The current owner had not succeeded in solving the flooding problem but convinced Edward that they could purchase pumps in Belgium that would dry the mine out. Edward went into partnership on yet another gold venture with this new partner, Mr. Smith, who was waiting for his money to be telegraphed from New York. In the meantime, the new partners met each morning for breakfast and talked over their plans before walking to a telegraph office to see if the money had come in.

One morning someone came rushing into the hotel and shouted there was a man in the street who wanted to see Mr. Smith. Outside was a cowboy, and as Edward and he stood on the porch, the cowboy asked which one was Mr. Smith. Mr. Smith acknowledged he was. It seems that Smith had broken the leg of the man's boss at a party the night before, so the cowboy killed Smith on the spot.

Now Edward owned the mine by himself, and he set about to make the venture pay. The pumps arrived from Belgium. He rounded up every ox and wagon in the county and took them 120 miles to Gage from El Paso. Incredibly, Edward was able to pump a lot of water out of the mine. Soon, he began to extract very high-quality ore from the ground.

By now, the mine had come to be known as King Solomon's Mine. He saw a bright future and included in it was the hope to marry a woman from a wealthy Chicago family.

However, her father immediately began to quash this love affair. He didn't want a Jewish name coming into their family and ordered his daughter to destroy all letters from Edward and end all contact with him.

Edward was crushed.

Her father had somehow failed to order her to destroy photographs she had of the two of them. Over the span of their lifetimes, Edward kept in touch with her, and in later years Spencer and Edward went to visit her in a nursing home.

She still had those cherished photographs.

But because of this tragedy and a broken heart, Edward was somewhat traumatized. He determined that this would not happen again because of his name and changed it from Edward Miller Solomon to Edward S. Miller, thinking there would be less prejudice against his Jewish name. However, it seems his corporations and other assets were often held in both names. [38]

As if a broken heart weren't enough, tragedy struck the mine as well. One night the foreman of the mine rushed to wake Edward. They had breached an aquifer and water was gushing into the mine with the roar of a thousand lions.

Edward's engineers soon broke the gloomy news to him. The only way to seal up that water, they told him, would be to bore a tunnel a hundred miles to the Rio Grande.

Edward walked away from the whole thing.

It was many years later that Edward met and married Louisa in Mexico. By then, Edward had lost and made several fortunes back East and in other parts of the country.

But once again, his fortunes waned. He and Louisa moved to Escondido, California, and were living there when Spencer reconnected with Louisa and met Edward for the first time. Edward loved plants and flowers. He had brought with him from South Africa the flower Proteus and he discovered that they thrived in California. Before long, Edward had introduced the flowers to California. Today they flourish all over the state.

When Spencer met him in 1974, Edward was in his 80's. Spencer liked him immediately and was entirely fascinated with his life story and how he had literally been on the front lines with Pancho Villa. The couple had two young adult sons, who at the time did not pay much attention to this old man and his stories. After all, here he was in a rocking chair.

But one night Edward had a vivid dream that he was operating that mine in Gage again, mining it and shipping ore. He had the exact recurring dream three times in a short span of time. He was determined at that point to get up out of his rocking chair, go to Gage, and open that mine again.

One of the sons reasoned that maybe if he and his brother took Edward over to Gage and he saw that it was in total disrepair after all these years—and that it would most likely still be flooded—then Edward would give up this idea. But his son miscalculated.

By now most of the mining stock had been sold off in pieces, so when Edward saw the mine in person again, he told his son they must drive north to the capital of Santa Fe that very day and research the current owners of the mine. The water table was much lower by now and he thought it could be mined again.

Edward found all the owners and for very little cost bought the land and the mine again and brought together investors to begin operations. Edward and his wife picked up their belongings from Escondido and moved lock, stock and barrel to Deming, New Mexico.

Enter friend Spencer. Around 1974 he invested thirty thousand dollars in the mine, and every two months he drove to Deming from California to assist in getting the mine up and going.

Edward sank a shaft looking for the veins of ore. He was told that he was using obsolete methods, but he didn't care. He was sure he could make the mine payoff; but with tremendous odds against it, the mine did not pay off.

Then soon, luck turned against him once again. He was told he had a heart aneurysm and that there were two choices before him: an extremely risky surgery to try to save him, or not have the operation and face certain death. The odds for either choice were not good. He courageously opted for surgery, but unfortunately, he did not make it.

After Edward died, the mining venture ended. As far as Spencer knew, it was still valueless.

But for Edward, and because of his courage in attempting to salvage the gold mine, and in trying to save his own life, he gained the admiration of his sons. One later attained a mining degree to follow in his father's path.

Louisa passed away sometime later.

For Spencer, this experience taught him the complications of owning part of a gold mine that did not produce. It was worthless.

However, for Spencer, and although it turned out to be a bad investment in the mine, the experience yielded something much more valuable.

The real treasure offered up to Spencer was not King Solomon's mine, but Juan Quezada. As the saying goes, all that glitters is not gold; and all that is gold does not always glitter. Juan Quezada was indeed a discovery of pure gold, although not of the glittery, metallic sort.

It was like this: many years after young Spencer and his family explored and then returned from Mexico—and many years after they had traveled with their friend Louisa—and many years after Spencer lived his life, and much later after he went to college, made great discoveries, and years later after he lived and loved, did he then buy a prehistoric pot which led him to his destiny, the prehistoric pot he bought for fifteen dollars at a yard sale!

Many more years later did his family's Mexico friend, Louisa, end up in California with her husband, who owned a gold mine in Gage, New Mexico, just west of Deming, New Mexico.

Even later, on a visit to see Louisa, did Spencer invest in said gold mine. And then, while making trips back and forth from California to Deming, New Mexico, Spencer would always check out the local yard sales and old junk stores in Deming.

One day, destiny played a hand and offered Spencer his future. He would wander into a junk shop to explore its offerings and find *the* magic pots.

Truly, only Spencer could really *tell it like it was*, as he walked, unexpectedly, back into Mexico again in 1976, and into a completely new life.

Chapter Eight

Mata Ortiz – Spencer Tells It Like It Was

"One Saturday morning I had exhausted all the small offerings of Deming, New Mexico yard sales, and thought I'd check out a store I had seen on the end of town, Bob's Swap Shop." After he entered the store, Spencer eyed three prehistoric-looking pots on a shelf. They were uncannily similar to the one that had been sitting on his piano for quite a while.

"I thought they were prehistoric, but the owner was adamant, no, they were not, they had been traded for used clothing several months earlier. I took the shop owner's words to heart and accepted that these pots had been "distressed," a term used which makes them look older. Later, after I met Juan, he told me he, himself, did not distress nor trade the pots. Someone else had distressed them to make them look prehistoric. Juan told me that he knew this was being done and he reasoned that he was a potter, and it was his job to make the pots. What others did with them after he sold them, he could not control," Spencer said.

"This only made practical sense to a man who had seven children and was very poor.

"At any rate, back at the junk store, the pots grabbed me and wouldn't let go. I remember walking around the shop all churning inside, and my best garage-sale-cool on the outside," he recalled.

Figure 16. *The Famous Deming Pots. Spencer's discovery of Juan Quezada's Deming Pot 1 of 3 Courtesy of Museum of Us, San Diego, California, November 2022*

Figure 17. *The Famous Deming Pots. Spencer's discovery of Juan Quezada's Deming Pot 2 of 3 Courtesy Museum of Us, San Diego, California, November 2022*

Figure 18. *The Famous Deming Pots. Spencer's*
discovery of Juan Quezada's Deming Pot 3 of 3
Courtesy Museum of Us, San Diego, California,
November 2022

145

"Then I realized that it didn't matter if they were prehistoric or not, just like my pot sitting on my piano.

"They were what they were, and it didn't matter at all. Finally, I bought them for eighteen dollars apiece. That seemed expensive at the time, but I couldn't argue that they weren't good quality. I took them back to Edward and Louisa's house in Deming. I'll never forget that evening.

"We were watching the Olympics on TV and I just loved watching gymnastics. But I couldn't focus, and after about forty-five minutes of the Olympics, I kept getting up to look at those pots. I was very taken by them.

"As I drove back to LA the next day, the pots were sitting on the front seat of my truck. I couldn't take my mind off them. I finally realized that in order to complete this experience I was going to have to find the potter. I called Bob's Swap Shop and asked if anyone there had any idea where they came from. The answer was no, but I was told that if I were going to look, I should try Mexico first. Of course, I knew that before I called them, but it was then, at that very moment, I knew I was actually going to Mexico to search for the potter.

"On my next trip to Deming, my mother was also visiting the Millers. I convinced her and Louisa to go down to Mexico with me on an adventure to find the potter I was searching for. They agreed! The three of us made plans and set out on the trip." Spencer thought it was significant that his mother was along for this adventure since, after all, it was she who had taken him to Mexico and encouraged his interest in archaeology and anthropology.

Still, it did seem uncanny that the three of them were headed into Mexico again so many years later. "I didn't want to take the pots with me and risk losing them at customs. So, I took photos of them with me instead. There was only one road going south into Mexico from Deming, so at each small village, out came the pictures. We asked everyone we saw if they recognized the pots," Spencer said.

"The name of the Mata Ortiz village came up a couple of times. We seemed to be heading in that direction so that by Saturday morning we had arrived at Nuevo Casa Grandes," Spencer said.

"Someone had suggested we check with a potter by the name of Manuel Olivas in Nuevo Casas Grandes. His grandmother had been a potter, and he had learned from her to make utilitarian pottery, but at some point, he had begun to make reproductions of the prehistoric pottery which had been found in the area, including effigy pots for which he became well-known." Effigy pottery is made in the likenesses of birds, animals, humans, and ancestral characters, and comes from the Casas Grandes culture which Charles DiPeso excavated at the Paquimé ruins in 1958-1961. [39]

"Because Manuel was making similar pottery to Juan's, he studied the pictures and immediately told me that he could make pots just like those. I explained that I was not looking for more pots, but for the potter who had made the ones in the photos. But he insisted he could make them just as good, maybe better! Manuel was an ingenious fellow. He showed me the kiln he had devised which he fired with sawdust obtained free from a lumber yard.

"He said he always fired at night. I asked why. He explained it made a lot of smoke and the neighbors complained. Even though he always fired at night, 'people be-

147

gan to notice the buildings around the plaza were turning gray. It was my firing.' He was using a keg of kerosene on a high tripod with a thin copper tube going down into a steel drum. By the time the kerosene went down the tube, it vaporized and that was his firing chamber.

"This all took place about twelve feet from his neighbor's fence and he was walking too close to it," Spencer laughed.

Figure 19. Manuel Olivas' firing methods using a steel drum, circa 2006 Courtesy of the Jon Samuelson Collection

"Manuel advised him to move away from it because the previous week he'd had an accident, an explosion, and a fire that burned the neighbor's pig—they had an unplanned BBQ! Manuel was a jovial person and very talented."

Figure 20. *Manuel Olivas' homemade sundial, circa 2006*
Courtesy of the Jon Samuelson Collection

After Manuel passed, his wife Maria, along with other family members, continued as highly successful potters. Manuel was the only *official* reproducer of prehistoric pottery for the Museo de las Culturas del Norte (Paquimé) in Casas Grandes for many years. [40]

His effigy pieces, along with the other prehistoric reproductions, and some of his children's more modern pieces, are hugely popular with anyone who visits the area.

Manuel Olivas was an important part of the Mata Ortiz and Casas Grandes pottery story.

He was born in 1940 and passed on May 3, 2007.

When Spencer showed up at his house, the was extremely helpful. He directed Spencer, his mother, and Louisa to Mata Ortiz, and the trio set out across the plains.

"The countryside was full of mesquite and not much more than a cow path for a road. It wound and turned with car tracks going off every which way. We got lost and a logging truck came along and directed us to Mata Ortiz," Spencer said.

Figure 21. *Kids on burros cruising the village*
in the evening glow, circa 2006
Courtesy of the Jon Samuelson Collection

"As we came into the village, we met a youngster about eleven years old on a burro. I showed him the photos of the pots and he said, 'Follow me'. It was quite a feat driving the truck slowly behind the burro, but finally, we were relieved when he motioned us to a house.

"I went up and knocked and Juan's wife, Guille, came to the door. She invited us inside. The house had three small rooms and seven children running around in it. Shortly, Juan came in the back door. I showed him the photos. He couldn't believe anyone would take photos of his pots, much less search him out. He confirmed that yes, he had made those pots about six months before." Spencer was surprised not only that he had found his potter, but also that he was a man. He had been looking for a woman, as most potters were women and he had made that assumption.

"Momentarily, there was a silence in the room. Juan misread me, and reacted by saying that he could do much better work than those pots in the photos.

"Then he took some pieces down off a high shelf and immediately I could see that I had found the very same potter who had made the ones I bought in Deming. Juan was nervous and volunteered an explanation that no one had been able to pay him to do his best work and he had a wife and seven children to support.

"The pots he just showed to me were very poor quality. Juan repeated that this was not the best work he could do. I told him I was only interested in his best, and that I would come back in two months. I asked him to make me samples of his best work. He replied, '*Seguro, que sí.*' Yes, of course.

"When I returned in two months, Juan and I had a halting, but long conversation about him, his family, his work, and his artistry.

Juan revealed that after years of experimentation he had made his first polychrome pot around 1970 or 1971. Juan and Guille remembered those times of celebration—

his first polychrome pot, and the birth of their son, Juan, Jr., in January 1971."

Juan soon discovered these pots had value. He gave them away as gifts to family and friends; but to Juan's disappointment, he discovered the same gift pots were being sold. It is not clear if any of these pots survived so many years later.

Another pivotal turning point occurred when Juan and a friend decided to walk to Palomas, Mexico, about a hundred miles, to find work. Juan carried some pots along to see if he could sell them. Indeed, he found a buyer; in fact, one that paid him more money for his pottery than he could have ever imagined.

Like most men of the village, Juan took a job working on the railroad to make a steady income, but he continued to experiment with pottery. During those years, he encouraged family members and friends to learn the art of pottery making. He always figured it could be good extra income for the entire family, and they always needed extra money. Eventually, his siblings Nicolás, Reynaldo, Reynalda, Consolación, Lydia, and Taurina learned from Juan, and began to make pottery.

Juan's pottery sales increased in increments, and he took a bold step in 1974. He had secured a large order for pottery from a company in El Paso by the name of Americraft, which handled Mexican imported crafts. He decided to take time off from working on the railroad to see if he could make a living doing what he loved to do, making pottery.

It was the right time to jump out of the nest and try his wings. He had hired five neighbors in the village to help him with this order.

"But by the time Juan and I met in 1976, he had already concluded that he could not continue this contract much longer because when producing volume like this, he couldn't maintain the quality—and Americraft wanted both quality and quantity. Of course, he found that to be impossible."

Spencer said, "Juan gave me a very brief explanation of how he did his pot-making, by draping clay over a curved plate or bowl to form the bottom of a pot. Then he built the pot from the bottom up by shaping a fat donut-shaped single coil of clay with his hands forming the pot from the bottom up. But he was not ready in that first meeting to give me more information.

"When later I met Professor Bill Miles from New Mexico State University at Las Cruces," Spencer said, "he had already traveled to Mata Ortiz before I found Juan myself. He had met Juan because it became known that there was pottery-making going on in Mata Ortiz. Because the area was economically depressed, Bill Miles had been asked to travel to Mata Ortiz to teach the potters the use of the potter's wheel. 'It was what was going on in Mata Ortiz in the way of art and they should leave it alone or they would ruin it,' Bill said. It seems that the government did attempt for two more years to get Juan to accept a diesel-fired kiln. The government wanted him to make mass-produced pottery, but he refused. He was not at all interested in anything he did not create himself. It had to be something he created and thought of himself."

Spencer reflected later that in the very beginning, neither he nor Juan could have imagined what lay ahead for them. They were forever linked from that moment forward. Not only linked but they were fascinated with each

other. Did they have any idea what lay ahead? It seems unlikely, but still, from the moment Spencer met Juan, he
knew something special was happening. "As time went on,
I came to understand that finding *that potter* of those three
junk store pots would not be the end of the Bob's Swap
Shop story, but only the beginning."

Spencer told Juan on that day in March of 1976 that
he would like him to make some of his very best pottery,
do his best work, and he would be back in a couple of
months to buy some pottery from him.

As promised, Spencer returned to Mata Ortiz in two
months' time; however, the pots Juan showed him were
essentially the same as he had been producing before. "He
had not believed I would come back," Spencer conjectured. "He had probably thought I was just a strange gringo who would never return.

"But even so, next an interesting thing happened!
Now that I had come back, he believed I *was* "for real." He
introduced me to his family members around Mata Ortiz.
It was a memorable day for me. As was the custom in Mata
Ortiz at the time, at each household I was offered hospital-
ity and meals. I must have had six meals that day.

"Through this entire period, my Spanish was very
poor because I had not spoken it for thirty years and had
forgotten it. Juan speaks rural Spanish which was hard to
understand. It was funny when I didn't understand what he
said, his response was to say it louder and faster. We com-
municated in a very basic way.

"But now that Juan somewhat believed in me, I was
able to emphasize, to help him understand, that I wanted
his "best" work, so I felt good that he got it, and we arranged for me to come back for a third visit.

"On the next trip, the third trip, I took photographer Bobbie Furst with me. Bobbie Furst was the son of the anthropologist Peter Furst who had done a lot of work with the Indians of western Mexico. Bobbie was naturally intrigued by this story. He photographed Juan making pottery and today these photographs are priceless. They are used over and again in books and at museums. [41]

"Juan had a number of pots ready to show me, and then proceeded to make a pot for us in the small kitchen of his little house. It was the windy season, and the winds howled and howled. A terrible sandstorm raged outside the house. All seven of Juan's kids were indoors. Their friends and other family members crowded throughout the small, adobe house. Bobbie set up his camera equipment. Even with all this activity going on, we watched Juan make that pot as if he were alone in the universe. It was mesmerizing to watch his hands at work. I could not take my eyes off his hands. I know other people also have that experience when they see him work. We sat there for two speechless hours.

"Still, even though his pots were somewhat better this time, I didn't think they were remarkably better. I asked Juan, 'Out of these pots you have lined up here, which one did you most enjoy making?'

"His answer floored me. 'Spencer, I have been so busy making pots I haven't had time to look at them.'

"I had wanted to buy everything he was making, even the broken and cracked pots. Here he was, a dirt-poor farmer trying to be a potter in a remote village in Mexico and suddenly he had this "live one" from L.A. buying everything he made. So, what was his incentive? It took me a bit to figure this out.

"But then I had a sudden realization. He thought it was to turn out pots by quantity, not quality.

"It was a long time before I knew exactly what my role in this adventure was. I was confused in the beginning. I knew that there in front of me was an extraordinary talent, possibly a talent as brilliant as any known artist on the world level, and I wanted to have a hand in helping that talent get off the ground. I wanted to be a part of setting him up in an environment that would be conducive to this end. I gave it a lot of thought. Very often when craft items are marketed the quality goes down because the distributor needs quantity. Eventually, this is reflected in the marketplace. Oftentimes the artist has no choice. They want to produce their art and in order to make a living the quality is sacrificed.

"On my next trip, I realized I needed to change the incentive for Juan. I told him that I had been thinking about it and proposed a different arrangement. I offered to pay him a stipend each month of three hundred US dollars for six months and he would give me everything he made. This money was a huge sum of money in those days in Mexico and would be equivalent to around fifteen hundred dollars per month in U.S. currency today. This would give him the freedom to pursue his art in any direction. He would be free to create anything he wanted. I encouraged him to experiment. I wanted him to explore and be free to use different materials. I said he would have time to look for new clays. And I told him that, sometimes what we look for the most often eludes us, and sometimes we have to let it come to us.

"I knew there might be some months there would be no pots coming from Juan. There was even the possibility that the art would not be ceramics because I knew he had also been doing woodcarving. At any rate, he happily agreed to the arrangement.

"My friends asserted that I had lost my mind and money. They hypothesized that even worse, 'you'll break the will of this human being, that real freedom is very difficult, and he'll want this relationship to continue, and you won't, and it could drive him to drink!'" Spencer laughed. "I wasn't worried," he added.

Spencer was proven out. He reported that when he returned on his next trip, the work Juan had produced was an order of magnitude better than anything he had made before.

"I returned every two months and this improvement continued for the first three years. It was just amazing. These were the "magical years," and they were extraordinary. It was as if this was the golden formula Juan had been waiting for all of his life."

With pots in hand, Spencer saw his role as one of communicating to the world this stupendous artistry of Juan Quezada and reasoned that there was usually no shortage of people who value quality art, although he certainly understood that oftentimes there is a distance of time, marketing, and availability between the artist and the buyer of fine art. It sounded simple, but it took quite a bit of thought to work this out. Driving back and forth to his home in Los Angeles, he had plenty of time to think this through, and about the genius of the young Juan.

During one of these road trips, Spencer met Anne Copeland. It was the late summer of 1976, and the beginning of a relationship that lasted about 6 years.

"It was early in the Juan project, towards the end of the first year, 1976. I was on the way back from Mata Ortiz to my home in San Pedro, California, passing through Phoenix, and decided to stop in and say hello and make the acquaintance of the people who published a small Libertarian magazine, *Freedom Today*."

Anne was the editor of the magazine, and she and Spencer were immediately attracted to one another. According to Annie, a very enigmatic Spencer came into her office. "He was very handsome and seemed extremely interesting, and I was instantly drawn to him."

Spencer felt the same, he said. "She was very good-looking, a redhead, and unbeknownst to me at the time, had set her mind to marry an archeologist or anthropologist someday. And here one appeared with a truckload of pottery up from Mexico, looking like an answer to her prayers."

Annie had just graduated with a degree in archaeology a few months before she met Spencer. She agreed they hit it off instantly. "I was titillated that he found me good-looking." Annie confirmed that she had dreamed of meeting an archaeologist or an anthropologist.

Spencer said, "I was so slim on my budget in those days that I had to sleep outdoors in the desert. When I told her this, the conversation led to something like my asking her, 'What are you doing tonight?'"

One thing led to another, and the two new friends camped out together in the desert that very same night. She remembered, "I went along joyfully because I was feeling very lost with the stressful dissolution of my marriage, and of course, I was also very attracted to Spencer. We did spend the night in a sleeping bag under the stars and Spencer, in his typical way, told me all kinds of neat stories about the stars. It was just immensely romantic. I knew I would love him from that very night. We awoke to see the sun rising with brilliant colors."

Annie had been separated from her husband for a while at the time she met Spencer. "I was married to an architect. We were still good friends, but our marriage was collapsing. He, too, was a libertarian. He had gone down a more dramatic road, becoming a tax resistor, and worse still, teaching others how to do it by forming a church organization. He had also given up practicing architecture. His personality changed when he went down this path. After we divorced, I think he was heartbroken, realizing what he had done to create the mess he was in. He finally returned to his architecture career."

On Spencer's next trip through Phoenix, they arranged to see each other again. Spencer used the same terminology as Annie in describing the beginning of their relationship. "It was so romantic, like a storybook meeting, and how it blossomed."

Spencer recounts that Annie was very important in the beginning of the project as he was getting his footing. He considered her as a key player in the early days. "She was personable, and Juan and his family gravitated toward her. Her warmth extended to all the other potters in the village, as well," Spencer said.

Annie recalled that those were very happy days. Her ex-husband and Spencer were both very mature and never harbored negative feelings toward each other. In fact, later Spencer asked and paid him to design the cover for a book by E.C. Riegle, *Flight From Inflation*, which Spencer had co-edited. Annie felt that she would always love her first husband for all he contributed to her life, and she would always love Spencer for all that he added as they went along.

Annie had experienced devastating trauma in her childhood. She had entered her previous marriage, and now this relationship with Spencer, with low self-esteem.

Her father had been abandoned by his parents at the height of the Great Depression when he was just 16 and had been regularly beaten by his father. He lied about his age and joined the Army. He met her mother and they married.

"Married life in the Army was very hard on both of them. Dad was gone much of our lives, first to World War II, and then later to Korea, and he served a couple of years in Okinawa after World War II before we were able to join him. It was a stressful life for everyone. In my memory, it seemed that women and children on Okinawa Island turned insane. Children, especially, really acted out in horrible ways. It was a nightmare for me every single day we were there." Over the years, much of the history of the psychological status of Americans on Okinawa has been published.

But the dream of Mata Ortiz and trying to fulfill Spencer's vision was difficult on her. "By the time I met Spencer, I was not an easy person to live with. I could not believe anyone could really love me and so I always questioned our relationship. . ." These emotional roller coaster rides impacted their relationship in a negative way.

Even so, Anne became a fixture on his trips to Mata Ortiz and helped him get the project off the ground. She was accomplished in many arenas and driven to learn new things.

Spencer encouraged her, as well, to branch out by starting her own graphic arts business or writing her Pumpkin cookbook, which she finally published in 2019.

Anne felt that Spencer and she were each other's best editors and could offer positive feedback about their publishing business, and the pottery venture.

For Spencer, the relationship was at times very difficult, and although Annie was fun to be with, she had a terrible fear that he wouldn't be true to her. Spencer had declared a very strong commitment, absolutely a life commitment, to her.

They were together during what Spencer dubbed, "the early, magical years" of Mata Ortiz. She went down to Mexico with him on several trips and still today there are people who remember her.

When she stopped traveling to Mata Ortiz with Spencer, it was natural for folks to wonder why. Spencer made excuses for her, saying that she was busy back in California. But there was a darkness inside of her that made her feel she was competing for his attention with the pottery project. Spencer could do nothing to keep her insecurities from manifesting out of nowhere. "She seemed to enjoy going down with me at first, but after a while, she just stopped," Spencer disclosed. "The beautiful relationship spiraled downward out of control."

She helped Spencer publish several of Popdaddy's works.

"I took care of the book orders, did the bookkeeping, and correspondence, and helped edit and even typeset one of the books."

She also helped him classify and put away the pottery and get it organized in his little rental garage.

Years later Walter Parks arrived on the scene. He became an avid Mata Ortiz enthusiast and the author of the very popular book, *The Miracle of Mata Ortiz*.

Published in 1993, the book has been an important resource for collectors of pottery for many years.

Walter became a good friend and helped Spencer document his pottery collection.

Anne remembered Spencer's little rental garage was the most fascinating place to go, for it was filled with all kinds of art, and in the middle of a very poor neighborhood with gang members hanging around who didn't have a clue about the dollar value of the art and pottery. Keeping valuable art in such a nondescript garage in a bad neighborhood was smart, for no one would think that there would be anything of value at all stored there.

Figure 22. *Walter Parks and Spencer MacCallum*
holding the three Deming pots in front the storage garage
Photo courtesy of the Walter Parks Collection

"Spencer was funny that way. He hid things in the most unlikely places," she said.

"Like carrying the pottery from Mata Ortiz in duffel bags across the border and, believe it or not, we never had a single pot get scratched or broken. He was always very low-key. He drove the same old Datsun pickup from the day I met him until long after we separated."

Spencer had a sense of class about him and demonstrated his knowledge of art by collecting very beautiful and unique pieces. Besides the large collection of Northwest Coast Indian art, he collected anything that caught his eye, and if it could be found at a garage sale, he would value it even more.

"When I met him," Anne recalled, "he had beautiful furnishings in his home and fabulous paintings on every wall. I still remember a favorite painting that looked like a piece from the Craftsman period. It was dark and mysterious. I remember he got it at a garage sale. He knew his art really well and always found treasures. Once he found a painting at a garage sale for ten dollars and later discovered its value at around two thousand five hundred dollars." Eventually, the couple decided they had more in common as friends helping each other than in a romantic relationship.

"The most important thing of all for me," Spencer reflected, "was that Annie eventually found certain healing and peace in her life. That was a blessing for her. And I was always grateful for her helping me, from the beginning."

Chapter Nine

Spencer Tells the Story of Juan Quezada and His
Incredible Artistry and His Journey of Discovery

When Spencer talked about the pottery, he liked to start at the beginning. Spencer shared his thoughts during in-depth interviews with the author during the first-ever joint interview, conducted by the author, with Spencer and Juan.

"I will start with Juan," Spencer explained. "He was a painfully shy man, which was ironic for someone who was also the all-time undefeated boxing champion of the village!

"I learned how shy he was, for example, from the story that his mother told me of when he would go up the mountain to cut firewood but would convince his brothers and sisters to sell it door to door for him because he was too reserved."

As Spencer got to know him, he began to understand that Juan had learned most of what he knew by experimentation and by studying prehistoric pottery.

He thought that Juan was astute, talented, and driven to be an artist. There were not many potters to emulate at that time, so he learned it on his own by trial and error.

Juan also did not know about the American Indians in the United States making pottery. In fact, according to Spencer, he didn't know they even existed.

"It was a couple of years before I realized that Juan had never had much input from the outside world, on any level. Each time I asked him a technical question he would tell me how he developed it. It was almost unheard of that someone like this did not learn his art directly from other potters. "

Figure 23. The first-ever joint interview of Spencer and Juan, 2005
Courtesy of the Jon Samuelson Collection

Although Juan had never visited the Paquimé ruins, he had picked up potsherds of prehistoric pottery by the hundreds over the years."

These he studied. So, in essence, his teachers were the ancient potters who lived in that area in the long ago past.

Figure 24. Juan signing the author's copy of
The Miracle of Mata Ortiz by Walter P. Parks, 2005
Courtesy of the Jon Samuelson Collection

"He figured out how to start a pot by using a bowl from the kitchen and pressing a tortilla of clay into it. This would be the base mold. Then he would make a fat coil of clay and put it on the mold and with his fingers press it all the way around. This doughnut would be the reservoir of clay for the pot. With his fingers, he would work the clay up to the height he wanted and then start forming it.

This method was unique to Juan and is known as the single coil method, as opposed to the Southwest Indians who used a continuous coil to make their pots.

Figure 25. *Spencer signing the author's copy of* The Miracle of Mata Ortiz *by Walter P. Parks, 2005 Courtesy of the Jon Samuelson Collection*

"If he were making a larger pot, he would add another coil further along. For the lip Juan would add a separate ring, saying that the lip was the *soul* of the pot—a delicate detail that gave the pot character. The single coil method was used in his neighborhood of Mata Ortiz for many years thereafter." Spencer reflected that as pottery-making began to catch on, there was no one who was more of a purist than Juan.

"He wanted the most uncontaminated clay he could get. He had broken and studied prehistoric pottery sherds and had detected particles of sand in the sherds. But he thought that was prehistoric carelessness. Eventually, though, he noticed that even in the best and finest of the pots this same sandy material was used.

Figure 26. *Spencer points to something of*
interest to Juan, 2005
Courtesy of the Jon Samuelson Collection

"As potters today know, when clay dries it shrinks a great deal if it doesn't have something known as a temper added to it," Spencer explained.

To temper means to bring the clay to the proper texture, consistency, or hardiness by mixing it with another ingredient.

"Without temper, ceramics break. The Southwest Indians use broken and crushed pottery shards as temper."

Figure 27. *Paquimé Ruins, Casas Grandes, Mexico, 2006*
Courtesy of the Jon Samuelson Collection

One day Juan's mother remarked that his deceased grandmother had indeed made pots in the old days, but his mother knew nothing about it, so she didn't know to tell him to add temper to clay. When pottery was displaced by ceramic ware, she was not interested in the old pottery making of her mother and aunts. Even though it took a while for Juan to make this connection, he eventually discovered the principle and worked out the formula. The microscopic particles of clay hold the water, but when it dries the particles come together and produce a lot of shrinkage. That shrinkage is counteracted by adding material that will hold the particles apart and keep the pot from shrinking. That is the principle of temper and he had discovered it himself, just before Spencer arrived on the scene.

Juan had been firing a lot of pots for Americraft. He used a big bucket of water and would put walnut shells in it to give the pots a patina. Next, he would put the hot pot in the water to cool it down. Juan had enough temper in his clay that the pot would not break, but eventually realized it was too much.

Later on, he began finding clay in the area that had its own temper of volcanic ash—he only needed to select the clay carefully. These clay deposits were available to any potter as they were surrounded by *ejido* land, community land. After the revolution, private lands were put into a community trust, usable by everyone.

Juan was also on the hunt for white clay for a long time. One day he said to Spencer, "Well, maybe this clay I'm looking for is not white in its natural state but turns white after it is fired."

He was always thinking about pottery and the clay and the paints.

"So it was that on a particular day, he was out looking for clay and Juan saw ants moving white pellets around on the ground. He dug around the anthill and suddenly there it was, the white clay."

Figure 28. The famous "T" shaped doors at
Paquimé ruins, Casas Grandes, Mexico, 2006
Courtesy of the Jon Samuelson Collection

In the beginning, Juan would burnish the pots using a spoon. Later, he began to use chalcedony agate stones which he would shape by grinding them underwater, then polish the stones with leather.

He also used deer bone and would specially prepare it. When he first fired the pots, he used wood, but that wasn't satisfactory.

He next tried firing the pots by burying them in a bucket with charcoal. When they were burning, he would swing the bucket up and down over his head to get air into the pot. When his arm was about to fall off, he would hand it over to his friend who was going to get a third of what Juan made from the sale of the pot. The pot would be fired just fine, but this method was burning holes in their pants and shoes, which they would have to replace.

Juan knew this was not going to work on a long-term basis. So, he looked around and decided to try dried cow chips, which worked much better. "Juan was able to tell me how he discovered each step in making pottery," Spencer explained. Juan told Spencer about his youth and how he discovered the pottery, an intriguing picture began to emerge. "I asked his mother some questions about his childhood and learned that he didn't start school till he was nine, but by the age of twelve, he was ready to leave school. Instead, you could find him roaming the hills and the mountains where he felt more at home than in the village. He began to collect wood to sell, and he would bring the wood down the mountain on the family burro, *El Minuto*, so named because of his smallness. Juan himself was young and not yet experienced, so one day he overloaded the burro. It slipped and tumbled over and over down the mountain," Spencer said.

Figure 29. Near the beginning of the relationship:
Younger Juan Quezada—Younger Spencer MacCallum
Courtesy of the Spencer MacCallum Collection

Figure 30. *Juan Quezada speaking to a*
tour group, circa 2007
Courtesy of the Jon Samuelson Collection

Figure 31. *A firing demonstration of pottery made by other artists at Juan Quezada's compound, 2007*
Courtesy of the Jon Samuelson Collection

"Juan ran after him down the steep slope and at the bottom, Juan thought surely the burro was dead. Crying, he unloaded the wood and went running home. Suddenly, just before he reached the house he heard "ee uh, ee uh, ee uh. He turned and saw *El Minuto* coming down the mountain to greet him. Never was a boy so happy," Spencer said.

His mother, Doña Paulita, disclosed that during his three years of school he learned nothing because he would constantly be drawing.

"From very early years, Juan was artistically inclined. He was not able to buy commercial paints or supplies, so he would experiment with egg yolks, green leaves, grass-hoppers, and anything that had color."

Juan would ask his mother to tell anyone who came looking for him that he was not home when in reality he was drawing on the walls in a storeroom where the children slept. He filled the walls with designs, and when they were all covered, he would take newspapers soaked in kerosene, laboriously clean them off, and start over. That is how he learned. He would draw anything, the railroad trestle, the hills and mountains, animals, and his favorite, the eagle design found on the Mexican coin.

When Juan spoke to tour groups during a firing demonstration in his backyard, he told his own stories, and especially a wonderful story of how he became interested in making pottery.

Juan said, "I was exploring a cave in the mountains and found two mummified bodies of a man and a woman. Beside them were two pots, one was white and one was yellow, and five other pots arranged around their feet. There were also other utilitarian pots that had been used for cooking, and they were full of beans, squash, roots, and other foods. But the painted, ceremonial pots intrigued me."

Juan explained that is where he had the idea that he could make one of those pots. "I had seen pieces of broken pottery in the area before, potsherds, but those pots in the cave were the first intact pieces I had found.

"I knew that the materials to make the pots had to be in the area and it was just a matter of exploration to find the materials and then rediscover that process.

"No one was interested in the first pieces I made. I didn't get any reaction at all! But three traders came to the village with clothing, shovels, and other items to trade which they had brought with them from the United States. I thought maybe if I gave them some of these pieces, they would take them to the United States, and perhaps some-one might take an interest. So, I asked them to take some of this pottery with them on their next trip.

"That's how it all started," Juan explained. "They were successful and came back asking for five, ten, or fif-teen pieces, and that's how it all began. Some of those pots that the traders took to the United States were probably the ones that Spencer found in the junk shop in Deming."

What is an absolutely amazing story within the story is what Spencer likes to call, "An unknowing woman's near miss at aborting the whole project."

In 2004, a woman approached Juan in Las Cruces, New Mexico holding three pots, which were similar to the ones that Spencer had discovered nearly 30 years earlier. She told a fascinating tale.

Apparently, six of Juan's pots had ended up on the shelf at Bob's Swap Shop in Deming. The day before Spencer appeared on the scene, this woman had visited the swap shop and had purchased three of those six. She took them home, showed her husband the find, and lamented that she had not purchased all six.

He told her not to worry. If she wanted them, they would go the next day and buy the other three. Enter Spencer and destiny.

He arrived at the swap shop early that next morning and purchased the remaining three pots on the shelf. When the woman and her husband arrived to buy them, they were gone. When hearing this story from the woman, Spencer and Juan were stunned. To think that if she had arrived there only an hour, or thirty minutes, or even five minutes earlier, Juan would never have become known as the master artist that he is today. It would have been very highly unlikely that today there would be over four hundred artists creating beautiful pottery, or that hundreds of family members would have benefited from better education and a better lifestyle, or that thousands of tourists today travel to Mata Ortiz.

As Spencer would always say, "life turns on the tiniest decisions we make each day of our lives."

Juan had shaken his head. "That story is just amazing."

Spencer agreed that from the very beginning there had been an almost magical essence to the chain of events. It was so intoxicating to Spencer that it took some time for him to understand his role on this side of the border. On the Mexican side of the border, it was important to support Juan and to help him bring to the village the concept of quality.

Spencer reflected, "Quality was a strange idea there at the time. Juan understood it and I understood it, but others did not. However, sometimes it only takes just one other person to give support to a new idea, in this case, the importance of quality. I stressed this mission, and I was able to play the role of guide to Juan, and in turn, to the village.

"Others came around to it reluctantly. His brother, Nicolás, was not turning out good work and I wouldn't buy it. Finally, one day he presented a nice piece, and I bought it. So of course, I expected everything to be good from then on. But it wasn't, and again, I wouldn't buy it. But gradually Nicolás came around to the idea of quality."

On the United States side of the border, Spencer's role was to promote Juan and the other potters. "After I had discovered Juan, I called Chuck Hillinger from the *Los Angeles Times*. He was the reporter who had written about the Narwhals when I became fascinated by them. "So, I introduced myself, and told him my Narwhal story—but then I revealed why I was calling him. 'You don't know me but I'm onto something you might be interested in.' A short time later he and I and a *Los Angeles Times* photographer were on the way to Mata Ortiz! Chuck was very interested in writing about my story of discovering Juan." In yet another "destiny moment" in Spencer's life, Chuck became his friend, and a willing instrument to spread the word of Juan Quezada.

"I wanted the story to be about Juan, but Chuck explained that I was an important part of the story, a bridge between the Mexican culture and our culture. Because of this, Chuck helped me to understand my role in the Mata Ortiz story, such as organizing shows.

"I had put together a traveling exhibition around 1979 and 1980. It would begin at California State Fullerton. To kick it off, Juan was invited to give a demonstration. I had taken Juan and Guille across the border at Columbus, New Mexico and we stayed the night with a rancher friend who lived just south of Deming. I contacted Bill Miles, the professor of ceramics at New Mexico State University at Las Cruces who had previously been to Mata Ortiz, to see if we could meet. He came to Deming and as we were talking, he commented to me, 'Spencer, I don't know of any artist, living at any time, in any part of the world, working in any medium, who has advanced his art as far as Juan has in a comparable period of time. And the most remarkable thing about it is that it has been totally self-directed.'

I think this was extraordinary.

"Some months later we traveled to Albuquerque to the opening of Mata Ortiz pottery at the Maxwell Museum. In my friend's BMW and my Datsun truck with the camper shell, we carried thirteen potters and boxes and boxes of pottery.

"It was a magnificent opening. The President of the University of New Mexico and the Mexican Consul attended. Everyone dressed up. It was wonderful to witness the reaction of Juan's parents, Doña Paulita and Don José, who saw for the first time what their son's art meant to the world. This was only three years after I had found Juan, so a lot had happened in a short amount of time.

"A highlight for all of us was a side trip to San Ildefonso Pueblo. Maria Martinez, (1887 - July 20, 1980), a world-renowned potter, had invited us, and I was so proud of Juan and the others that we could meet this great artist.

"We also had the gift of a wonderful side trip to Acoma. Lucy Lewis (1890 - March 12, 1992), another world-famous potter, and her daughters invited us to a specially prepared dinner at Acomita. Meeting both potters was a special occasion for Juan. [42]

"As a treat, Juan and one of Lucy's daughters tried each other's brushes and clay.

"We were served bowls of blue corn meal mush and large bowls of red chile salsa were passed around. This is a meal served to special visitors. As we were parting, Lucy's granddaughter who was eleven or twelve years old grabbed Juan's hand and held it hard. 'So that I might be a great potter, too,' she told Juan.

Her mother had tears coming down her face and was saying a prayer over Juan in the Acoma language.

"About five or six years later, Juan and Lucy Lewis and her daughters were demonstrating at Idyllwild and I suggested to Chuck Hillinger that he write a follow-up story, one which I have used many times over the years. He had noticed that Lucy and her two daughters were watching Juan work and Lucy was talking quite a bit to her daughters. She was telling them that she liked his work. After another pause, she spoke some more to her daughters. She was saying that Juan must be an Indian, or he would not have been able to handle clay as well as he did.

"After a bit more, she insisted that his ancestors must be Acoma Indians. She referred to a time when a Catholic priest at Acoma traded some young women into Mexican slavery for a church bell. She was convinced that he had to be a blood descendant of one of those slave women!"

Juan's career blossomed and he seemed to be enjoying his life. "But I wanted him to branch out a little."

Spencer said that for a long time he had wanted to ask Juan to make a very big pot, even though it would require a large mold for the tortilla base. He wasn't quite sure how to approach the subject with him.

"One day while I was in Los Angeles, I went out to where they make big propane tanks to see if I could get one of the ends. They did give me one, "for the cause."

"I was very happy, and we tied it with ropes on top of my camper shell. It was the funniest looking thing. By now, I had learned a thing or two about Juan, so I knew enough not to take it to him directly. Instead, I took it to his brother, Nicolás. I suggested to Nicolás that perhaps he might be able to use it when he made chitterlings. He was very pleased and helped get it off the truck.

"On my next trip to Mata Ortiz, I was very pleased to see it in Juan's yard, which is exactly where I wanted it. He then began to talk about making a big pot, but he never pursued it. I think at that point I did casually mention this project to Juan, but it never got off the ground."

By now, Spencer was in full swing promoting Juan, but he knew the time would come when the pottery would have to sustain itself.

Spencer visited many museum directors' offices, introducing himself with pots in hand, setting them on the director's desk, and allowing the pots to speak straight to the director in the language that Spencer had already learned. "These articulate pots that had spoken to me when I first saw them now took care of everything. Introduction, explanations, everything. I was just along for the ride."

Spencer recalls that there were many extraordinary events with Juan's pottery. The pots seemed to be instilled with a consciousness of their own, and that somehow the pottery touched people in many unexpected ways.

Just prior to the first US exhibition, Spencer had traveled to Mexico to bring Juan back with him to California, and to arrange for his family members to meet them later in Deming, New Mexico.

He was excited about this trip.

When he arrived in Mata Ortiz, a totally unexpected and remarkable thing happened. Spencer went to Juan's house and there were eight or nine large pots ready for the show. They were all about the same size, about a foot in diameter and perhaps eighteen inches in height.

When Spencer laid eyes on one particular pot, he had an encounter he has not had before or since in his life. "It was an extraordinary experience. My eyes fell on one particular pot, which has since been dubbed the "levitation pot," and I felt my body go light.

"I suddenly had the sense that my body was about twelve to fourteen inches above the ground. My first thought was to look around to get the reaction of other people who were close by. But they didn't notice that I was off the ground!

"My next thought was wondering if I was going to lose my balance and fall. I was seeing the world from a unique vantage point.

"When the experience was over, I looked at my watch and about ten minutes had elapsed. For the next couple of days in the village, I could consciously turn my thoughts to that pot, and instantly I would sense that I was off the ground for a moment.

"I experimented with this several times to test it, to see if this had been a real experience." And yes, it was, well it *seemed* real.

Spencer took it at face value.

It was real, at least to him, but what caused it? Was he sick, or dizzy, or had an illness? He could not get an answer, whether it was "real" or not—so he finally accepted it for what it was, that it was a phenomenon he did not understand. And he also understood that *real* events in life are different for everyone.

There was no explanation for it, then or ever. He could not explain it. When he revealed this experience to others, he spoke about it as if it was almost a normal thing to have happened—that it was so unusual yet fell into the realm of possibilities that sometimes only Spencer could fathom.

It was so odd, just as was the story of Juan Quezada and Mata Ortiz, yet it was hard to not believe it. People just accepted it.

After he and the entourage left the village for the traveling expedition, this experience never happened again. He felt that this occurrence was a culmination of the first three "magical years," and that it was also a commencement for Juan, a beginning of a new chapter in the Mata Ortiz adventure.

Spencer was elated and perplexed at the same time. Three years earlier he had been open to the emotional fulfillment of finding those three pots.

It was as if it was something he needed or wanted, but he didn't consciously know it, so he wondered if this event was somehow providing the emotional completion he had been subconsciously looking for.

But he moved on and concentrated on Juan. "I felt that Juan was now in his stride and could go forward without me. In a way, it was an ending and a beginning for me. I had been a willing instrument for this project. However, during the experience with the levitation pot, I had the feeling that I was being released if I wished to be, or I could choose to stay with the project if I chose. I did choose to stay with it for over four more years."

Years later, Spencer's private collection went to what was then the San Diego Museum of Man, now the Museum of Us after a name change in June 2020. [43]

In 2006 Spencer arranged for the author and Jon Samuelson to be hosted by Grace Johnson, a curator at the Museum of Us at that time. She graciously arranged and presented a viewing of the three Deming pots. The Levitation pot was on display at the Museum during the visit.

Spencer reflected on this levitation pot. "It was the last one I could part with." Although the collection is not on public display at the Museum, it is available to researchers.

Occasionally one or more of the pots from Spencer's collection will be displayed, just as the levitation pot was on special display in the summer of 2006.

Figure 32. *The author and the "Levitation Pot"*
at the Museum of Us, San Diego, CA, 2006
Courtesy of the Jon Samuelson Collection

Spencer never was able to reconcile this experience with The Levitation Pot, either to himself or to others.

The experience was just too far out of the norm.

During the first three years of the project from 1976 to 1979, Spencer recounts that he had many other amazing coincidences associated with the project, such as a time getting papers in Juarez. "Juan and I were in a large, crowded room at the border getting his papers in order to cross. We were running out of time and were told that Juan needed one more character reference, written on a business letterhead. Our hopes were dashed of getting his papers in time for our journey, when suddenly I heard someone call out my name." Turning, Spencer saw a friend who happened to be a Mexican businessman in Juárez.

Figure 33. The "Levitation Pot" By Juan Quezada as displayed at the Museum of Us, San Diego, CA, 2006 Courtesy of the Jon Samuelson Collection

Spencer relayed their problem and the man quickly replied, "My office is only three blocks from here. I'll have my secretary type the letter and we'll have it to you in thirty minutes." Another unique coincidence was when Spencer was driving in the night back from Mexico to San Pedro, California. Arriving about 5:30 a.m., he wanted to get some breakfast before going home. He parked in front of a restaurant that had not opened yet. He thought he'd take a little catnap while waiting.

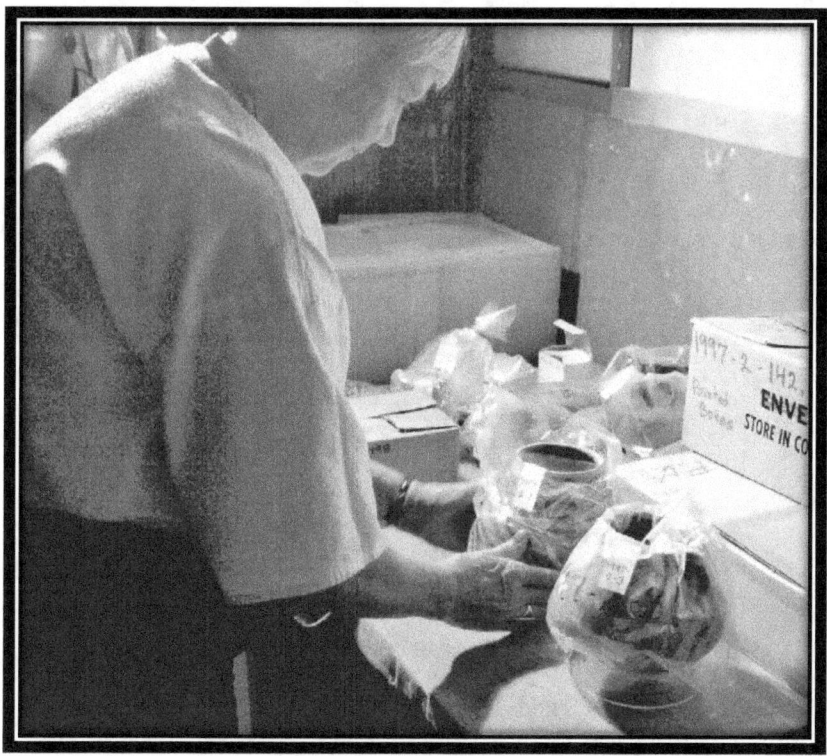

Figure 34. Grace Johnson, a curator at the Museum of
Us, carefully unwraps Spencer's donation of the
Deming pots, circa 2006
Courtesy of the Jon Samuelson Collection

Figure 35. Two of the famous Deming pots made by Juan Quezada on display at the Museum of Us, 2006 Courtesy of the Jon Samuelson Collection

He parked, but the next thing he knew a wheel suddenly came off his truck and rolled down the street ahead of him.

He had been traveling at high speeds across the desert all night long and this shook him up. What if he had been traveling the highway at rates of speed when it came off? He was grateful it had not, but nonetheless, still shaken.

Another time he and Juan's family members had been traveling to Juárez. Several of Juan's family members were in the back of the truck. Spencer had been hearing a whomp, whomp, whomp. As they came to the outskirts of Juárez, he felt sleepy and decided they should all take a catnap.

Starting again, he was only going about 10 miles an hour when the rear axle of the truck broke loose and flew up toward the steel bed of the truck. It ruptured the bed but did not come through and did not hurt anyone.

Spencer was convinced that traveling at their normal rate of speed as they were before he got so sleepy, the axle would have come through like a projectile and seriously hurt someone.

But, then, what to do next?

Guille settled him down and said not to worry. Her sister's husband, an automobile mechanic, lived two blocks from where they were.

So, once again, they were saved.

For Spencer, these incidences were always more than coincidence, and they all contribute to what Spencer has termed "the magical years."

During that time, and later on, Spencer felt that the work spread because of Juan's efforts to teach and share his knowledge of the pottery with members of his family and village.

Eventually, there were over four hundred potters in the village.

"Juan was very generous with teaching and imparting the knowledge of pottery-making to others. This gave birth to more potters, which in turn sprouted more sales, and then the word spread faster and faster.

Figure 36. Museum of Us curator, Grace Johnson, and the author
admire the Deming pots made by Juan Quezada, 2006
Courtesy of the Jon Samuelson Collection

"He was so generous in everything except his paints. He very closely guarded the recipes for the paints. Nicolás knew the secret, but no one else. Why? Juan felt the future of the village depended on quality," Spencer said.

As long as they were doing their best work, he would let them use his colorants.

Spencer said that Juan did not want them to yield to the temptation of turning out mass-produced junk.

"If he felt they were slacking off, he would withdraw his colorants. That was his quality control for the potters and for the future of the village during the first three years. As time went on, others learned to make the paints themselves."

It is noteworthy that both Juan and Spencer were vigilant of quality control in their vision for the village. Juan and Spencer always had the best interests of the village in mind. The number of potters in the area remained about the same for the first six years.

The duo reasoned that not everyone would or could be a potter. Why not branch out into other creative endeavors? Juan wanted the village to manufacture ceramic wall tiles.

He would design them, and this would allow others who could not be potters an opportunity to make a living in a new cottage industry.

Spencer contacted a tile company and off he and Juan went in his Datsun truck on a two-day trip to Saltillo. They toured the tile factory but before this endeavor got off the ground, many others in the community began to take up pottery. Soon an amazing wealth of talent sprang up.

During the decade of the 80's the number of potters exploded. Spencer thinks that it took that long before the role model of farmer/cowboy-turned-potter was totally accepted and understood. Culturally, this was a courageous move on the part of Juan to shift the macho image from cowboy to that of artist.

In the beginning, people from neighboring villages would sometimes tease and make fun of the artists in Mata Ortiz. However, that soon changed when the villagers began to see that they could make an excellent income from it. Also, since Juan himself was a cowboy, they saw that the two images could blend and live well together in the same person. Juan and Spencer insisted that the villagers learn to understand the importance of quality.

As the receptivity for Juan's work increased, Spencer was able to introduce his pottery all over the United States.

But Juan's reaction to traveling outside of his comfort zone was a mixed bag of positive and negative experiences.

He and Guille saw many things for the first time, but for Juan, the first time was enough to be the last time.

"Juan loved the hall of Greek statues at the Metropolitan Museum in New York. He was fascinated by the precise anatomical art form. I offered to arrange for him to spend some time in the hall on his own, but his family would not consider leaving him there. Everything was so foreign to them.

"When we went to Tucson for an opening of his work at the University of Arizona, neither Juan nor Guille had ever seen an elevator and they were startled when we got into it, the doors closed, and it started moving. It was all so new to them! That particular event was a beautiful evening, with a harpist playing and lots of dignitaries circulating through the crowd. It was a wonderful experience. The people were captivated by Juan. The University itself had only a very small budget for an opening such as this, therefore many people dipped into their own pockets to make it happen. It was very touching.

"The following day was Sunday. We had been invited up to a private home in Phoenix for breakfast. Our hosts showed us around the house, and we noted the incredible collection of Native American art. There was a lot of pottery. I was curious to see Juan's reaction to some of this pottery and found he was mainly interested in one particular pot. I thought it would be interesting to see if our host could determine which pot Juan really liked but decided against putting that forward to avoid embarrassment to our host.

"But the pot which spoke to Juan was a very old Hopi pot. The potter spoke across the years to Juan. The renowned Hopi-Tewa potter, Nampeyo (1860-1942) was simply amazing in her artistry." Nampeyo is famous for her Sikyatki-revival-style pottery. Sikyatki is the name of an enormous ancient Hopi village on the east flank of First Mesa that was abandoned about 1500. The abandonment of Sikyatki is told in Hopi oral tradition as due to a dispute with Walpi, whose descendants still reside on top of First Mesa, which resulted in the destruction of Sikyatki. Sikyatki was partially excavated by Jesse Walter Fewkes of the Smithsonian Institution in 1895. His excavations focused on the Sikyatki cemetery areas, as well as the rooms.

Nampeyo visited the excavation with her husband, Lesso, and was extremely inspired by the finely made, impeccably decorated jars and bowls of pottery that were being removed. [44]

Spencer was not at all surprised that Juan connected with the artistry of this amazing potter. From there, the group traveled to San Pedro, California. "I had a potter friend who used a potter's wheel and Juan was shocked to see it. My friend asked if he wanted to try it out and Juan was adamant, no!

Also, during this trip, Juan talked on the telephone for the first time, and he would talk and make noises on the phone.

In the Mexican countryside, you don't go up to the front door and knock. "You stand outside and call out.

'Hup! Hup!' Then you just wait until someone comes to the door. So, he was making this sound into the telephone.

"But following that trip, Juan became ill. He was stressed to be out of his country and away from his home. He finally confessed to me that he thought someone was trying to work magic against him."

Spencer was sympathetic. He told Juan he would see what he could do because he knew someone who just happened to know a Chihuahuan witch. Maybe they could get some insight. Spencer wrote all of Juan's concerns down and went to see her.

"She told me that whoever was witching Juan was an amateur. She instructed us to find a piece of tiger's eye stone and a couple of other items, and to tell Juan to do certain things with these items."

Spencer presumed that Juan followed the instructions because as far as he knew the problems were solved, even though thereafter it seemed more difficult to convince Juan to journey away from Mata Ortiz.

By now, other emerging artists were willing to take up the slack and do whatever was necessary to be successful themselves.

As they each came into their own, the story of Mata Ortiz evolved into what is now known as the amazing phenomenon of Mata Ortiz.

Chapter Ten

Juan's Siblings and Other Artists of Mata Ortiz and Casas Grandes, Mexico

Juan's prosperity was evident, and stimulated artistic expression in Mata Ortiz because people saw his success, and because he shared what he knew to encourage family members and many promising artists. Remote villages such as Mata Ortiz offer very little economic or creative relief, so the new day that dawned in Mata Ortiz was an opportunity as none could ever have imagined.

For many of the years, when Spencer worked with Juan, he was also helping other potters get off the ground. Most of them, like Juan, had started by making pottery for Americraft.

Although there have been as many four to six hundred artists in the area who became amazing potters, there were a few that Spencer especially noted in the interviews. "I would like to recognize a few of the friends I have made over the years. This story would not be complete without acknowledging not only the great artists of Mata Ortiz but of my friendship with so many.

"I guess you could say they are representative of the magical years in Mata Ortiz."

He spoke of them not only individually, but he felt it was important for people to understand the amazing progress that happened so quickly to many of the artists. Spencer developed enduring friendships with many of them, including Juan's siblings.

There were nine children born to Juan's parents, Don José Quezada and Doña Paulita Celado. One died at a very young age and the remaining siblings were Juan, Nicolás, Reynaldo, Reynalda, Lydia, Jesús, Rosa, and Consolación. Today there are many potters with the name Quezada, as that name is taken by anyone who marries into the family. Juan's brother, Reynaldo, began working in pottery and trying new innovations, and as a good artist will do, he searched for new expressions of his artistry.

Spencer recounted this story. "One time Reynaldo and I were on the train going to Juárez and he asked me if I thought he could ever be as good as Juan or could ever excel him. I've always regretted that I wasn't prepared for that question. Other than Juan, I thought Reynaldo had more talent at that time than anyone else. He had a true artist's spirit of searching for reassurance, or even for a level of artistry that he might have deemed inaccessible, but that was there all the time. I felt I should have said something, such as "sure, if you apply yourself, you'd have a good chance of doing as well or exceeding Juan."

But instead, Spencer said, he felt caught off guard and did not respond. Spencer never quite exactly understood why he did not answer in a positive way to him. He felt that he should have used that moment in time to give him more encouragement.

"However, it was indeed Reynaldo Quezada who was later responsible for a number of technical breakthroughs, such as the *tejido*, the woven design. He discovered this method when one day he left a pot to go do something else. Returning to the pot, he worried it might have set up too much and become too dry. He pressed the clay with the end of his knife to see how stiff it was. Then, he reversed direction and crossed the knife the other way. He liked it.

"He continued around the pot, producing a rope-like, woven design. It became Reynaldo's signature trademark and style that is instantly recognizable as his." In *The Many Faces of Mata Ortiz*, more information can be found in this wonderful, full-color, coffee-table book that shows exquisite pottery and details about many of the artists in Mata Ortiz. [45]

"Another day, while working on a pot, he ran out of the clay he was using," Spencer recounted. "Well, Reynaldo had some different colored clay handy and he put the two together and made his pot. When he sanded it, he saw this wonderful mixture of clays, now famously known as the marbled look. There are many other innovations that can be attributed to Reynaldo."

He was the first to sand the pots. He desired to achieve an ultra-smooth surface. Spencer notes his pots were as smooth as glass. Another one of Reynaldo's significant breakthroughs was painting the pots after they are dry.

The sanding and smoothing made it possible to paint extremely fine lines on the surface. Using fine grades of sandpaper, Reynaldo sanded the pots before firing.

The sanding was very important. The potters learned that if you spread a drop of oil over the dry pot, then use a slightly damp cloth over that, the oil helps the burnishing stone to glide over the pot. The oil also keeps any moisture from the cloth penetrating the clay.

The art of Nicolás, another of Juan's brothers, was also extremely popular. Spencer told them all that he would only buy the best pottery, and word got around.

When Nicolás brought Spencer a beautiful pot, he bought it. When he brought him one that was not the best, he would not buy it. The potters learned that Spencer was serious.

As Nicolás began to understand that quality pays the best, he taught other potters and had a following of collectors and many students.

Juan's sister, Lydia, was more cosmopolitan in her spirit than any of the rest of the family. Just after Spencer began his association with Juan, he also offered a similar financial arrangement to Lydia, Nicolás, Reynaldo, and Felix and Teodora Ortiz.

It was the same monthly stipend of three hundred dollars per month. When Spencer invited Lydia to breakfast at the Hotel Hacienda in Casas Grandes to discuss the monthly arrangement, she was very reserved. He thought that she was shy and really didn't know what to make of Spencer, but they struck a deal.

Spencer was extremely happy with her work and thought that Lydia never plateaued, but that her work consistently improved over the years.

"To many collectors, she seemed to have a more personal style than Juan and became a favorite. She developed her own following. I admit I favored Juan's work in the beginning, but now the work of each one is exquisite and beautiful. However, it was almost like she and Juan had been destined to be the best of the potters for quite a long time." Lydia was considered by traders and collectors to be one of the very best potters in the Mata Ortiz tradition. She has always been an innovator of many new styles, such as the black-on-black, as well as the special tulip lip, which has been widely copied. Her children are also potters and have been very successful also.

Spencer had a fond place in his heart for Lydia and felt she was pure talent. One time in the early days, he took Lydia and some other potters to Idyllwild for pottery demonstrations.

Figure 37. *Lydia Quezada Celado Talavera with her amazing pottery at her home, 2005*
Courtesy of the Jon Samuelson Collection

Spencer arranged for a pilot friend to give them a flight in his light plane. None of the Quezada family had ever flown before.

"I cautioned my friend to not try any fancy maneuvers. But when we were way out over the ocean, he spotted a fishing boat he recognized, and wanted to buzz his friends!" Spencer remembered with a laugh. "Everyone hung on to me for dear life and I thoroughly enjoyed it!"

Figure 38. Spencer and Lydia Quezada Celado Talavera, 2005
Courtesy of the Jon Samuelson Collection

Lydia married Rito Talavera. "I've always liked the sound of her name: Lydia Quezada Celado Talavera. I think it's very poetic," Spencer said. When they married, Lydia asked Spencer to be her *padrino*, godfather. She in turn became his *ahijada*, goddaughter. "I remember inquiring about the responsibilities of *padrino*. I was supposed to get the bride to the church on time and help with the expense of the band.

"I was married to Annie at the time and on the day of the wedding, we had left Casas Grandes on the way to the church at Mata Ortiz. Annie and I were dressed to the nines for the wedding and came to Colonia Juárez.

"Instead of turning right and going through the village, I thought I'd take a shortcut, which would take us to the left and across the river. I had gone that way many times before.

"But I didn't know there had been a storm and it had reconfigured the bottom of the river. Suddenly, in the middle of the riverbed, the truck dropped into a deep hole. The water started to come in through the door.

"Everything that was on the floor started to float. Annie got up on top of the seat and began to freak out. I was observing this situation and secretly thought it was a hoot. I climbed up onto the cab of the truck to analyze the situation.

"In a nearby house, I could see someone peek out from a curtain, watching these crazy gringos stuck in the river. On the bank across the river was a kid on horseback. I called out to him to get us some help.

"I called out, "*Andale! Andale!*" He just sat there on his horse. Finally, a few other people arrived and then suddenly, by coincidence, one of the Mormons showed up with his pickup truck with a winch and called out, "Do you want some help?" Did we want some help? Of course!

"He turned his truck around, waded out in the river, attached his cable, and wound us up. As soon as we were out of the river, we opened the doors, and whoosh, the water rushed out. Amazingly we were still pretty dry because Annie had been on the seat and I was on the roof, and equally astounding, the truck started right up.

"We made it to the little church that is still there in Mata Ortiz just in time. It was a really long service, but afterward, there was a huge party with a barbecue and dancing until dawn!

"The festivities continued throughout the night and then the family served breakfast. When it was over, the very nicest part began. In the United States culture, the bride and groom are exhausted at the end of the celebration, then travel off on their adventure. But after the dance, Rito returned home to Anchondo, the village where he had grown up; and Lydia went home with her family. Everyone went to bed to rest. About noon they rose and bathed and Lydia's family, and a few others of us, took her in the direction of Anchondo. We traveled to a very beautiful hot spring and stopped to picnic.

"We continued on to Anchondo to Rito's family, where he was also refreshed with sleep and food. At this point, the family delivered their daughter to Rito. That was a nice civilized way to get married. They each had their last time together with their family, rested, and then began their new life together."

Lydia's husband was known for his blackware depicting reptiles such as lizards and snakes.

Spencer remembered that Lydia's honesty with customers was legendary.

"In the past, there might have been a time when I would shortchange myself when trying to keep up with what I bought from them, but she would always correct the records. It was totally refreshing. I liked that. She was always recognized for having integrity."

When Spencer was away from Mata Ortiz, he would receive Christmas cards from her. "It was always something that really touched me. This did not seem to fall in the range of usual things for people in Mata Ortiz to do. But I've never forgotten how close we were. Given the different culture and different circumstances, it was really very moving for her to always have included me."

Another protégé of Spencer's during that time was Taurina Baca who lived directly across the street from Juan. Taurina was beautiful and vivacious and had a great sense of humor. "She had an inner knowing of herself, and did not conform to everyone's expectations.

"When young, she was working in the business world, but after Juan taught her to make pottery, she never returned to that environment. She became a well-known potter. With the proceeds of her first pot she bought a stereo console and invited me to dance. I was tongue-tied and embarrassed, but thought it was wonderful."

Over time, Spencer fostered many relationships with artists and their families. He considered the artists as family, and they in turn with him.

His relationship with Reynaldo was called one of *confianza*, confidence. He explained to Spencer that in a village where everyone is related to everyone, it's always beneficial to have a confidential relationship with a nonfamily friend. This is to keep each other informed of what's going on in the village that might affect the other.

Spencer explained, "One of the rules of the friendship was that neither was allowed to take offense at anything the other person said or did. We could talk on anything, including cultural differences. Reynaldo was quite interested in that. One day we were crossing the desert in my Datsun truck heading toward California. We had not been talking much when out of the blue he exclaimed, 'You know, a lot of Mexicans, especially along the border, think that Americans are stupid!'"

He went on to explain that Americans let themselves be taken advantage of, and other people of the world considered this to be stupidity. "People tell stories about it and joke about it," he said. He told Spencer one of the stories about an American who stopped in at a little village cantina and fell quickly into a warm relationship with a fellow as if they had been friends forever. This went on for a while, and they were drinking and having a good time when the fellow told the American that there was something in his home that might interest him.

"Would you come with me?" he asked. The American said sure and went with him, and when they got to his home the man brought out a human skull. Now, it was a widely known folklore story that after Pancho Villa was assassinated and buried, someone dug up the body and stole the head. That actually happened. His widow hoped until the end of her days that before she died, she would be able to restore the head to the body, but she never did. So, the fellow brought out this skull and he told the American that it was the skull of Pancho Villa. "It has been in our family for many years, *señor*." The American was impressed with this, thought about it, and asked, "It wouldn't be for sale, would it?"

The Mexican replied that his family had this skull for many years, and it meant a lot to them. "It is important to us, so we have never thought of selling it. If we ever should think of selling it, though, it would have to be to someone very special to us, someone with discrimination. Someone like yourself." The deal was made.

The next morning the American is walking down the street feeling very pleased with himself, for now, he had Pancho Villa's skull in his possession.

A neighbor, having heard of this windfall, fell in stride with him and told him he had something to show the man.

They went to his house, and he pulled out a small skull and he claimed that it was Pancho Villa's skull.

The American was smug. "Well, it just so happens that I have Pancho Villa's skull, so this couldn't be it. And besides, what do you take me for, this is a child's skull!" The man then replied, "*Seguro, que si*, yes, of course, but this is Pancho Villa's skull when he was a child."

Then the American asked him, "It wouldn't be for sale, would it?"

"That was the end of Reynaldo's story. We went on driving and after a while I asked him, 'Reynaldo, you were talking about Americans being naive. Yes, we generally make the presumption when we meet a person that they would be trustworthy. And of course, we are sometimes mistaken. But that is the assumption we make, and it's productive because most of the time it works out. But in Mexico, you don't trust anyone outside of the family, or maybe close friends."

At this, Reynaldo added that they often don't trust family, either.

Spencer explained to Reynaldo that in the United States, it is by making this assumption that allows people to do more business, have more exchanges with others, and create much more wealth. This inherent trust makes many more partnerships possible.

"We drove on for a while and then finally Reynaldo said quietly, 'Spencer, I have learned something this afternoon.' That made me feel so good. So, we talked then a lot about cultural differences and from then on, he was always interested in this subject.'"

Spencer said that Reynaldo really enjoyed discussing the many cultural differences, and a significant one was Mexican men's attitudes toward women.

It was a game with them, trying to get a woman's attention, trying to get her to acknowledge him in some way.

"We were at the opening of a pottery exhibition around 1979 which I had organized. Reynaldo was there, and he had a fine sense of feminine beauty, so when he saw a young, gorgeous Japanese woman, he approached her. She gave him a very nice, warm handshake. For a vision like that to give him this kind of handshake, well, he was climbing the walls. I had to tell him to calm down, Reynaldo, calm down. It does not mean what you think."

Reynaldo later went to live with Spencer in San Pedro where Spencer had rented an old barracks building and converted it into an art gallery.

Fort MacArthur in San Pedro had been demilitarized and there were empty barracks along the marina. In 1978 Spencer managed to get a space from the Harbor Department and set up a gallery with displays of Juan's and other potters' work. He rented a complete barracks, in an H shape with a lot of space, and then subleased one wing to a very fine artist and woodworker who made impressive wood furniture.

Spencer had partitioned off the space in the upper story for separate displays.

Juan's, Lydia's, and Reynaldo's pottery were in individual display spaces. He bought some new cardboard boxes, painted them brick red, and set pottery on them. He had painted the walls and made an attractive gallery out of it. "All of the pottery belonged to me as per the agreement I had with each of the three artists, so I wanted to introduce their work to the world in any way I could.

"I had two bowls made by Juan on display. They each had very realistic black widow spiders at the bottom. I did not particularly like these bowls because I liked his imaginative artistry more than realism. These turned me off, but I put them out on display anyway. One day two artists came and spent practically the whole afternoon trying to decide which of the two to buy.

"They really liked them. Whenever I would sell a piece of art, I always tried to reassure the customer they had made a good choice. I think this brings to completion the venture of buying a good pot.

"But when these customers finally selected and paid for their bowl with the spider at the bottom, I could not say anything. The words stuck in my throat. I was just so glad the pot was gone. It was a funny experience—I couldn't really explain it."

Spencer operated the gallery for a few years and would also display the pottery at various Native American art shows.

The sales would just cover the booth rent, but he would get the attention of anyone who came within thirty feet of his booth. Spencer said he would give them the whole story of Mata Ortiz. As they became interested and enthusiastic about Mata Ortiz pottery, he'd ask them to sign his guest book.

In this way, he accumulated quite a mailing list. Using this, he would invite them to an exhibition at his gallery.

"We would have a demonstration of pottery-making and Reynaldo would cook and serve Mexican food. I would give a talk with slides. We would make a lot of sales.

"We discovered that doing a demonstration while exhibiting was exciting to people and stimulated sales. Around 1981 Reynaldo and I were exhibiting at the Pomona County Fair. The fair was ten days long and we were working our booth for about nine hours every day. It was pretty rigorous. Reynaldo was doing demonstrations, and we had a nice exhibit of pottery for sale."

The Mata Ortiz method of firing takes a short time, unlike the Native American pottery firing which requires several hours. Spencer and Reynaldo did a firing each evening at seven o'clock. A Hopi potter had a booth just across the way from them and they became well acquainted. He was intrigued with the Mata Ortiz methods. He had been making highly polished black ware, but he was intrigued that the Mata Ortiz black ware was so thin. He thought it must be very unusual clay. They showed him how to make a pot in his customary way by using Mata Ortiz clay, and he found it worked out fine.

Then Reynaldo made a pot in the Mata Ortiz way using Hopi clay. With a short firing time, the pot came out with a fine burnished black surface that met all the Hopi standards and expectations. "It was an excellent pot, so we all saw that it was not the different clays at all, but it was the firing.

"Reynaldo would produce the firings with great showmanship. He would fire the same pot using both the reduction firing using no oxygen to the fuel, and oxidation firing when more oxygen is used. People would ask where do you get the black clay? It was not the clay, but the way it was fired. The iron that is in most clay gives it its reddish and brown colors. Naturally occurring iron oxide is Fe_2O_3."

Spencer memorized that little formula which when fired produces a natural color of red or reddish brown. By heating Fe_2O_3 in the absence of oxygen, the molecule will lose two oxygen atoms and simply become FEO. It's still iron oxide, but now has the natural color of black.

When the pot is fired and starved of oxygen in a way that air cannot get in and circulate around, it will produce a black pot. Because this is a chemical change, it is not just black on the surface, but if broken open, it would be black all the way through.

The graphite method of firing pots uses graphite and kerosene applied to the outside of the pot to produce a fine black metallic finish, but the black color does not go all the way through the material. It is basically like painting a pot.

To achieve this result, it is necessary to starve the pot of oxygen. And to produce a brown, tan or red color, the pot is then fired again but, in this process, the air is circulated around the pot.

This reverses the process.

A pot can be reversed as many times as is desirable, making for a fine pottery firing demonstration at the art shows Spencer was hosting. People were absolutely fascinated by it. To produce a metallic finish, horse or cow manure was used in the firing process. It produces a brilliant shiny finish to the pot.

This reduction firing produces the famous blackware.

The artist makes a small bed of powdered horse manure and when it gets hot enough to ignite, it starves the oxygen from inside the chamber. This produces a gunmetal effect by setting the pot right on top of that bed and covering it with a metal bucket, making sure that no air can get in. Then cow chips are built up around the outside into what looks like an old-fashioned beehive. For oxidation firing it is the same process except the bucket is up on chocks or bricks, as well as the pot, so that the air can circulate around the pot.

Spencer explained, "We would prepare a reduction firing before people would arrive. But the pot that Reynaldo would put in there was painted with polychrome bright designs. As people gathered around, they would eagerly wait twenty minutes for the firing. Then we scattered the ashes and lifted the bucket and voila, here was this black, burnished, gleaming gem. And we would hear this nice satisfying "ahhhh" from the audience.

"No color would show at all. Then Reynaldo would say, 'For those of you who can wait, I'm going to fire this again and you will be interested in the result.' They would go away and come back in about twenty minutes. The second time we opened the firing, there would be magic to behold! Now, there was a bright, polychrome pot that just minutes before had been a black pot! It was great showmanship. We would do that demonstration every evening and it was great fun. "In the meantime, I would be giving the presentation to everybody within thirty feet without letting up. Nobody got away. It was 1981 and a man named Tom Fresh, a teacher at Idyllwild School of Music and Arts in Idyllwild, California, came by and saw all of this and was swept away by the exhibit of the pottery and the story that went along with it.

"Tom invited us up to Idyllwild. At that time, I did not know about Idyllwild. The school was called Isomata, for Idyllwild School Of Music And Arts. [46]

"Tom Fresh was a teacher at Idyllwild and was the director of the Mother Earth, Father Sky program of indigenous arts. He had developed that program for all ages, and it was excellent. His policy was to invite Native American artists to come there to teach, especially those Native Americans who were in actual contact with the ceremonial life of their people, and who could teach the style and techniques of that ceremonial artistry to others.

He understood that the cultural environment of any place is an inherent part of its art. For instance, you would not think of going to Paris to study art and ignore French language and culture. And so that's what he wanted, a place in the southwest where students of southwest art could learn and practice."

Idyllwild had living facilities for its students. At that time, it was a summer campus of the University of Southern California but has since been renamed Idyllwild Arts.

"On the next trip to that area, I was in touch with Tom. He soon suggested that Juan teach a class at Idyllwild during the summer session. They would pay all of his expenses for lodging and meals at the school, plus an honorarium.

"Tom was an interesting person, a painter in his own right, and had made his living as a commercial artist.

He had taken all of his savings and bought this beautiful piece of land up in the San Jacinto Mountains near Idyllwild and donated it to a Buddhist monastic organization. He reserved for himself a little corner of the property to build a cabin on it. He wasn't a Buddhist; he was just Tom Fresh.

"Over time, we would take Juan, Reynaldo and many others to Idyllwild to teach."

Spencer continued to operate his art gallery in San Pedro, but he was racking up debt with the expenses of food and transportation for the potters to and from Mexico traveling to art shows, Idyllwild, and other destinations. He was running up a huge deficit and operating at a tremendous loss.

Still, and to his satisfaction, people finally began to come to these events at his San Pedro gallery and a certain buzz got going about the pottery. It started to sell.

"We had events at my San Pedro gallery two or three times a year."

Reynaldo had a comfortable living space at the gallery complex and settled in very nicely. He met and became friends with a potter in Santa Monica who had a studio.

Reynaldo accepted a job and a loft area as a living space, so he worked as a security person at the studio for extra income and was able to use the studio space to make pottery.

He also developed some classes teaching pottery. Spencer helped him to develop publicity for his classes. Things were great but he decided to go home to Mata Ortiz for a visit. However, once there, he decided to stay in the village. He never returned to California again.

"Basically, Reynaldo was my best friend for a long period. I had much affection for Reynaldo. He helped me a lot with my Spanish, and I was often reminded what a good friend he was." Spencer also sponsored Felix Ortiz for a while, and even though the money was running out fast, he wanted to see more potters get off the ground.

Felix was one of the first potters in Barrio Porvenir, the southernmost barrio in Mata Ortiz.

As Juan's reputation began to grow, the villagers in Porvenir took an interest and began experimenting. They began by using a continuous coil method as opposed to Juan's single coil. This technology was more like those of the U.S. southwest Indians. Felix continued and became quite excellent in everything he did.

Spencer was not aware the barrio existed until about six months after he first arrived in Mata Ortiz, and then Juan introduced him to Felix, who had a very different style. Felix and Juan had sometimes been a bit at odds over the question of quality.

Juan asked Spencer once if people liked disordered designs such as Felix's work.

Spencer often contrasted them, saying Juan had a classic mind and Felix a romantic mind.

Felix would sometimes get inspiration in the middle of the night and get up and work.

Spencer sponsored him for a time because his pieces had a liveliness that was very interesting, and he would include Felix in the exhibitions of a variety of potters' works because he wanted to promote the area as a whole.

Macario and Nicolás Ortiz were two brothers also from Porvenir who became well-known potters after abandoning their careers as musicians.

Their band was known as The Rebels of Rhythm, or *Los Rebellos del Ritmo*, and they would travel to California to visit relatives. But when their instruments were confiscated at the border, they embarked on their pottery careers.

Macario was the first who made quality graphite in Porvenir. The rabbit is his trademark. Nicolás also sculpted rabbit effigy pots.

"In the early years, collectors took an interest in Nicolás Ortiz. He was an incredible sculptor of stone and that would have been his chosen path, but he needed instruction. When I was promoting him in my early talks, I was trying to find someone to send him to school for proper training."

He would go up into the mountains and bring down Cantera stone from the ruins of an old church.

He only had a chisel and a claw hammer to use. A sculptor normally uses a mallet. He often would say that his hands would get bloody, but then they would heal and he would begin a new piece.

Spencer recalled, "Of the first five pieces he ever attempted, the third piece was of five human figures and had more open space than almost any you'd ever see in a sculpture. It was amazing.

"When I would show this piece amongst the pottery slides, I'd pause and ask my audience, 'Do some of you think I have a wrong slide here, and people would say, yes.'"

Spencer lamented, "Of course, Nicolás Ortiz needed classical training in anatomy, but it never happened. As a potter, his figures were sculptural in nature, and he also used a lot of animal motifs in his work. "I remember Nicolás once made a little sculpture of two figures copulating. He would sell these in the bars. They were attractive. He fired one of these pieces while I was at his home and his mother came out and asked how the firing was going. It was interesting that often in Mexico there was a much more realistic view of humans and their activities than in the states."

Spencer believed that much of the excellent levels of artistry found in the area was due in part to Juan stimulating others in the village to be creative. Rather than secrets, Juan openly encouraged others to become skillful and dedicated to the art.

The more Spencer became fascinated with his project and the potters, the more he became involved with their lives and they with his.

But Spencer could see the writing on the wall. Not only did he run out of money and could no longer sponsor the potters, there seemed to be a coming shift of relationships on the hot desert wind.

Perhaps it was inevitable that eventually, the bloom on the rose would fade.

As the mercurial dance of human dynamics wound its way around and through the relationships, financial woes, and the incredible budding artistry, the rose started to wither and blow away.

Chapter Eleven

Spencer's Relationship with Juan and Guille;
Traveling to Exhibitions; The Dream
Unravels; Through the Gate

Spencer had to consider not only Juan's personality in how he conducted and saw himself in this project, but also another very important person, Juan's wife, Guillermina. For Spencer, at times and over time, these became increasingly confusing relationships for him. Often, he could not sort out conflicting 'messages' he would get from both of them.

He did not always understand the complexities of either of their personalities or why things seemed to happen the way they sometimes did.

Spencer saw the Mata Ortiz project the same way he viewed art: unique, valuable, inspirational, and breathtaking.

All of which required an enormous structure, organization, presentations, artists, and paying the bills.

Spencer struggled with what he intuited to be some animosity toward him, some reluctance to be cooperative, and a relationship that had been open and caring seemingly closing in on him, and to him.

But he pushed on and set aside this complex mix of emotions and innuendos.

Regardless of confusing messages from both Juan and Guille, Spencer felt he still had a decent relationship with them.

He inherently understood that they were also navigating the dynamics of the unusual trio; however, they all continued to be hospitable to each other, just as was his friendship with Juan's parents.

Juan's mother Doña Paulita and father Don José were close to Spencer. "Don José was quiet, so I had more conversations with Doña Paulita. She would tell marvelous stories of how Juan as a child covered the walls of his bedroom with drawings. I asked her, 'Were you angry he messed up the walls?' Her response was, 'I was proud.' That endeared her to me."

Their handshake agreement had worked all right for both Spencer and Juan in the first year, but a little more than a year later, Spencer and Juan agreed to get a legal, contractual agreement for their partnership.

Spencer reflected afterward that he himself would not have asked for it, but Juan and Guille wanted it. Spencer had an intuition that it was an omen for what came later. "In Latin American countries there is a suspicion that lawyers twist the words around," Spencer said.

"Therefore, they don't trust the legal process. Most people would have much preferred a verbal contract, so I was surprised that they wanted a legal contract. However, I wanted to abide by their wishes. What they wanted was more money in the monthly stipend."

Spencer knew someone had to have been talking in their ears, but still, he was fine with it. However, he could not quite get a grip on what was exactly taking place.

He never was in it for the money anyway. For him, his primary motivation was the art of discovery and the discovery of art!

His lawyer in Los Angeles drafted the contract for him.

"I raised Juan's monthly stipend to five hundred dollars, plus a royalty of ten percent on sales. This agreement provided for an annual year-end review, and an arrangement where Juan became a full partner. Therefore, I would never make more money than him. I then had it translated into Spanish by one of Mexico's most distinguished lawyers.

This lawyer was highly respected and someone whom Juan and Guille knew and trusted.

"On October 28, 1977, the three of us went to the lawyer's office in Juarez and signed the document."

As they exited the lawyer's office and headed for his truck parked two blocks away, the police suddenly descended on the trio and took them in separate vehicles to the police station. The police were making a huge deal out of having arrested them and were treating them very roughly.

When Spencer mentioned the name of the lawyer they had just visited, the police immediately backed off. Spencer showed the lawyer's business card to the police, and they replied that they had not understood who they were. They apologized and that was the end of that.

Spencer never knew what the incident was about and suspected it was mistaken identity, but they were very glad to be out of Juárez and on the way home to Mata Ortiz.

Driving back to Mata Ortiz, Juan and Guille were in the back of the truck. Spencer had placed a five-inch foam mattress on the truck bed. Juan and Guille seemed happy and playful in the back of the truck. Spencer thought it was great that he was carrying such happy cargo. They were all content, they had all signed the contract, and all was well. For services rendered, the Mexican lawyer took some of Spencer's inventory of Juan's pots in payment. He asked for several more than Spencer had wanted to pay, but Spencer reasoned it would be worth it in the end.

Later, Spencer heard a rumor that the "Juárez lawyer" pots may have been pawned years after their transaction, and that the pawnshop owner had them hidden away somewhere for safekeeping. Pawnshop? Bob's Swap Shop? Spencer thought there was some irony somewhere in that story and contended that photographs of those pieces would be a valuable addition to the record and history of Juan Quezada and Mata Ortiz, but none were taken. He never knew the destiny of that pottery.

Over the years, Juan shared his knowledge throughout the village of how to make pottery. "Juan was generous. How did he teach others? He didn't *teach* really, the knowledge is passed by observation, which he freely allowed others to do. The homes of the village are centered around family. Pottery making then becomes natural when children grow up with it."

When they were doing demonstrations and pottery classes across the United States, Spencer worked up a presentation of how Juan made his pottery. One day Juan took him aside. "Spencer, don't tell them so much."

"Why not?" Spencer asked.

"Those that are going to get it will get it by observation, and when they get it that way, they've made a discovery and they will make it their own."

Spencer realized that this was brilliant logic on Juan's part and a truly sophisticated understanding of the learning process. "This is so different from learning by teaching. Juan's technique was to help people learn, not be taught.

"People talk about the creativity of Mata Ortiz potters. How can so much creativity be accounted for? People say it must be something to do with the gene pool, but that is impossible because Mata Ortiz has no historic depth. The village was first known as Estacion Pearson and a lumber mill was established in 1909. People came from all over the area to work, so it was a random population." [47]

Spencer would often lecture that in the fine arts tradition in Europe a young artist learned by being an apprentice. "They would begin, for example, by sweeping the floor. They were told how difficult art was and that it would take years, a lifetime, to achieve anything of merit. But in northern Chihuahua, no one has ever told them it was difficult. They have a real and sometimes urgent economic incentive. They have a multi-faceted legacy. One of the benefits of Juan sharing with others is that they have learned the ingenuity of experimenting, of problem solving, of trying different clays.

"You hear various potters around the country, even the Southwest Native Americans, say that they are running out of clay. That is mostly an erroneous psychological perception.

"In Mata Ortiz, they have totally opposite views. They look for clay everywhere and because of this, they

220

are always discovering new and different clays. Mexican potters understand that you could never run out of clay from Mother Earth.

"It was truly a matter of perspective," Spencer said.

"During a symposium at Santa Fe, potters from Mata Ortiz and Southwest Native American potters were asked what they are thinking while creating pottery. Mata Ortiz potters commented that they are thinking of ways to develop their own expression in art, so their pieces would not be confused with other potters in the village. However, a Native American pueblo potter may try to make pottery in the same way as her grandmother, including digging clay in the same exact place, even though eventually you would run out of it."

To Spencer, this showed a polar shift in how these artists viewed the process. Although he appreciated both, he thought the Mata Ortiz potters had a better chance of expanding their concepts and their work.

No one was a better champion of these emerging artists than Spencer, but there had already been dark storms brewing on the horizon between him and Juan and before too long, the partnership between the two men bubbled down into a meltdown.

As a forerunner to this, and to Spencer the most disappointing experience of the entire project, was when Juan and Guille had their eighth child. Laura was born and Spencer had hoped to be her *padrino*, *compadre*, the godfather. This is considered to be a real familial relationship. This association establishes a *compadre* relationship with the parents. [48]

Spencer wanted very much to have been compadres with Juan, but they gave that honor to another American who had befriended them. Spencer was deeply hurt at the time, and still, many years later, he confessed he never got over it. It was confusing and he could not understand why it happened. Although his being her *padrino* was not openly discussed, his feeling at the time was there had been a general expectation that he would be asked. Things were said, hints given, muted and vague talk, a small discussion here or there. The bottom line was that Spencer expected it. "I intuitively felt that they did not want this for some reason. At times they were warm and at times they seemed cold. Eventually, I began to feel something very negative was afoot, and I felt thwarted in all of my efforts regarding the project or anything with the potters. For example, when I would write to Juan about the project, I wasn't sure that he received the letters. I wrote the letters in Spanish and Guille would read them to Juan, but I think she held some of them back."

Spencer started to feel he was being pushed away. He was giving his life and his money for this man and his family, and he felt that something was working against him. He confessed he just did not know why. It became difficult and uneasy for him to be around their family. He, at last, discussed it with Juan, who told him that he could not control what anyone said or did, but he offered no solution to Spencer.

In only just a few years, and just as Spencer was facing serious financial problems, his relationship with Juan and Guille slid further down the slippery slope of expectations.

He knew they were headed toward the bottom of the vortex when he and Juan entered a separate, small business deal on the side. Spencer had been working on securing a weekend teaching project for Juan at Idyllwild school and he and Juan agreed that they would settle the business finances that weekend. The teaching weekend was arranged in Idyllwild, but Spencer's truck broke down midway there and a friend came and rescued them. His truck was taken to be repaired. Juan taught the class the next day and all was well. The plan was that Spencer would drive Juan and Guille back to Mata Ortiz on Sunday morning. Juan had cashed his check for teaching while there, but did not approach Spencer with the money for the business deal. Spencer reasoned they would be driving to Mata Ortiz the next day and there would be plenty of time on the long drive to bring up the subject.

Spencer went to retrieve his truck in town and arrived early the next morning to pick up Juan and Guille. He was shocked to discover that they had already left for Mata Ortiz on the bus! Spencer was mortified. They didn't even tell him they were leaving, nor tell him goodbye.

He instinctively knew that this scenario was a warning of where their partnership was headed, even though Juan did eventually put in the money on the deal. But their aloofness toward him was disturbing.

In another area of contention among the three, Spencer had repeatedly cautioned both of them that they should not accept down payment money for pottery pre-orders. In his opinion, this created a burden on Juan who was then pressured to fulfill those commitments. Spencer called it "debt slavery." Spencer had explained that Juan was not a burro, but a racehorse. "You don't work a race-horse day after day, the way a burro works."

Juan certainly did not need pre-orders, as by that time, there were many people waiting in line to buy his pottery. Spencer always felt that he had much more creative ability than he had accessed up to that point. Juan's creativity emanated from his spirit, but as long as there was a debt burden, he was not free.

Spencer felt that by taking pre-orders, he would not be able to catch up, or be able to accumulate a collection of pots for a show, or to work in another medium, such as wood sculpture.

If they accepted deposit money for pottery, then no freedom. On reflection, and as the years have gone by, Spencer concluded, in part, that there were just too many new sensations and experiences that frightened Juan and his family. For instance, whenever Juan left Mata Ortiz, he was miserably out of his comfort zone. He became quite physically ill.

Perhaps the Quezadas felt the pressure in a way that was not really understood by Spencer or anyone from the outside. It was just too much of everything.

Or perhaps they felt the money was so unbelievable that they felt a need to take it while it was there. Collectors and buyers of all types were literally forcing money into their hands—standing in front of them paying extra U.S. dollars in cash for pots that had already been commissioned by someone else—which at this point was several thousands of dollars for one pot.

And then there was the fame, the press, the reporters, TV producers, and the rich and the famous. By now, Juan's artistry exceeded that of many great pottery artists around the world. It was called sublime, outstanding, exquisite, and unsurpassable.

But even a dream come true can have a nightmarish side to it, and a negative effect on the dream. Visualize a

Juan Quezada pot: Juan and Guille standing on one side of it and Spencer on the other. Looking at each other in confusion, expectation, wealth, fame, attraction, and distraction. Where did they go from there?

Finally, their arrangement began to more than unravel, it began to shred around 1982 into 1983. Spencer was not only out of funds by this time, he was in serious debt.

Around this time, he had met Peter Tellini in California who owned an art gallery in Switzerland. "It was one of the very best galleries in that country, and he was always looking for new talent to present to the European art world," Spencer related. They traveled together to Mata Ortiz on several occasions and Tellini developed an interest in collecting Juan's work. "He had good ideas and he wanted to produce and maintain a catalog of all of Juan's work. This would have been wonderful for future research and reference. If a question ever came up as to the authenticity of a piece of Juan's work, one could refer to the catalog. He had really excellent ideas on how to preserve the integrity of the work of Juan and other potters, and he was devoted to presenting the potters to the world at large.

"By this time, I had no choice but to face the music. I had run out of capital and could not continue to promote the potters."

Spencer and Tellini agreed to become partners in the Mata Ortiz project because Spencer knew he could provide the much-needed capital.

The plan was that the two of them would represent Juan.

"Tellini naturally wanted a clear contract in writing with Juan, Guille, and me, of course. He wanted the contract to clarify that he and I would exclusively represent Juan, because he was willing to fund the project.

"But Juan would have no part of it and told me he was afraid of it. He just wasn't comfortable."

Figure 39. *Exquisite Juan Quezada pot*
Courtesy of the Walter Parks Collection

Spencer felt that his relationship with Juan was imploding, but he hung on with desperate hope to see where it all went.

"It seems that my exclusive arrangement with Juan became a tool for collectors and traders to undermine my partnership with him."

Traders began to present Spencer in a dark light to Juan and Guille.

Spencer said he was not surprised by this.

They planted seeds of doubt, they offered more money, and it became obvious that they began a negative campaign against him which became more intense.

Spencer thought that Juan and Guille caved in and began to sell to outside sources.

Figure 40. *Sophisticated Juan Quezada pot,*
taken to a world-class level
Courtesy of the Walter Parks Collection

Of course, it is likely that none of those people would have ever known about Juan if not for Spencer.

And even more likely that if they had, his work would not have eclipsed the tourist trap ceramic quality or attained the value that it had by that time. This dark force energy continued, to the detriment of both Spencer and

227

Juan. What had been a beautiful and simple enterprise took on water.

Spencer began to find pieces of Juan's work turning up elsewhere that he had not seen himself. "It was in El Paso that for the first time I found a piece of his work myself in this manner.

Figure 41*. Black on black, Juan Quezada*
Courtesy of the Walter Parks Collection

I immediately turned around and drove all the way back to Mata Ortiz to confront Juan and to express to him how upset I was, but he brushed me off. He did not seem concerned at all. So, I acquiesced and let this incident go.

"But right after that, Juan, Guille, and I traveled to the Ghost Ranch in New Mexico to attend a workshop. Soon, Juan and Guille began to hang out with a Santa Fe gallery owner, and then the three of them would go out to dinner without me.

"After the workshop was finished, I drove Juan and Guille to the bus station.

"As Juan went through the gate, he spun around and said flatly, 'Our contract is over,' then turned his back on me and kept on walking at a fast pace to the bus."

Spencer was stunned. Juan disappeared into the bus and Spencer stood there in shock.

He never forgot that moment. In remembering it even years later, it was obvious that those few seconds had burned an image into his mind that refused to be forgotten.

Or lessened. It was a traumatic moment in time and space for Spencer.

Because Juan was on one side of the gate and Spencer on the other, there was no opportunity for Spencer to respond or question Juan.

Just like that, Juan was out of his life, and Spencer was out of the picture.

Those four words somehow devalued the many years of Spencer's hard work and disenfranchised this man who had given Juan and his family all he had—and humiliated and hurt Spencer beyond the four words that had just been spoken.

On top of this devastating situation, he now had accumulated over fifteen thousand dollars in credit card debt and his inheritance was spent.

Still later, however, Spencer maintained an it-was-for-the-best-attitude. "I know it was probably just as well, as I knew in my heart and soul that I just could not seem to let go of Juan and Mata Ortiz otherwise.

"Of course, I had seen that something was going down with the other trader because they had become so secretive and chummy, but I didn't expect this.

There were lots of other smaller incidents and tell-tale signs.

"And I knew that Juan and Guille were not happy with the idea of my partnering with the Swiss gallery owner, but even after all of that, I had no idea that they wanted to end our relationship completely.

"That was the end—when Juan went through the gate."

It was 1983.

"On some level, I felt a bit of relief, and even though Juan was not willing to go forward with a new partnership, I had no more resources and could not have continued anyway. So, what could I do? "After that abrupt ending, folks felt that Juan treated me badly, and maybe so, but I have always tried to see things in a more positive light. No relationship is perfect. I could not blame Juan or Guille. I was in an untenable situation. This was an opportunity to release the child to whom I had given birth. Juan could now be on his own, and it was time to let go of the mentored and cut the apron strings for both of us. It was a release for him as well as me.

"But there is no denying that when a break like this happens, it's hurtful. Even so, still, and this will surprise a lot of folks, the most distressing situation of all with Juan and Guille was not being chosen to be *padrino*, the godfather to Laura. It was really sad. Although the possibility had not been overtly discussed among the three of us, there was a great expectation of it, at least on my part. I had really hoped for it, and the denial of that honor was far and away the most painful episode of my time with them."

Spencer shared this tender misgiving, and it was like opening a door to another world within his life. In that admission, Spencer showed more of himself as a human, not the anthropologist, than at any other time, perhaps, in his life.

For him, what mattered was connecting. He wanted that link to Juan and Guille.

He had grown to love them and was very fond of their family. In fact, he took on the role of Grandfather, godfather, father, mentor, nurturer, uncle, in short, family member, long before he expected to be considered *padrino* to Laura.

In his mind, he already was one of the family, completely, in every way except by blood—and he erroneously thought that not being blood didn't matter and that he would always be safe with his adopted family, the Quezadas, and also the extended family, and the potters of Mata Ortiz, as well. They would always be his and he would always be theirs.

But not being chosen as *padrino* had been a wake-up call that he should not have ignored.

Today, there is still a perception in the public by some people that Juan treated him badly. It's out there. It's in the consciousness. But Spencer wanted to set the record straight and he reiterated that he thinks about things differently. Spencer reframed it this way.

"It wasn't with malice of forethought, and I couldn't have continued anyway."

Spencer said that he was able to walk away and was fine, even with the emotional letdown. He felt released.

In his very astute mind, Spencer knew that he needed this forced separation. He could not have done it himself otherwise.

It worked for the best of all concerned.

Spencer reflected, "It obviously was the time for it to happen. In retrospect, what else could have happened?

He wouldn't accept my partner and Juan did not know my financial situation and that I was, in fact, overextended.

After we parted, the gallery owner in Santa Fe became his exclusive representative through his gallery, but their arrangement fell apart very quickly." Spencer was able to move on.

Back in California full-time without challenging road trips to Mata Ortiz and all over the country, he managed to take time for himself to heal from the mental and physical exhaustion of it all. It was a sorting out time, a reflecting time, a time for nourishing himself.

However, the next turn of events in Spencer's life could not have been more unforeseen.

Here's how his new life came about.

Chapter Twelve

Life After the Split; A New Business;
Emi; Writing; Lucie; Return to Virginia

A new opportunity appeared around 1985 and lasted until about 1996. Spencer was able to extract himself from a dire financial situation and, more importantly, from living out of a storage building.

He had a friend who owned a small window-washing business near San Pedro, California. "He had about twenty-five clients and one day asked me if I would help him out for a week. He was short-handed and it was good, clean work, so I said yes, and to my surprise, I found I actually enjoyed it. Soon, my friend wanted to sell this business, so we worked out an arrangement for me to buy it."

Spencer was at first terribly self-conscious. He was never snobby or had an attitude, but after all, there he was, a Princeton graduate, an anthropologist, a great thinker, a discoverer of great things and great people, and now, he was a window washer! But he found that by doing this work he was literally grounding himself and discovering a new Spencer. He felt more connected to the world than ever before. In his new profession, he learned how to appreciate himself, his family, and others. He set out to expand the business. In his "Spencer the Discoverer" fashion, he found it was as much fun to collect new customers as it was to collect almost anything else. He built the business up to one hundred and fifty customers and even purchased a *super ladder* for a princely sum of five hundred dollars. This ladder "could stand up and do tricks," Spencer laughed. "And it was amazing the times people would stop and ask me the best cleaning solution to use for window washing." He always told them, "The best formula is a capful of Dawn in a bucket of water." His life as a small businessman was cathartic, and he found these years to be extremely maturing and self-nurturing.

"Years after Juan and I split, some people told him that I was cleaning store-front windows for a living. He was astonished at that. He then had a new image of me as a window washer, even though I was really proud of my window-washing business. Not only that, when I did finally see him again, and he learned directly from me that at the time of our split I was in debt, he was shocked. Really shocked, and dejected. And I knew he sincerely felt very badly for me. He could not understand why I had not discussed this with him. He was truly perplexed. He just didn't get it.

"He, and many others, never seemed to comprehend what it took to make Juan Quezada and Mata Ortiz happen as they did. The time, the money, the energy. He had an erroneous belief for all those years that I had become quite wealthy, when in fact, quite the opposite was true.

"Much later on, I had an opportunity to tell Juan that I wanted him to know the eight years I did window

234

cleaning was a very maturing experience. In fact, I was indebted to it, and it was an extremely rewarding time in my life. I was proud that I was able to do that kind of work. He seemed to understand, but he was still bewildered. I don't think he ever got over it."

At any rate, Spencer felt that those years with his window washing business gave him a new understanding of humanity, and in fact, this new maturity helped him to grow and serve in other ways that were unimaginable. Soon he moved out of the storage garage where he had been so frugally living and into a small apartment, also taking a part-time job there as a security officer. Things were good. He now had a home again, a thriving business, and extra income from the security job. Then an even more wonderful "life event" came knocking on his door.

It was 1986 and he met Emi. In graduate school, Spencer had a special friend by the name of Judy. They had stayed in touch and now Judy's cat became instrumental in Spencer and Emi meeting. Living by the ocean in Alaska, Judy's cat would often present her not with a mouse, but with beautiful feathers. Seagulls and bald eagles would often clash over the delectable fish in the shallow ocean waters and occasionally these birds lost their feathers on the beach. Judy's cat loved to collect eagle feathers and bring them home. Judy asked Spencer to find homes for them with his Native American friends who used them for ceremonial purposes. And, by the way, her friend, Emalie, would be taking a trip to Los Angeles soon and could deliver them.

Emi was a nurse serving in Alaska villages on the offshore islands and had decided to attend nurse practitioner training in Los Angeles. She contacted Spencer to deliver the package. He had planned to do some serious searching at yard sales the next morning, and he seldom went to less than thirty on a Saturday morning.

Figure 42. *Spencer and one of his yard sale treasures, 1986*
Courtesy of the Spencer MacCallum Collection

He didn't want to miss his Saturday outing, so he asked Emi if she wanted to go along. She did.

Spencer's lifelong passion of discovering new things and people, in this case, was the catalyst to serve up the best treasure he could ever have hoped to find, and that was Emalie.

Spencer distributed the precious feathers to grateful Native American friends. Years before, Spencer had been told by a psychic that he had an Indian guide who had helped him many times in his life. He often wondered if his Indian guide was instrumental in arranging that meeting.

Spencer was not shy about his feelings for Emi and would confess that meeting her had been one of the greatest blessings in his personal life.

She was a strong personality, was hugely likable, and was an all-around good person. Her life had been full of adventure and heartbreak as well. Emi felt that the two of them had a lot in common. She said, "Spencer and I were both unattached. I had been a widow for a few years, and my children were grown."

Her late husband, George, had been a bush pilot and a jet aviation mechanic. They had moved to Alaska where she had taken a position as head of nursing at a small hospital. "My first husband and I had gone to Kotzebue, Alaska. I was the Director of Nurses at the hospital. We had been in town for a few days trying to get situated, but then our furniture and belongings had been delivered to the wrong house.

"On my first day at the hospital, my husband began moving our belongings from the wrong house to our new house. He was fifty years old at the time and had been carting our belongings between houses when someone let him know that there was a snowmobile down the road he could use. So, he walked a mile to get it, but when he arrived there, it didn't have any gas, so he walked a mile back to the house to get a gas can, then a mile back to the snowmobile.

"Then tragedy struck. The weather was brutal, minus 65 degrees. I was being given a tour of the hospital when we received word that there was an incoming arrival.

When we got the call at the hospital that someone was coming in, it was reported to be a sixty-year-old male.

"This man did appear to be sixty years old. He was unrecognizable to me. What did look familiar was his belt buckle. I blurted out, 'Why, that is just the kind of buckle that my husband George wears!'"

Saying it, Emi suddenly realized that it *was* her husband lying on the gurney. The incoming patient was George, but at first, Emi did not recognize him as his complexion and features had been completely distorted by freezing.

Emi continued, "He dropped dead while pull-starting the snowmobile. The three miles of strenuous walking in those extreme temperatures was just too much.

"He was dead on arrival. I was literally stunned. In total shock. But it's fortunate he could not be revived because he would never have been the same. In those days, there were rarely, if ever, autopsies performed up there. I later reviewed the symptoms of cold shock that can cause the heart to fibrillate, then stop. This appears to be what happened.

"I stayed in Kotzebue after that, even though I thought about going back to Sitka immediately where I had a lot of friends. But I thought to myself, Emalie, you need a challenge, so stay here and see what unfolds."

Emalie decided to stay in Kotzebue and give it a try. She knew that working would be a good thing to help her with the sudden shock, grief, and depression. She had made a commitment to that job, and she felt she should stay.

"I wanted to do something worthwhile. I'm a Virgo, very tenacious and strong.

"So, I stayed in Kotzebue for about a year.

"Then things proceeded to get even tougher. Because there was no mortuary there, one of my duties was to allow people to view the bodies of their deceased relatives. I didn't like that. It was too hard for me to be the acting mortician. Also, managing the hospital was difficult. I was the supervisor to the nurses who came to Alaska who wanted to idealistically live in the wild, and to be bush nurses. But they wanted to play, to take a dog team and scamper out in nature, and they often would not get back to their shift at the hospital on time, so I would have to cover for them."

The politics of the hospital were significant. The doctors expected a lot from her and because of her position, she was basically on call full-time. "I don't think anyone should have to be on call full-time, so I proposed that the most experienced nurses take over when I was off duty. However, the boss in Anchorage said no to that proposal. It just became too much.

"Eventually I left and did go back to the Sitka hospital where I had previously worked. Later they offered an internship in Los Angeles for nurse practitioner school, which is why I first landed in L.A. When I first met Spencer, I thought: he's fun, and let's see what happens."

From Spencer's point of view, he said he loved Emi immediately! She was interested in him and his life, and she was always up for an adventure, such as going to yard sales with him.

From Emi's point of view, she also fell for Spencer right away, even though he was pretty shy.

She said he was funny, very witty, knowledgeable, friendly, and very endearing.

"He had not been in a relationship since Annie, so he was in San Pedro just working, hanging out, and doing his thing." They began to date.

Emi was going to school and was extremely busy, attending twelve-hour days of classes and study. She wondered why she was pressing herself at that stage in her life. There were many times she wanted to quit but didn't. After completing those studies, Emi returned to Sitka to fulfill her commitment to the hospital because they had sponsored her internship.

During that time, she was able to put her skills to work in a very productive environment.

Taking a twelve-hour ferry ride out to the villages to spend weekends managing prenatal care was extremely rewarding to make sure there was a good outcome for the babies.

But Emi also felt the pressures of being expected to work extra shifts when already exhausted. Hospital administrators never seemed to understand nurse-patient relationships.

She considered continuing her studies to become a doctor, but life, in the form of her new relationship with Spencer, intervened.

After she fulfilled her Sitka commitment, Emi moved in with Spencer. It was not too long before Lucie, Spencer's mother became ill, and they decided to go back east to help her out.

Spencer related, "We had gone across the country to take care of Lucie. My mother liked the idea that her youngest son had come to take care of her and devote his life to her during her last years, but another woman in the picture did not fit well; although Emi, as a nurse practi-

240

tioner, was far more capable than I to tend to Lucie's needs.

"Lucie made life difficult for Emi, and at one point she was treating Emi as if she were a servant. She would agitate Emi enough to cry, and Emi would respond by saying that she only wanted to be treated as a member of the family. One day, my mother spoke very harshly to Emi that there are only two ways to be a MacCallum: one is by birth and one is by marriage. I overheard this and went into the other room and from the doorway I motioned to Emi. 'Let's get married. We'll call her bluff.'"

Emi agreed. Spencer thought of a very special place to hold the ceremony, imagining he would like to have a ceremony in a Quaker Meeting place. His Grandfather Popdaddy was of Quaker extraction and there was a charming Quaker meeting house, built in 1726, up at Princeton set in a little clearing. [49]

"I had always enjoyed the Quaker meetings. When I attended Princeton, it was expected that students attend a church service on Sunday, and I used to bicycle out to this little Quaker service. So, I called a friend at Princeton. He was a professor of pre-Columbian Art and was well connected with a lot of people."

The professor was eager to help and told Spencer that he had several Quaker friends he would contact. He reported back that normally the meeting house would not be lent out, but he gleefully asked Spencer, "When can you come? You may use the meeting house for your wedding, and I'll make all the arrangements. You'll stay with me!"

"We went up and stayed overnight with him. On the way, we traveled through the beautiful Amish country. We needed a wedding ring for Emi. I had found a silver band I

241

could use, but we needed one for Emi. Not having much money, we stopped in antique shops along the way. The little shop lady said she did not have any wedding rings, but then she exclaimed, 'You know, my husband died five years ago. I have always worn this ring, and I don't have a need for it really. If you would like, I will sell you this ring.' Spencer asked, 'Was it a good relationship?' She smiled, "He always called me his angel.'"

Spencer knew then that it would be a good ring, so she took it off and it fit Emi perfectly. "So now we had the ring. We went on to Princeton and stayed with my friend. The next morning at about seven o'clock he took us over to the meeting house. A Quaker member had already been there and opened all of the wooden shutters and built a fire in the fireplace. Smoke was rising out of the chimney now, the sunlight was streaming through the clearing in the woods, and it was absolutely beautiful. We stood in front of the fire and I had penned some appropriate words to say. But in Quaker services, there is little or no speaking at all. I stood looking into the fire and thought that when the time came, I would know what words to say. But somehow the time never came for words. Finally, I felt I should put the ring on her finger. And that was it. And we were married. Pretty soon the Quaker man came and I helped him snuff out the fire and close the shutters.

"Then my friend showed up and drove us back. That was our ceremony. You could not ask for a more beautiful wedding, really," Spencer said.

"After the ceremony, we went back down to Virginia. We wanted to stop in and tell the antique shop owner how happy we were, but we could not find her place! Later on, we made other trips to that country, and made dedicated searches for her and that little antique shop! But no matter how hard we tried, or who we asked, or how much effort we put into it, we could never, ever find it again. It was as though that little shop and the sweet and generous woman had never existed."

It was yet another complex mystery, certainly as full of mystique as everything else about Spencer, that never was solved.

The happy couple returned to Virginia, but Emi's new status as Spencer's wife seemed to have little effect on Lucie's attitude toward her.

They stayed in Virginia for almost six years taking care of his mother.

They had traveled there with the original intent of staying for only six weeks and had planned to make arrangements for someone to come in and take care of Lucie.

"I had sold my window washing business and put things in storage. Our plan was to get her situated and then do something different. Because Emi was a nurse, she'd been thinking of working with the Peace Corps. But instead, we moved up to Frederick, Maryland, about thirty miles away, and leased an apartment. My mom was in her late eighties at this point, and due to age and illness, she was antagonistic."

Emi reflected, "One time I was sleeping upstairs, and Spencer was downstairs. I decided to go down to him. I was on the way downstairs when she came out and asked where I was going. I answered, *I'm going to sleep with Spencer.*

"She looked at me and said, 'Well, I love him, too.' I was shocked. She wanted Spencer to herself, without me in the picture," Emi said.

Figure 43. Emalie and Spencer MacCallum
on their wedding day, 1988
Courtesy of the Spencer MacCallum Collection

Spencer explained, "Lucie had never really accepted any women in my life or in my brother Crawford's life. She never remarried after the bitter divorce from our father. "She could never get over either being married to, or divorced from, my father. She did have opportunities, but in her mind, she was still married to my father." During this time, Spencer's brother Crawford would return to Virginia to see the family.

By now, the two sons realized that Lucie had never taken a grip on her life after the divorce. They asked her why she had not moved to Santa Fe years ago, a town she had loved, and she responded that she had wanted to keep a home for them back East. They pointed out that since they had lived for many years out West, the answer did not make sense to them, but she had maintained that erroneous vision, despite what might have been best.

Spencer recalled that before she died, he told her he would always remember her as she was in Mexico, not in the dreadful days and months leading up to her death. She was grateful to him for that. "She had always hoped to age gracefully, but unfortunately she did not."

She had wanted to die at the age of eighty-six, the exact same as Popdaddy, but life wasn't cooperating. Because of severe osteoporosis, her rib cage had slipped into her pelvis. "She had thirty-six fractures, and it was agonizing and difficult for her."

Attending a last annual New Year's party, she wanted to go home early because she was hurting so much. She realized then that there was no quality of life ahead for her. The doctor had told her she had a strong mind, heart and lungs and would live a long time, but she responded with, "Don't tell me that." She was in a nursing home during the last year of her life, but Spencer knew it was Lucie's wish at that point to just die, and at home.

Lucie relied on Spencer to follow her wishes.

She had decided that if her mind was indeed her strongest asset, then while she still had it, she would use it to make her own decision to stop taking any food and medicine. She asked to be taken out of the nursing home to her own home. She also reconciled with Emi close to the end, joking with her that it was time to get rid of all the old rugs and all the old antiques, meaning herself included. Then she would tease Emi, "You and I will go to Florida and get some new things with bright colors."

Lucie was home, and had expressed her gratitude to Emi, "You did it, you brought me home to die," and they cried in each other's arms.

"So, at the end, she gave in to Emi," Spencer said. She appealed to Spencer and Emi to not take her to the hospital at the very end. "It took about three weeks for her to die. She didn't feel hunger after a few days, and she didn't want to see friends who might encourage her to eat."

Spencer's brother came from Albuquerque, and they took turns sleeping by her bed at home. The night before she died, Spencer found a bottle of wine his father had made years before. He had become a very good vintner. They opened it and though Lucie wasn't speaking, they all had a sip, held hands, and sang Amazing Grace.

Lucie was dressed in her MacCallum tartan and clan pin, sitting up in the four-poster bed with the canopy around it, the French doors opened to the garden.

Spencer said that as his mother was passing, he tried not to feel an emotional reaction, explaining that as always, when something really touched him, it would manifest in stuttering, so he had learned how to curb his emotions. This was the secret he held deep within himself that few people knew about.

Figure 44. *Lucie, Spencer, and Emi at Lucie's home in Virginia, circa 1988*
Courtesy of the Spencer MacCallum Collection

"She died around seven a.m. the next morning. My brother remarked that all our family members of that generation were gone, and it was up to us now to carry on."

An era ended for the family and then, after six long years, Spencer and Emi were ready to move forward with their lives. They had managed to keep up with Emi's adult children and their families, but taking care of Lucie had monopolized their time. The couple now turned their attention elsewhere. Emi's three children were scattered, and they could now spend some time with them. Spencer felt lucky to have had a close relationship with them.

The couple decided to move to Tonopah, Nevada in 1997. Friends of theirs touted the wonderful climate and naturally, they liked the idea of being back in the Southwest. They visited the town and immediately fell in love with it. It was quiet and unassuming and seemed a good place for Spencer to write. Emi took a nursing position at the local hospital.

Spencer and Emi had always been in sync about their ideas regarding social organization. Tonopah was a peaceful place to put more of those ideas on paper. "Emi and I both shared many of the same views and publishing these ideas became our joint priority. She has been a wonderful partner to me," Spencer smiled.

"Emi was the best person I could ever meet to help me pursue new ideas. She had a fine philosophical mind and was a good editor. We've had quite an adventure together. We are opposite in so many ways, but it was wonderful how well we got along."

As they were enjoying living in the peace of the Nevada desert, he had an opportunity to edit and publish a book about Somalia.

Spencer noted, "This country had not had a central government for many years. They were undergoing an economic boom, though the media did not report it. Why? Many people cannot understand how a nation can survive without a government."

Spencer became involved when he heard about the author, Michael Van Notten, who was working on these ideas. Spencer tracked him down and they instantly became friends.

Michael Van Notten was a Dutch lawyer who married into a clan in Somalia and studied the customary law of the Somalis. There was no statutory law, so customary law held society together. According to the book, various clans lived according to customary laws that can handle the complex needs of society. (50) Michael spoke eight languages and had been intrigued with customary law and went to Somalia where he met his future wife, a high-ranking cousin of a chief.

"When Michael married," Spencer said, "the bride's family asked him how many camels he would give to the family if he ever left. The normal figure would be between thirty and fifty, but Michael claimed he would give two hundred camels." The Somalis embraced Michael and viewed him as a stepping stone to the modern world.

Spencer never forgot when Michael brought the Chief of the Samaron Clan to visit Spencer and Emi in Tonopah, Nevada. "The Chief was tall, he had beautiful ebony skin and a very regal bearing. He knew men, cattle, and the stars. On his first visit to the United States, Michael and the Chief had traveled to Las Vegas to investigate the new cattle feeding procedure that trained cattle to eat leaves and branches like a giraffe. It must have been quite shocking for him to see Las Vegas spread out before him like a universal galaxy against the night sky."

Michael had asked Spencer to help him publish his ideas. Although Michael passed away not long after making this request, Spencer kept his commitment to Michael and continued to edit and publish the work. Published by the Red Sea Press, *The Law of the Somalis, A Stable Foundation for*

Social and Economic Development in the Horn of Africa, edited by Spencer Heath MacCallum, was published in 2005. [51]

In 2003, Spencer and Emi found themselves moving to the village of old Casas Grandes in Mexico, only a short drive from Mata Ortiz itself. Spencer and Emi's original intent was to live modestly and do some writing. For Spencer, it was a homecoming back to Mexico, for that is where he felt his true roots began to grow. They both felt comfortable with the prospect of living in the Mexican culture.

Once they made that decision, they began to look at housing. "Our interest was an old adobe ruin that needed a lot of work. It would have been impossible to live in it in the condition we found it."

But soon, there was an opportunity to buy another nearby house that was ready to move into and had a small pecan orchard. "We bought the second house and got cold feet about contracting to rebuild the first house, so we almost sold it. Then we met Luis Tena, a local builder, and we hired him to rebuild the old adobe. Things began going so well on the remodel that a neighbor asked us if we would buy his house, a real ugly duckling. But it was charming and had those old high ceilings and vigas, so I asked Luis if he would help us with it. He answered, 'I will help you with any project for the rest of your life.' Then we got another, then another."

The MacCallums never had the intent to remodel and rent houses. But that is what happened, eventually naming all six houses the Pueblo Viejo Courtyards, Extended Stay Rentals. They called their rentals "The Adobe Experience."

They enjoyed renting them to archaeologists, researchers, writers, tourists, and people who were going to the area for any number of reasons. As far as Emi and Spencer's societal views were concerned, "We saw a natural order to things," Emi said. "I can see things in a global context. Spencer is quite linear with his thinking, but I can see around an issue, all the angles."

Spencer had talked about being able to present to the world some of his and Popdaddy's ideas. Emi reinforced that idea. "He had this commitment to Popdaddy because his grandfather told him that the only thing in life that would disappoint him is if Spencer didn't think further than he had about these things." Emi agreed with Spencer's mission. "We did this together. I supported and encouraged his economic ideas."

Explaining some of these views, Emi said that you didn't have to have a total crash of a system to make new ideas work. "Spencer pointed out that a new system already worked with shopping centers, hotels, and other multi-tenant properties. What is required is infrastructure. You don't have to have such heavy taxation on the people to make a system work. It can work with the money that is earned. We just wanted to promote new ideas and positive ways of looking at reorganization."

When Spencer and Emi moved to Casas Grandes, Mexico, they wanted a place for people to meet and talk about ideas and do some writing.

They then realized that their house rentals were a way to enhance the overall development of the community and help provide parttime employment for folks in the area.

"We wanted to take part in other peoples' projects," said Emi. "But we loved the idea of restoring these adobes. We were putting into action some of our ideas. We were landlords, and some of the money we received from the rentals went into the common areas, such as the museum and art gallery. We believe in private management, rather than a subdivision with a homeowner's association. These ideas are just one of the things that Spencer and I had in common when we met," Emi said.

Emi was a source of strength to Spencer. Her presence in his life was inestimable. Smart, funny, and sociable, she was like a reflecting pool back to Spencer. She could condense and edit his and Popdaddy's scholarly ideas and thoughts into everyday patter.

A uniquely special gift, she could see the big picture of everything they were doing together from the day they met.

Her sharp mind cut through the ifs, ands, and maybes and laid the truth out in front of everyone. She was also a happy soul. More than anything, perhaps, she brought Spencer the gift of joy. She was the partner he himself said was perfect for him. Her clarity of mind showed Spencer how life could be lived with purpose yet peace of mind. Reflecting on various topics of their lives together, Emi was philosophical.

Emi thought that Spencer going into Mexico at an early age gave him that vision and background, and "Lucie was amazing that she allowed them the freedom to explore Mexico on their own, but yes, she seemed to harbor a lot of personal issues," she stated. "I don't think she acted in a mean way at the end because of her illness. No, she had her mental facilities all along. It was just that she was a very interesting, complex woman."

Lucie's unresolved issues seemed to revolve around her denial of her failed marriage. She never accepted the divorce from Ian, and she had a very difficult relationship with her father. She loved him dearly, but Popdaddy was so strict.

It was in 1898 that Lucie's mother, Johanna Maria Holm, married Popdaddy, her father.

"Popdaddy ruled the roost, and was Victorian," said Emi, "and not only to his wife but also to his three daughters. Evidently, Lucie was the apple of his eye, but it was a tradeoff. She would get a lot of attention, but she had to walk the line.

"Lucie and her sisters were not allowed to wear regular children's shoes or fashionable shoes for young ladies. He had them wear the sturdy kind of shoes that would last."

Lucie's childhood with Popdaddy set the complicated background for Spencer and Crawford, and set up a deeper, driving force that always motivated Lucie.

"The worst time I had with her was when Lucie heard a program on the radio about elder abuse. She called the social worker. The social worker came out and Lucie lied to her that she was being starved. When I heard this, I confronted Lucie and she replied, 'Well, do you remember one day you got me all ready to go to a fancy $100 per plate meal? We didn't eat until two p.m.!'"

Emi also reflected about Crawfish, Spencer's brother. "It seems that for him to get his doctorate was not enough for Lucie. She wanted him to get the Nobel Prize! As Lucie herself became very domineering, just like Popdaddy, Spencer's brother Crawford rebelled to an extent that he and Lucie did not speak for over twenty years."

But there were other undertones swirling around these four people. For instance, apparently Spencer did not know that Crawford had harbored feelings of incurable jealousy of his brother, although it seems everyone else did know!

According to Crawford, "This was the reason that for many years I was not close to Spencer. I knew then that it was my problem, but it was incurable." However, Crawford has been complimentary of Spencer and extremely proud of him, of what he accomplished, and especially of his marriage to Emi.

Emi reflected that the first time Spencer took her to meet Crawford, he told Spencer, "Marry her."

Emi confirmed that she and Lucie did reconcile at the end, but it was a bittersweet ending for Emi, and one that was preceded by a lot of personal pain inflicted on her.

After Lucie passed, they fixed up her house in order to sell it.

When they did, it was another commencement in their lives, one which released them to move on and do the things they had planned all along.

Emi reflected on Spencer's life and what brought them together.

"Spencer had given his all to the Mata Ortiz potters, and when he left the project, there was a great opportunity for him to mature when he went into business for himself. And the years that we spent taking care of Lucie were very difficult. So, I have always admired him as someone who takes care of others first in his life. Who else but Spencer was driving thousands of miles to sell the pottery, spending thousands of dollars to do so, and talking thousands of hours to museum directors, or coaching and coaxing and building true friendships with the people of Mata Ortiz?

Who else but Spencer was spending every penny in their personal bank account to help farmer-potters become full-time potters?

"What is a fact is that by the time other traders and buyers arrived en masse on the scene in Mata Ortiz, Spencer had already laid the foundations for success. He had already put thousands of miles on his Datsun pickup to promote this project."

Emi continued, "He had already given his life to help Mata Ortiz happen. It was Spencer that encouraged the pottery-making that was already ongoing there and encouraged all the potters to be better and better. But greedy traders just wanted to swoop in and take the cream of the crop and did not want to acknowledge that years of work by Spencer are what was behind this success.

"But even so, as it is known now, by the time he left the project he had spent everything he had, his inheritances, savings, everything trying to maintain the Mata Ortiz potters, the exhibitions, and the brokering of sales to the museums. I reiterate this because the energy and effort he put into making other people's lives better and more productive and more creative have been greatly underestimated.

"I was always amazed at how people thought it was so easy, but it was extremely difficult for him to have done what he did. People have a way of filtering complex activities down to the simplest of terms, either not wanting to know, or perhaps out of jealousy attacking Spencer and the true facts, or they just have a desire to destroy a good man's reputation, refusing to honor what it took for Spencer to create a Mata Ortiz movement from virtually nothing and take it somewhere beyond imagination."

Visionaries rarely see the balance of money on the ledger of life. Putting their life energy into a project, such as promoting an unknown artist to the world, requires an understanding of the role that is played on a grand scale versus our own lives. It's easy to see this visionary thread in all of these people.

But it took more than vision, it took an extreme amount of work.

"Spencer had that vision of Juan," Emi reflected, "and after all, who but someone like Spencer would have seen that genius in those distressed pots he found in the Deming junk store? How many people in the world would have seen that?"

After the couple moved back to Mexico, Spencer worked on several writing projects.

Emi continued, "Popdaddy had a lot of ideas on inspiration and religion. He gave a set of talks that were recorded, and I edited that material and worked it into a book. He had his own thoughts and insights into aesthetics and religions. Sometimes people make a big deal about belief in God; however, they never ask others to define God. Sometimes people are against something, but they have never defined what they are against. Worse still, they have never defined what they are for."

Emi liked to explain that she and Spencer were not libertarians with the capital 'L', as would define the Libertarian group itself. However, they did believe in the philosophy of individual responsibility and allowing everyone the freedom to express their own spirit.

"In that way, yes, we were libertarians. We don't like to use the term because you get pigeonholed. Labels are counterproductive."

Along with writing, and running the rentals, they found they had become "support staff" to the potters in Mata Ortiz and Casas Grandes. "For years, there were still many people who could not write a letter. You would see storefronts with flyers advertising the service of letter writing. Many potters would come to Spencer for help. We wrote letters for them stating that they were going to a show. Spencer had to fax a list of the potters to the border. We also wrote hundreds of letters of recommendation for potters applying for a United States Visa. These were the kinds of things we did for people."

But during the Virginia years, the MacCallums never completely lost touch with Juan and Mata Ortiz.

Juan turned to Spencer for help, asking him to come to Mata Ortiz to help him with a difficult situation. He traveled by air and car in a rush to get to Mata Ortiz in what turned out to be an extremely interesting experience.

Here's what was going on with that, and in Mata Ortiz during the years that Spencer was in and out.

Chapter Thirteen

*Tom Fresh; Walter Parks; Dr. Richard
O'Connor; A Call for Help From
Juan; Selling the Collection*

One thing Spencer was thinking about in the decade after he and Juan and split was how he might help in continuing to promote the large number of exhibitions of Mata Ortiz potters and pottery as he had done in the past. "Juan's contract with the gallery in Santa Fe ended after a very short time, so he was on his own. Over time, I had some contact with him after the split. Emi and I had traveled from Tonopah to Mata Ortiz on occasion, and I wanted to maintain a connection with Juan and some of the other potters. Juan and I would warmly meet and shake hands, and I felt that we both had moved well beyond the split. I told him I would be there for him if he ever needed me, and he seemed comforted to know I was not completely gone out of his life. I also wanted to somehow promote more shows and museum exhibitions."

During this time, Spencer started an online Mata Ortiz newsletter sending it out from Tonopah, Nevada. Not only had there been few shows or exhibitions, but there had also only been a handful of demonstrations and many folks didn't know what was going on with the potters or the collectors. A newsletter would let people know what was happening.

At that point, he considered putting together shows or exhibitions, but his true desire was that the Mata Ortiz phenomenon become self-perpetuating. "For instance, I put forth the idea of a European tour of Juan's work. I naively figured that I would only need to plant that seed in a few places, and it would take off. But it didn't work out that way."

It appeared that Juan himself did not have a large amount of pottery for exhibition, but there were collectors who told Spencer at that time that they would make their personal collections available for viewing.

"Folks in England, Spain, and Germany were very interested. It was something I had envisioned doing for a long time, and I really hoped it would come together, but it was taking too much energy and effort, and I was beginning to feel very hesitant to take on this kind of activity again. So, I dropped it, and once in a while I would plant that seed where and when appropriate hoping someone would take it up."

Tom Fresh of Idyllwild had become more and more involved with the potters, as had Walter Parks, a consultant for the Idyllwild Campus.

In 1993 Walter published *The Miracle of Mata Ortiz* which was called by Spencer, "a significant historical work. He covers the story of Juan who was a very complicated person," Spencer said. "Thankfully, Walter and Tom continued for many years to promote the potters and the pottery of Mata Ortiz. *The Miracle of Mata Ortiz* helped a great deal with the continuation of the pottery, and I heartily encouraged the book." [52]

Tom, Walt, and later Dr. Richard O'Connor were pivotal in keeping exhibitions and pottery demonstrations going.

Not only that, but Tom and Walt's enthusiastic roles in the project helped spur a meteoric rise in the number of potters in the mid-1980s. There were many discussions about why this happened. One obvious explanation was that in the years getting the Mata Ortiz project off the ground, children were growing up around their adult family members who were making good incomes as potters.

This gave them an inherent understanding that it was OK to be an artist, if so desired. These young potters had by then established good relationships with Juan and other successful adult potters in the village. They had been taught pottery-making skills at a very early age and had a head start.

Also, by the mid-to-late1980s, Juan was attracting buyers of the highest caliber. One was a noted woman collector from Japan.

Spencer recalled, "One day, I received a phone call from Juan explaining that he'd had an inquiry from the Japanese to buy his pottery. He was greatly excited about this overseas venture."

Someone Juan knew had become the intermediary broker for these negotiations, but Juan had rapidly become concerned that the Japanese required a smoother touch than he and the broker were able to provide. He asked Spencer to help.

Juan paid Spencer's airfare to Albuquerque, New Mexico, and he was met at the airport by Juan's broker who was handling the transactions. Right away, he began to tell Spencer how business was done in Mexico—that there was the law, and there was reality.

The reality was that a business from another country had to have a partner in Mexico. A company would make an application to transact business in Mexico, then the Mexican government would select someone to represent that company in Mexico. That person would become, in effect, the company's partner while doing business in Mexico. He told Spencer that's the way it's done, and he was acting on behalf of the Japanese in this endeavor.

Spencer was aghast and wondered if the only reason this man had secured this Japanese connection at all was that he, not Juan, had designated himself as Juan's representative. Even though the man knew Spencer's role in the Mata Ortiz story, he ignored Spencer's value in these negotiations.

Spencer was wondering why he was telling him all this, but soon realized that the man wanted to find out if Spencer was willing to play the game, to go along with his double agent role, and (to Spencer's mind) crooked way of doing business. The man immediately reminded him of a seedy character. Spencer later discovered that he had indeed been living in Albuquerque under an assumed name.

Spencer stayed at the man's house, which contained a beautiful collection of Juan's pottery. He showed Spencer all his various art and artifacts of this and that, and Spencer was not impressed at all. "He must have seen that I was bored to tears."

The next morning was a Saturday, so he asked Spencer what he would like to do. Saturday morning? There was only one thing to do. Spencer told the man that he would like to go to yard sales. So, in Albuquerque on a sunny Saturday morning, the man drove Spencer around in a huge black luxury sedan. "The entire time the guy was shouting on his mobile phone to his clandestine buddies about *the business*. They'd pull up at a garage sale and Spencer would jump out and do his sleuthing for treasures. It must have been a sight to behold. "In the next day or so, I made a future appointment to meet the Japanese representative in San Diego for a date a few weeks later. Juan's broker was supposed to travel to California and meet with us, as well. I began to think, however, that before I went any further with this situation, I should try to find out something about him. I then returned to Virginia and decided to ask a friend of mine about him. He held a very high position with U.S. customs enforcement.

"He reported back to me that I should avoid him at all costs as there was an arrest warrant out for him in California. Turns out that the government had not known of his address in Albuquerque, so they were grateful for the tip!

"My original plan with this man was to meet up in San Pedro and from there we would drive together to San Diego. However, I was told that under no circumstances was I to get in a car with him.

"I contacted him and suggested that instead of meeting him in San Pedro it would be easier to meet in San Diego. He agreed but didn't show up. When I contacted him later, he accused me of breaking the appointment by claiming I had the wrong date! But I think he was on to me.

"Soon he was picked up by the authorities. He told everyone that I was responsible for tipping off the authorities and he threatened that 'he was going to get me.' It was a great relief that shortly after he got out of jail on bond, he was assassinated in a gangland killing!"

The "broker" was now out of the picture and the Japanese were still pursuing a deal with Juan.

It was revealed that the client was Mrs. Horiguchi, head of the Fuji Project Company, Ltd.

She was a collector of fine art from around the world and was interested in building the Tokyo Fuji Art Museum and would place Juan's pottery there. [53]

"Juan was excited about this project. He was doing some of his best work ever. As coincidence would have it, or maybe not, I had heard of someone who had married into the Japanese royal family and through mutual friends, I asked for an introduction and help to learn the proper Japanese etiquette and protocol. He was delighted to help me and gave me invaluable instructions. For instance, the Japanese have different degrees of bowing and if you're not sure of the status of the other person you bow lower. It's the benefit of the doubt. This is just one little protocol that you must know. So, I was ready when I finally did meet with the Japanese representatives. They were very appreciative and courteous, and we proceeded to establish a line of communication between all parties so that they could purchase some of Juan's best pottery.

"By the time Mrs. Horiguchi came along, Juan had already gained fame and popularity with collectors around the world, as well as with his fellow countrymen and dignitaries. Mrs. Horiguchi ended up with a great collection of his pottery. She owned properties around the world, including the Banff Lodge in Canada, and she placed much of his pottery there at that time." [54]

As time went by, Juan's business relationship with the Japanese and the sales, deliveries, and accounting became very muddled.

Juan asked Walter Parks, an accountant by trade, if he could figure out the Japanese sales. With the painstaking acumen of an accountant, he looked over the contracts, the agreements, and payments, but the numbers did not match and could not be completely straightened out. Walter relayed to Spencer that he thought Juan had been handsomely paid, but he could not verify the paperwork.

During those years, Juan's reputation as an artist kept growing, and his sales were steady when he had pottery to sell. His stature zoomed to the very top.

"When the Pope visited Mexico in 1998, he toured Mexico and the state of Chihuahua. The officials wanted to give him something special. They gave him three Mata Ortiz pots, one by Juan."

By this time, according to Spencer, both he and Juan had mutually reestablished a comfortable friendship, if not a business relationship. Spencer said he was very comfortable with Juan at that point and felt that the past was past, and they had both grown since those events of the partnership and the consequent split.

So it was that Juan reached out to Spencer again, but this time not for help, but as an invitation.

In 1999, Juan was given the prestigious *El Premio Nacional de Ciencias y Artes* Award in Mexico City, the highest award that could be conferred on a living artist. [55]

He invited the MacCallums to travel with him to Mexico City to receive the national award. He wanted Spencer and Emi to accompany him as his guests. "We worked our schedule so that Emi could arrange to be off her nursing duties at the local clinic in Tonopah. We were elated to be going, but at the last minute the President of Mexico had to change schedules, and then Emi could not change her work schedule again."

Spencer traveled to Mata Ortiz. Juan had rented an entire bus to take thirty family and friends to Mexico City. Spencer said that the trip took thirty hours to Mexico City. "It was great fun. We had children and babies everywhere. You know, it seems that in the states you'd hear them squealing and crying all the time, but it seemed there was not one sound the whole way down or back. How you explain that cultural difference, I don't know.

"We arrived at the hotel in Mexico City and went to a plaza where they had mariachi bands. Juan bought all the drinks and refreshments and was so generous to everyone. The ceremony was in the national palace and a thousand people came. There were various award categories for art, music, and science.

"Juan was presented the art award. He didn't wear a tie but wore his cowboy hat and boots. When embraced by the President of Mexico, Juan's hat made him appear much taller than the President.

"When I first met Juan, he was shy and retiring and very uncomfortable as a star. But then, I was very pleased to see that Juan had grown in maturity, and of course stature as a world-class artist, so that he was very much at ease in front of the lights and cameras. I remarked to Juan, 'Even though we have not seen each other much over the years, it is extremely satisfying for me to see how easily today you are able to talk in front of the cameras, knowing how shy you have always been.' "He smiled at me, 'Spencer, I learned that from you.'" Spencer said that

Juan had always been very generous in giving full credit to him, and to others.

In December 2003, Spencer and Emi moved to old Casa Grandes, Chihuahua, Mexico. He and Juan saw each other frequently.

Spencer said that during that time, he and Juan were at ease with each other. It was a relationship that was friendly and courteous.

Spencer noted that Juan was not a warm and fuzzy person and had a complex personality. He was not interested in understanding cultural differences. At that time, he had not once attempted to speak English because, in Spencer's opinion, he was basically shy and would not want to stumble around and make mistakes. But by the time Spencer moved to Casa Grandes, he could see a distinguished maturity in Juan's actions and thoughts, and although this was true, there remained the basic core values of his culture.

"To explain some of the cultural differences I will tell you a little story about a woman journalist who was doing a series of interviews with Juan. She began to feel comfortable with him, and one day she playfully touched the brim of his hat. That was the last time she had access to Juan. He would not interview with her again. Although she had made this innocent gesture, to Juan and to many other Mexican men, this was a highly offensive gesture. This is one reason Juan does not get too involved with other cultures. He doesn't understand the foreign nuances, and he's pretty certain that most outsiders do not understand his."

During the years when Spencer had been struggling to get out of debt, he had kept his entire Mata Ortiz collection in a garage in San Pedro, California. It was a totally untenable situation as far as the risk of theft.

In the mid-1990s Dr. Richard O'Connor in San Diego heard about Spencer's collection. Dr. O'Connor was a medical doctor and a collector himself. He was also on the Board of the San Diego Museum of Us. According to Spencer, he was a person who got onto something and wouldn't give up.

"Evidently, Dr. O'Connor learned where I was keeping the collection and had called the San Diego Museum of Us to see if they were interested in it. Their focus at that time was on Latin America, so they were.

"He called me out of the blue and asked if I was interested in selling the collection to the museum. The collection of one hundred and fifty-one Juan Quezada pots contained Juan's pottery from the beginning. It was a fine teaching collection of his work for the first three years in chronological order, and it showed the development of his style."

Spencer also had one hundred and fifty pieces of pottery from other Mata Ortiz potters in their early years.

The collection was appraised at that time at one hundred and twenty thousand dollars. Spencer decided that he would donate a large part of the value to the museum as a gift/purchase with only fifty thousand dollars paid to Spencer.

Why would he sell it at all? A few years earlier, Spencer had been virtually homeless and literally lived in a garage with his personal belongings and his marvelous collection. He had just managed to pay off fifteen thousand dollars in debt by starting up the window washing business. "However, it was difficult to think about letting go of this thing, this Mata Ortiz project," Spencer reflects. "It had a tremendous grip on me. And I was holding onto the pottery."

He had not been able to afford insurance to cover the collection and it had greatly concerned him that he could not properly care for it.

Here was an opportunity to keep this fine collection together. Although he had needed money, he had persevered in not selling it off piece by piece. He couldn't bring himself to do that, but to see the collection go to a museum was ideal. It would be well cared for.

Dr. O'Connor set about raising the fifty thousand dollars. "Then, I sold the entire collection to the Museum of Man (now known as the Museum of Us.)

"The levitation pot was the last one to be delivered to the Museum of Us, and when I took it, the museum thought that maybe the Levitation pot wasn't included in the sale, but I assured them it was. But on reflection, I often thought that maybe they were giving me a way to hang on to that pot. They knew how important it was. They said, 'Do you really want to give us this pot?' I did say yes, and I never regretted it, because I knew it would always be in a safe place."

Today the collection is well cared for in the Museum of Us. It is stored in a subterranean chamber and is available to researchers, or those who are writing about the Mata Ortiz story. To describe the collection, or its value, is almost impossible. It is an amazing testament to Spencer that he held onto the pottery when he was deep in debt as even the sale of a few pots could have helped him to move out of his storage-garage living situation. Certainly, if the many potters who Spencer had helped for so many years had known of his situation, they would have and could have easily, with the sale of only one pot each, lifted him out of a desperate financial situation, as he had lifted them out of poverty. But he told no one.

And to be sure, it is even more stunning to think of the value of his collection then and now, and that he did not receive even fifty percent of the value for himself. The collection at that time was valued at one hundred and twenty thousand dollars and he would only take fifty thousand dollars. The value today is inestimable.

Over and over again, it is clear that the integrity of Spencer MacCallum was unquestionable. In fact, the more that is learned, the more there is to be grateful for about Spencer, and his life.

Chapter Fourteen

Return to Mata Ortiz, Casas Grandes and the Past; Ron and Sue Bridgemon

After the MacCallums moved to Casas Grandes in 2003, Spencer had many opportunities to deepen his friendship with Juan, and they discussed several times in what direction Juan wanted to take his art.

"He wanted to branch out and have more freedom to pursue other creative projects. Juan was a complex person, and as such had a wealth of abilities, talents, and mediums in which he could work."

Also, surveying their new home surroundings of Casas Grandes, Spencer speculated that someday a bright future for Mata Ortiz and Casas Grandes could be centered around tourism. The area offered cultural focal points for Northern Mexico, such as the history of the Inland Camino Real, the Hacienda de San Diego, and the old Janos mission built in the 1600s. Also of great interest were the Mormon colonies, the Mennonite colonies, and good restaurants and hotels.

Add in the Paquimé ruins and one of the most interesting museums in the world, the Museum of the Cultures of the North, located at the Paquimé ruins. All this remarkable history was a bedrock for the Mata Ortiz pottery and the potters. Together, there was a consensus to capitalize on this almost unlimited tourism aspect of the area.

In addition, the cultures of southwest and central Mexico had been studied for years, and archaeologists were looking more intensely at northern Mexico to provide answers to the prehistoric relations between central Mexico and the southwestern United States.

As far as the artists were concerned, Spencer had a lot of ideas to expand and capitalize on their natural talents. Silversmithing and any kind of jewelry-making were important additions to the area's economy.

Innovative jewelry, such as using potsherds in the settings, was very attractive, reasonably priced, and quite popular with tourists.

Both Spencer and Emi at that time viewed themselves in a kaleidoscopic vision of being active more with the people, the potters, the artists, and other creative ventures than in promoting just the potters and the pottery. They soon were very busy. So many wanted and needed their help. They were actively involved in encouraging new art forms in the area and were a vital force in enlivening the area with creativity and ideas.

Spencer and Emi were soon discovered by a whole new generation of potters. The MacCallums encouraged and helped them when possible, such as writing letters that helped them cross the border to display their pottery at galleries and shows. They always understood that their help was very much appreciated.

Spencer revealed that he had a moderate case of face blindness or prosopagnosia. "I would repeat to folks that there were many new potters who knew me, but I didn't know who they were. I explained to them that I walked around without a memory of them. It was difficult, but that's the way it was. I even told my old friends, 'When you see me, please speak and tell me who you are.' And they did. I said this out of self-defense so that people would know what was happening with me." Spencer laughed nervously, but he was not shy about discussing these aging issues.

"I have never been particularly good with faces and names, but at any rate, these were not the same faces that I left behind years ago and there were a lot of years on those faces by then."

Spencer enjoyed discovering new talent where he found it, not just in Mata Ortiz. For instance, in one of the outlying villages, he discovered a young man making imaginative figures. The artist gave him some pieces, and Spencer told him he would direct visitors to this young man. One day, he went to Spencer and told him that a tour bus of forty people had appeared at his door and bought everything he had!

"The figurines were of all kinds of animals. They were made out of clay and then painted. He was so grateful about this, and he always wanted to do something for us. Take us out to dinner or something like that. Finally, I suggested that we would rather enjoy dinner in his home. He arranged a dinner party for us and also invited the people who introduced us, and who continue to be friends and fans of his. We went to his house where they sat us at the head of the table. I then realized that he and his family were not going to eat with us as I imagined they would. I protested, but they said, no, no. They were doing this for us, serving us, and the whole family was doing the very finest cooking they possibly could. It was really a beautiful, very formal occasion. I told him that the only word for the occasion was elegant. It was truly elegant. It was so nice of his family to do this for us."

While in Casas Grandes, Spencer and Emi attempted to continue to publish the monthly email newsletter they had begun in Tonapah. The newsletter had been an encyclopedic effort to track everything relating to the village with about six hundred and fifty subscribers at one time. But when the MacCallums moved to Mexico, they found they could not send bulk email from Mexico. It just was not working, so the email newsletter lapsed for a year.

Eventually, they were able to put up a website.

However, to Spencer and Emi's relief, Ron and Sue Bridgemon picked up the Mata Ortiz Calendar newsletter in 2011 and religiously published it via email subscription until 2021. Having led ecoadventures into various areas of Mexico since 1988, Ron and Sue fell in love with Mata Ortiz, the potters, and the area, and made over of two hundred roundtrips to Mata Ortiz (and still counting) leading enthusiastic collectors of the pottery.

Spencer felt their volunteer efforts were priceless, as they almost single-handedly linked the news of the Mata Ortiz potters to collectors and buyers from around the world.

The Bridgemons published a wonderful book, *The Magnetism of Mata Ortiz,* in 2010, and became entrenched in Mata Ortiz. Spencer was forever grateful for their involvement. "The help from Tom Fresh, Walter Parks, Dr. O'Connor, and the Bridgemons helped to keep Mata Ortiz alive. All of us are forever grateful to them."

"Some of the news that was being sent out included personal news about the potters and their families. For instance, when Emi and I were still publishing the newsletter," Spencer said, "it included a small social column announcing *quinceañeras* and other interesting family items. I wrote about Reynaldo's daughter's *quinceañera*.

"Reynaldo came to our house in Casas Grandes when he was planning the *quinceañera* (15th year of age celebration) for his daughter, Lucie, who was named after my mother. [56]

"He asked if I would be *padrino* and Emi *madrino*. I understood that our major responsibility was a financial one. He was asking us for fifty dollars, and he would ask about five or six others to help. Reynaldo and I did not have a *confianza* relationship at that point because I had been gone for many years. However, we became close again when I became *padrino* for Lucie. I felt quite comfortable with him.

"Once you are a *padrino* you are always a *padrino*. I had been honored when they named their daughter Lucie. When Reynaldo was living in San Pedro in the barracks, my mother had stayed there for a time.

She had been delighted with the barracks because I hung fine paintings in all the bathrooms, and I had put up paintings on the walls and decorated the place with antiques. She was really happy with this, and she had her own room, and I mine, and Reynaldo had his. He would bring Lucie coffee in the morning. She just dearly loved being waited on this way. Reynaldo had fine manners and they got along great. Reynaldo visited her once in Waterford, Virginia. So, he named his daughter after her. "Time went by, and he came by our house a few days before the event

274

for the fifty dollars. On the day of the celebration, we dressed in our finest to go to the church, but we were late and arrived just as everyone was coming out of the church.

We missed the church ceremony, but the wonderful dresses and the setting were just beautiful. We went to their house in a procession of cars that ran through the village. They had tented over part of the street by his house.

"The dance was a beautiful affair, with twenty-five tables of flowers, and on each table was a bottle of brandy. As people arrived at the entrance to the dance, they were formally announced. Lucie entered dressed as a bride and was met by her father. He took off her right slipper and put on her foot a high heel shoe, then he did the same with her left shoe. This was the symbolism of maturing into adulthood. Everyone danced. The villagers who were not invited watched everything. I danced with a number of people because it was the social thing to do!"

Spencer adapted to his various roles during those years with enthusiasm. He claimed he was more comfortable living in Mexico amidst all their friends than anywhere else he had ever lived.

He was described as an icon, and on a website someone else had created, they put up his photo with the caption: "Godfather of Mata Ortiz". He laughed, and was perhaps timidly embarrassed about it, but he revealed that he enjoyed his new status as the Godfather!

"I was always cautious not to mess up my new status! Sometimes I would be traveling here or there, and I would hear someone call out my name. 'Spencer!' That happened frequently."

Part of Spencer's charm was always his accessibility. Just like his complete and utter confidence in the universe—he remarkably had complete faith in other people. He believed that it was part of his role from the beginning of the Mata Ortiz project to be the communicator, to relay to the rest of the world the outstanding talent he had found in Mata Ortiz. He said that the communication piece was always primary.

"Early on when I was casting around to discover my role with Juan, I knew it would have to do so with creating an environment that would be conducive to the blossoming of Juan's talent. I was confused for a while as to how to do this, but gradually I hit on the idea of my role as communicator and that of giving Juan total freedom to create.

"In thinking about quality, there is a tendency for it to deteriorate when crafts are produced for a mass market. Traders want to deal in volume. So, they place a large order, and the vendors want to fill this order, but they can't fill it without some sacrifice in quality.

"Eventually the pottery commands less in the marketplace because the quality is going down. And the trader has to come to the potter and say look, I am awfully sorry, I'm just not getting enough for this now. I cannot pay you as much now. So, the craftsperson then thinks, oh, my gosh, my standard of living is going to drop, what can I do about it? The only thing he can possibly do is increase his volume. Make more with a little more sacrifice of quality, you see. This process then is a gradual, relentless spiral downward to the point where finally it is just trash being sold along the highways.

"I made the assumption that there is no shortage of people in the world who value quality and are able to pay for it—if they know it exists. Now there is the rub. The people in Mata Ortiz were in no position, for language or cultural reasons, to make contact with collectors or with the art world in order to get the word out that they have quality pottery. No way they could do that. That became my role, then, to be the communicator."

Spencer and Emi had several reasons to move back to Casas Grandes. It was not primarily for the pottery, or for the potters. In fact, they never considered for a moment living in Mata Ortiz. As in any small town or village, there are crosscurrents of intrigue, it is clannish, and they did not want to live where they would be asked to take sides in conflicts. They did not want to live in that environment.

But Casas Grandes was a town with real historical depth and culture and seemed attractive for that very reason alone.

There was a real tranquility about it. "Whenever we told someone in Mexico that we lived in Casas Grandes they inevitably used the word *tranquilo* to describe life in Casas Grandes."

The MacCallums had some long-term issues to think about as well. "Emi had pointed out that when we would need elder care, we would not want to go into an old folk's home. But in Mexico, we would be able to have someone live with us, for example, instead of having to live in assisted living homes. This would be much more appealing to us, of course."

To Spencer, there was a sense of coming full circle. It felt good to them, and with their many friends nearby, it was a comfortable life. Spencer and Emi had a bit of status and that helped ease them into the community. They built their rentals, did some writing, enjoyed visitors and friends, and lived in a tranquil environment.

The ultimate last chapter to Spencer was talking to tour groups about his life as the Mata Ortiz/Juan Quezada "finder." The audience could tell this was a role he was made for, the "communicator" between the potters and the world, as Spencer would say. Many tourists were tripping through their house, wanting to meet the famous Spencer MacCallum. And to fulfill a vision of earlier times, in 2013 more exhibitions began to manifest again. As he had been hoping for, it perpetuated itself organically without much effort from him. Spencer and Emi were smack dab in the midst of it all. They were the hub. Spencer felt that he promoted not only Mata Ortiz but the entire area and Casas Grandes.

As mentioned earlier in this book, Spencer had an unending trust in the Universe, that it would somehow provide for him and his, that no one could ever really know what's down the lane, but we must all put our best foot forward to reach out to others. This trust extended to the human family, as well.

If one word could sum up Spencer's life, it might be "nexus." He was a connection between a prehistoric culture that was buried and settled under the sand, and all that made Mata Ortiz and Casas Grandes what they are today. He was able to span the age gap between Popdaddy and himself. He touched people from all walks of life and helped them to link up with their true and creative nature.

In Mexico, he related to people and places from all spokes of the wheel: the potters, the museum, the Paquimé ruins, the old and the contemporary culture, traders, tourists, collectors, and the local people themselves. Spencer spoke to thousands of tourists throughout the years about the pots in the Deming junk shop, about finding Juan and other artists, and even about the gold mine fiasco. He showed rare and precious slides and poured out his heart to the crowd. His was a feast of memories, and the tourists gobbled it up. He could talk forever, and the audience could listen forever.

During these talks, Emi would sit in the back of the room and act as the timekeeper. She kept an eye on the clock and at the appropriate time, would raise her arm and point to her wristwatch. Spencer would see her signaling to him over the heads of adoring eyes. He didn't want to stop, no one wanted him to stop. But he heard Emi in his head, the voice of reason.

The tour group was tired, they'd been in the village all day buying pottery; they'd had enchiladas and tortillas for dinner and powerful Mexican margaritas; and they wanted to go to bed to dream about their magical day in Mata Ortiz.

But, did they want to stop? No, not really.

Because for this—for a couple of hours with Spencer— none of them cared about sleep, or tummies stuffed with Mexican goodness, or the need to bubble wrap their pots for the trip home tomorrow. No, this was a moment in a magical time with Spencer.

Outside, the honking horns of old Mexico were never heard. For the past two hours they'd been mesmerized by this man standing in front of them in his MacCallum family tartan, sewn lovingly into his tie and tam.

And now, their lives had crosscut with his.

They didn't want to leave because they had so few moments like this in their lives, because they all knew, that right then, at that very moment, and maybe just once in their lives, they were all touching greatness.

Epilogue

Othtli Award; Then They Were Gone

In 2015, Spencer was presented with the Ohtli Award, Mexico's highest cultural award, at 6 p.m. on Tuesday, May 5, at the Mexican Consulate in El Paso. There is no better way to explain what this meant to Spencer than to include here an email sent out, dated April 23, 2015, announcing his award, which included an invitation to attend.

This was Spencer summing up his Mata Ortiz work, his life, joy, and satisfaction, all rolled together in a single email. This award reflected the true greatness of Spencer MacCallum, with the many challenges, ups and downs, victories and failures, and magical visions all rolled into one. The email follows:

From: Spencer MacCallum
To: Mata Ortiz Friends
Thursday: 4/23/15 9:13 a.m.

This Cinco de Mayo, on May 5, 2015, will bring a beautiful close to my work with Juan Quezada, now so deservedly a Mexican icon, and the other artists of Mata Ortiz whose art has so much strengthened and added to the cultural identity of northern Mexico. The government of Mexico, through its Secretariat of Foreign Af-

fairs, will present me the Ohtli Award, Mexico's highest cultural award, at 6 p.m. on Tuesday, May fifth, at the Mexican Consulate in El Paso. Following this ceremony, which will be part of their Cinco de Mayo celebration, Adair Margo, Chairman of the President's Committee on the Arts and Humanities under George W. Bush and a longtime aficionado of Mata Ortiz, will host a supper party.

Now going on 84 years old, I deeply appreciate this poetic conclusion to my 40-year Odyssey with Mata Ortiz and Casas Grandes. But the award goes to all of you. Neither Juan nor I alone, or the two of us together, could have done any of this without you— my wife Emi and my former wife Anne, museum people, traders, collectors, gallery owners, artists of many kinds, photographers, educators, writers, students, tour operators, archaeologists, media people, friends and facilitators both Mexican and American, all of whom lent their time, inspiration and so often perspiration to this. You have been the Mata Ortiz extended family not just in name, or as a figure of speech, but in active fact. Bless you all and thank you all.

Those who would like to attend this ceremony are most warmly invited. A number of places are available for the supper afterward on a first-come basis. If you are interested in attending the supper, please let us know as soon as possible so that we can reserve a place for you and Adair can plan accordingly.

Spencer and Emi

Then Spencer Was Gone
December 21, 1931 to December 17, 2020

It was in December of 2019 that Spencer and Emi traveled to Deming, New Mexico to run errands and transact their financial and other business in the States.

The report said that Spencer was in a marked crosswalk between the gas pumps and the convenience store when a vehicle ran him over. Apparently, neither Spencer nor the driver of the vehicle were paying attention to what they were doing nor saw each other.

Spencer suffered internal organ damage and multiple broken ribs and bones. He was airlifted to a hospital, then after several weeks was released to return to Casas Grandes. But only a year later, in December 2020, he left Mexico and all of us for good.

In this book, when Spencer told me the story of selecting the worst of his beads to give to his mother so she could make a necklace, and then he got those same beads back when his mother passed, he commented, and laughed, "Well, there must have been a karmic lesson in this somewhere, but I don't want to think about it."

When he passed from this earth, I wonder if he softly smiled and thought, "Well, there must be a karmic lesson in getting run over in Deming, New Mexico — where the Mata Ortiz project started — but I don't want to think about it."

He could be so matter-of-fact one minute, then completely mystical the next.

He always seemed to manage, or to compartmentalize, so many aspects of the various aspects of his personality, but then he could bring them all together in the most unexpected ways that would turn your head around.

Figure 45. *Spencer checking out pottery at the*
the author's home, 2007
Courtesy of the Jon Samuelson Collection

To Spencer, I say thank you for looking over my shoulder as I wrote your story. Yes, I could hear you . . . when you would say, "how about writing it this way—or that way?"

I could sometimes even hear the exact words.

And I would then reply to you, 'Thank you, Spencer, of course, that was just right." And we shared a few laughs along the way getting here, too! I was proud to know you, and honored that you shared the stories of your life with me, and although you are not here in the physical anymore, you are still in all our hearts.

Godspeed and adios, my friend, and someday I hope to see you "there," wherever "there" may be.

*Figure 46. Spencer and Jon Samuelson, 2007
Courtesy of the Jon Samuelson Collection*

Then Juan Was Gone
May 6, 1940 to December 1, 2022

As this book was nearing publication, and just about two years after Spencer left us, shockingly Juan left us also. In this book is perhaps a Juan Quezada that was not really known to many people.

Although one thing is true, there will never be enough words to capture either Spencer or Juan. I am privileged to have known them both, to have interviewed both, as well as their first interview together, and to have shared them with you herein. As with Spencer, Godspeed and Adios, Juan.

I am blessed, very fortunate, that it never entered my mind, not even an inkling of a thought, to touch your hat.

Figure 47. *Adios, mi amigo, 2008*
Courtesy of the Jon Samuelson Collection

Then Emi Was Gone
September 3, 1937 to December 29, 2022

In the same month and year as Juan passed, so did Emi on December 29, 2022, only a little more than three weeks later after Juan. She had been having health concerns and was taken to Las Cruces, New Mexico, and then to Arizona for treatment, but she did not overcome her physical health challenges.

Figure 48. The author and Emalie (Emi) Caley MacCallum, 2008. It was a blessing to know you. Courtesy of the Jon Samuelson Collection

Jon and I visited with Emi and her family at a Las Cruces hospital in December 2022, just a few weeks before she passed. Although she had previously read the book, I asked her if she would like me to read to her from it. She eagerly sat up in bed as I did.

She smiled at me and said, "Your book about Spencer is really wonderful. And very important. I am so happy it is finally being published. Thank you very much for doing this."

When we were leaving, I went over and gave her a hug, and said so long. She seemed content. I didn't know that would be the last time I would see her on this planet.

To say she was Spencer's bedrock is a vast understatement because she was so much more than that. Anyone that knew her sensed her joyful nature, her keen insight, and her truly infectious laugh.

Conclusion

When my husband, Jon, and I met Spencer, Juan, and Emi, we were associated with Geronimo Educational Travel Studies International, headquartered in Douglas, Arizona.

Geronimo continues today as a contractor for Road Scholar, an international travel leader for over forty years, offering six hundred worldwide programs in educational programs for adults. Along with Frank Ortega, we worked about seven years taking tourists and pottery collectors on trips originating in Arizona down to Mata Ortiz.

Figure 49. Front Row: Guillermo, Jon Samuelson
Back Row: Charmayne Samuelson, Frank Ortega,
Hotel Hacienda, Nuevo Casas Grandes, 2006
Courtesy of the Jon Samuelson Collection

One could be so lucky in life to ever find a kinder, gentler soul than Frank. He has encouraged this book for as long as it has been an idea.

Those were lively days filled with color and sunshine; history and *nopales* (prickly pear leaves) for dinner; super strong margaritas; and music by our friend Guillermo who played guitar and sang songs with a loud husky voice for our evening entertainment. My husband Jon never failed to request, *"Mi Linda Esposa,"* and Guillermo never failed to make a giant production of it, with a huge grin, as he sang it directly to me.

To everyone I have known that has made this book possible, I thank you sincerely and do so with much gratitude and appreciation.

As Spencer would say, it has been quite an adventure, which is "not something you do, it's a mindset." I know Spencer would be proud.

Charmayne Samuelson, July 2023

Appendices:
Interview Transcripts

Candid interviews seem more engaging when one can read the transcripts themselves.

Because of this, the following is a fascinating look at the major players in Spencer's life while he was involved in Mata Ortiz. The following are bonus interview transcriptions conducted in 2005 and 2006. Some of these interviews took place with a translator.

For clarity of reading, the following interviews are transcribed in a direct question-and-answer format and are edited for punctuation and grammar.

Appendix I

First Joint Interview Ever Conducted with Both Juan and Spencer

Charmayne: What did you think about Spencer when he first arrived on the scene in 1976?

Juan: I couldn't understand what he was doing. I knew why he came here, but I couldn't understand what he really wanted.

Spencer, laughing: I didn't know what I was doing either.

Charmayne: Juan, how do you think your life might have played out if Spencer had not arrived on the scene?

Juan: I think my life would have been totally different if I had mainly just made sculptures. Because I like to sculpt. But when Spencer came here, I already did know about the different kinds of clay and what was here. I had been exploring and looking for new clay for years. I knew the clay already. If I hadn't succeeded with the pots, I would have changed back to making sculptures out of clay. And paintings on bones. From way back, many years ago, I have sold them; and if I didn't sell them, I bartered to buy pigs, corn, beans, and chickens. That was my life. Yes, I think so, I would have changed back, because I really like sculpture and painting. Actually, what I like the best. I have always liked doing those things because making pots takes so much more time and I only have so little time these days.

Charmayne: Are you doing any sculptures now?

Juan: No, I don't have time.

Charmayne: Would that be your first love over pottery?
Juan: *Si, Si!!*

Charmayne: That's a bombshell. That is really very fascinating. (Juan and Spencer look at each other and smile at my comment.)

Charmayne: Well, I want to ask, what did you think about Spencer then, in those days, and what do you think about him now?

Charmayne: We just talked to Lydia and she said that Spencer is the little angel of Mata Ortiz. What do you think about that?

Juan: Not an angel exactly to me, but a person with the wisdom to bring the town forward. I think we all are grateful to Spencer; the whole town is grateful.

Charmayne: Juan, I want to ask you about the levitation pot and if you are familiar with the experience that Spencer had with one of your pieces of pottery.
(Spencer explains which pot.)

Juan: I think that the piece was a very pretty one, so it was natural to have a strong reaction to it, but I didn't know Spencer had that experience.

Spencer: I felt like I was floating in the air for about 10 minutes. At the beginning of that experience, I asked myself, what must other people be thinking about this, because I am floating in the air? And I looked around, but everything and everyone else seemed very normal, and then I thought, I'm going to fall but I didn't fall. It was a very rare experience. Did you know about this, Juan?

Juan: No, I didn't know about that. (Juan was visibly confused with Spencer's explanation, as he had never heard this story before.)

(Following, Spencer is further explaining in Spanish his experience, which he said felt like it was a graduation of the "school" of Mata Ortiz.)

Figure 50. Juan Quezada Painting on Bone, *located at the
Museum of Us, 1998. Animal vertebra with red painted
decoration and with the eyes circled for emphasis.
Courtesy of the Jon Samuelson Collection*

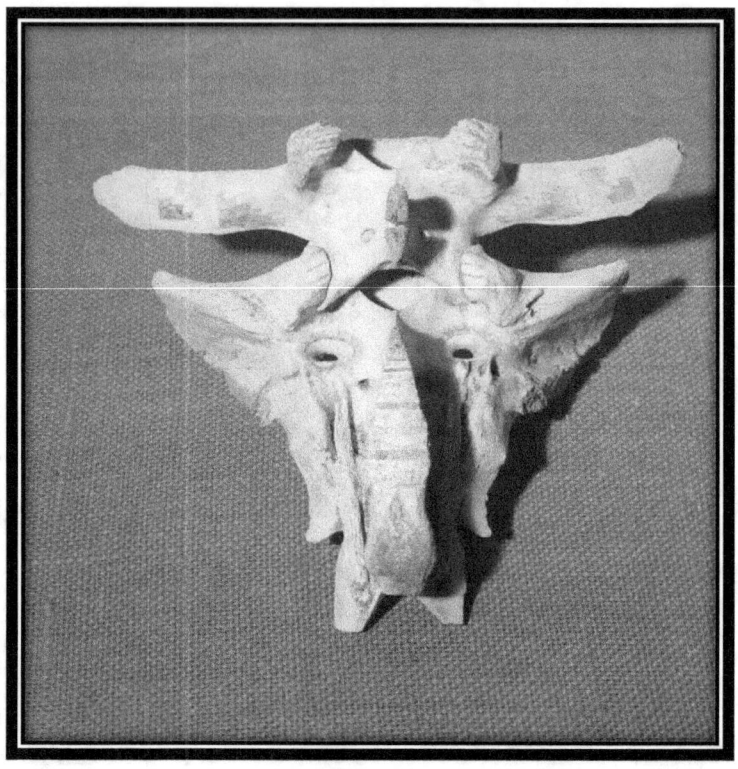

Figure 51. *Juan Quezada Painting on Bone*, *located at the Museum of Us*, *1998*. *Animal vertebra with red pained decoration.*
Courtesy of the Jon Samuelson Collection

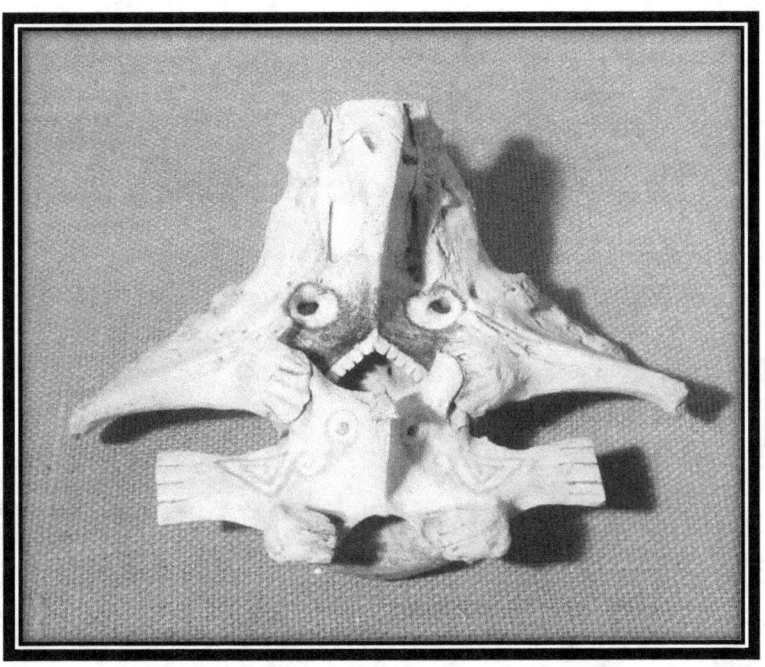

Figure 52. Juan Quezada Painting on Bone,
located at the Museum of Us, 1998. Animal
vertebra with red painted decoration.
Courtesy of the Jon Samuelson Collection.

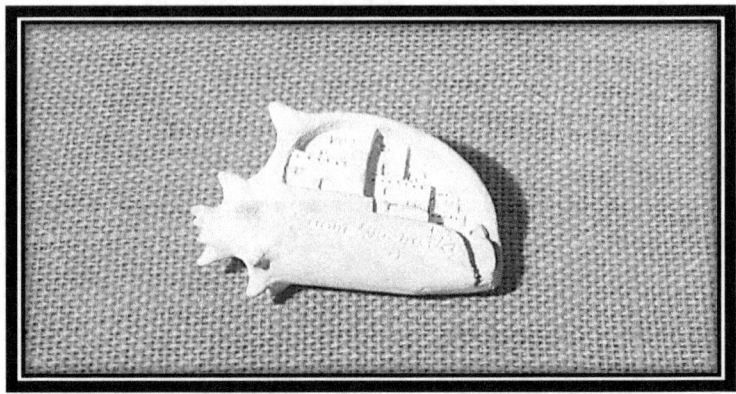

Figure 53. *Juan Quezada Carving, located at the Museum Of Us, 1998. White figurine in the shape of a shell, with cliff dwelling carved on one side.*
Courtesy of the Jon Samuelson Collection.

Figure 54. *Guille, Spencer and Juan during their first joint interview, 2005*
Courtesy of the Jon Samuelson Collection

Spencer: It was a very curious experience. I haven't had this experience before or after that one, which lasted a few days. For about two days here in town I was experiencing that levitation. I just needed to think about that pot for a moment, and it would happen again. But once I left the village, I never had this experience again.

Juan (mystified): No, I didn't know you had that experience. (Juan seemed nervous and did not seem to understand what Spencer was describing.)

Spencer: Just thinking on that, I asked, "Why? Why? What is the meaning of this?" Well, three years before I had come here looking for the end, the culmination of the adventure of finding those three pots. But that was not the end, it was only the beginning, of who knew what. And looking at the beautiful pot, I thought I was having that experience. "Now, this is the culmination of what I had come here looking for three years ago." But there is more. I felt like... in English, we say commencement, the graduation of school when life starts. I had the same feeling of completion with you, Juan, that you had begun to move away from me. I felt like there was a greater power than us, and that power said to me, "You can leave this project now, Juan is on the right track—or you can stay in the project if you wish." Well, what should I do then? It was such an extraordinary experience.

(Juan does not answer Spencer. He does not appear to know how to respond. He was showing distress. There was silence for a few moments, until I asked the next question.)

Charmayne: Juan, have you ever had a levitation experience with your pots?

Juan: No, I haven't had any extraordinary experiences like that one.

(Again, a couple of silent moments, but then Juan speaks to Spencer.)

Juan: But remember that strange experience in Deming? That woman in Deming leaving those three pots at the junk store…I think that was strange. And you bought them and then that woman went back to get them, to Deming to buy the other three pots. But you had bought them already.

(Both of them laugh and shake their heads. Then Juan addresses Spencer again.)

Juan: Only that I was very lucky that I had a big step forward in life. You know, our economic situation was that we were extremely poor and today I cannot say today I am rich, but I have some land, some cattle, I am healthy. I have work and it's marvelous.

Charmayne: Juan, it seems that Spencer has an almost spiritual connection with you and the people from Mata Ortiz.

Juan: Yes, of course, definitely. If not for Spencer, I think we wouldn't have what we have today in Mata Ortiz.

Charmayne: Juan, you have a light in your eyes when you talk about Spencer.

Juan: Yes, of course.

Charmayne: Juan, do you ever get tired of talking about pottery and doing demonstrations?

Juan: Never. To go to the mountains looking for clay and for minerals, and talking about pottery, is fascinating for me. We are going back soon to California, Pomona,

Silver City, and Aspen, Colorado. So, we have a lot of work, thank God.

Charmayne: Do you have any good stories to tell?

Juan: I remember when we went to the Rhode Island School of Design. One of the students asked, "What is the difference between our city and Mata Ortiz? I answered that I noticed the crows don't have the same call. But what surprised me is that people wore the same clothes there as in Mata Ortiz. Also, there were many types of trees and woods there, which we don't have in the desert. I remember Guille commenting that they had lots of firewood! Another experience I will never forget is when we went to Princeton and Spencer's friend gave us refreshments in a glass that was many, many years old.

Spencer: My friend was a curator of the Princeton Art Museum and we stayed with him at his home. He served us wine in a fifth-century Greek ceramic goblet. It was in perfect condition, and we were almost afraid to touch it.

Juan: I will never forget that. Another time, something really funny happened to us. We went to a house where we had been invited to dinner. So, Spencer and I didn't eat anything that afternoon because we were supposed to have dinner at that house. We arrived at the house and we talked for a while, and we waited and waited, but there was no dinner. As it turns out, it was the wrong day for the dinner invitation! I was so embarrassed.

(They both laugh, with a twinkle in their eyes, at this remembrance.)

Charmayne: Juan, do you think that you and Spencer could go on another trip sometime?

Juan: Sí! Yes, of course!

Spencer: Juan, people want to know what do you think when you are making a pot, creating art? What is your feeling during the process?

Juan: I feel very good. For me, it is marvelous sitting down and starting to paint. Sometimes I am a little nervous, and as soon I start painting, all those feelings go away. I try to work for an hour or two at a time, and it is wonderful.

Charmayne: What do you consider the highlight of your artistic career at this point?

Juan: They had a ceremony to honor me, with mariachis and festivities. According to the Governor, this was the first time an honor was presented of this magnitude. Also, whenever we are in the United States, we have received a lot of support from all the people.

Charmayne: Anything else you would like to add about Spencer?

Juan: I just want to say as I have many times. Spencer, to me, is the most honest person I've met in my life.

(Guille walks into room.)

Charmayne: Guille, what do you think about Spencer, about Juan, and about Mata Ortiz?

Guille: To me, they are treasures of Mata Ortiz. That's how I feel.

Charmayne: Do you have a good story to tell about Spencer?

Guille: We always felt very comfortable with Spencer, and if it wasn't for him, we couldn't come as far as we have done with all this.

Spencer: Guille, I am sure you remember how many times I got into town and I would be really hungry and you would fix potato soup for me.

Guille (laughing): Yes, I know how much you love potato soup.

Charmayne: Juan and Guille, are you glad that Spencer moved back to this area?

Guille and Juan: Yes, of course, of course!!

Appendix II

A Conversational Interview with Juan, Conducted at His Friend's House

Charmayne: Juan, is there anything else that you might have thought about and would like to add for this book? I'm touched by your statement that Spencer is the most honest person you have ever known

Juan: *Si, si,* again, I always say this is so. To me, Spencer is the most honest person that I have ever met in my life.

Charmayne: Are there any other stories about Spencer that would be good to put in this book?

Juan: I remember once that he and I went looking for white clay. Someone had told us where to find it near Cuauhtémoc, Chihuahua. Spencer suddenly said, "Let's go! Let's go!" So just like that, we took off for that little town. When we arrived there, Spencer and I left Guille and one of the boys in the car, and he and I went walking and walking through the countryside. We were on ejido land (community land). After we had walked a very far distance, Spencer noted that it was now late, we didn't find the clay, and we needed to return to the car. He looked at me, 'Juan, you think you can run back to the car?' I laughed! 'Yes, of course, I can.' Then we took off running and I got to the car long before Spencer. When he got there, he fell down gasping for breath, and said, "I never saw a deer that could make pottery."

Charmayne: Do you see a lot of new innovations today by the potters of Mata Ortiz?

Juan: Yes, there are a lot of innovations. But we are going to have to look at how the pottery is being sold. There is going to be a meeting to talk about the future of the pottery. The future of the pottery is not so certain because a lot of potters are on the streets now selling their pots. They stop the visitors and make demands that they buy. And that is very annoying.

Charmayne: Is the pottery on the streets of a lower quality?

Juan: Not necessarily. It's that the potters don't know that we have to respect our work and respect the persons that come to visit us. I always have been against presenting our pots on the streets to sell.

Charmayne: Because of the quality?

Juan: Yes, sometimes it is lesser, but most of it is very good. So that is not the issue. The thing is, a lot of people come here to just visit, not necessarily to buy. But the street sellers stop them here and there throughout the village and then the tourists are not able to just visit because they are hounding them to buy.

Charmayne: Are there more people selling on the streets this year than before?

Juan: Yes, and that's bad for Mata Ortiz, for the pots, and for the prestige of the pieces of Mata Ortiz, because a good piece is never to be offered on the street.

Charmayne: If those potters are just trying to make a living also, what then is the solution?

Juan: I don't think there is any. For instance, we have had meetings with the mayor of the city asking to renovate the train station. He did renovate the station, then gave it to the community with the stipulation that they wouldn't sell on the street. But they don't stop selling on the street. They are always there. So, I don't think there is a solution until tourists lose interest in the pottery being sold that way, and also let it be known that they don't want to be bothered so much. Many of the Americans that come here know where all the potters live, and some of them like to visit only the potters they are interested in. They can see a lot of variety and it's fun because we don't all work the same way. The worst thing is to go to the street to offer the work and then say, "Want to buy this?" And they are asked what is the price, and the potter replies it is worth one hundred dollars but he will let the tourists have it for fifty. That is not good for any of us.

Charmayne: On another subject, Juan, are you satisfied with what you have created so far, is there hunger to keep creating?

Juan: I am always creating new things, always trying to get better. I really enjoy what I am doing. I am always looking for new paints and clays, and trying to get better.

Charmayne: You mentioned before that you would have preferred to be a sculptor and carver rather than a potter, if it hadn't been for the intervention of Spencer.

Juan: Yes, but I never had enough success, even though I made my living for a long time making sculptures there on the mountains. I was making sculptures out of wood, lamps or other pieces with various animals on them. I liked hardwood such as ironwood, and was making my living by trading for food. This is what happened, I did not sell them for money very often. When my mother-in-law went to sell them, they would tell her, "We don't have money, but we like them, so we can give you a pig, one chicken, beans, or corn. So, we were always bartering.

Figure 55. Juan Quezada carving located at the Museum of Us, 1998. A horn bird figurine, resembling a crane or heron, standing with a curved neck, carved from two sections of cow horn when he was a child Courtesy of the Jon Samuelson Collection

Figure 56. Juan Quezada Carving, *located at the Museum Of Us, 1998. Wooden crucifix composed of two crossed naturally shaped, unworked wood with carved figure of Christ attached with nails. Courtesy of the Jon Samuelson Collection*

Charmayne: Now, Juan, if you start making them, they would sell like hotcakes.

Juan: Yes. It made me so happy one time when I was doing a demonstration at a school at Aspen, Colorado. The director asked me, "Juan, if you want, we would like you to make a sculpture of a model. We will pay for the model." I told him I had never used a model before.

"Okay," he told me. "Juan, when you come back if you would like to do this, the school can pay for the model."

That made me feel good and was encouraging. Maybe someday I can do more sculpture.

Appendix III

A Joint Conversation with Lydia Quezada Celado Talavera and Spencer in Lydia's Home

Charmayne: You are almost as famous as Juan. You are an accomplished artist in your own right. [57]

Lydia: We all owe so much to Spencer. (She smiles brightly)

Charmayne: What do you think about us writing this book about Spencer?

Lydia: I think you could write many things about him, because Spencer is an intelligent person. He has more experience than his age reflects.

Charmayne: I think that's very insightful on your part.   Lydia: That's how I feel.

Charmayne: What was your first impression of Spencer when he came onto the scene in 1976 and what did you think about him taking on a project like this back then?

Lydia: I didn't think he was much experienced. I wasn't sure what was happening at the time.

Charmayne: Spencer said he didn't either. What did you think of Spencer's arrangement with Juan?

Lydia: I remember when he came to the village. The family talked about it a lot. They said that Spencer wanted to express himself and say things in Spanish, but it was very difficult to converse in Spanish with him. We all valued the effort he was making to communicate with us. I somewhat sensed that he was going to help things change.

Spencer: I remembered the time my mother and I took Lydia to breakfast at the Hotel Hacienda to make the same arrangement with her. She seemed uneasy about it. Folks were still not certain about these arrangements.

Lydia: Yes, I was, it was all unknown ground for me, as well.

Charmayne: How would your life have played out if Spencer had not appeared?

Lydia: It would have been very difficult. My life was not as hard as my brothers, but my mother had told me that I would have to work very hard. By the time I was ten I was selling little milk candies door to door.

There were many young girls in that situation in the village then. It was really a nice family time back then, but it was difficult. Now that I have my own family, I value those times even more. And then by pure good luck, and the grace of God, Spencer, the angel, arrived in the village.

Charmayne: What does it mean to you for Spencer to be your *padrino*?

Lydia: Mexicans feel that this relationship is a real commitment and I feel fortunate that I have a *padrino* such as Spencer because not everyone has such. First of all, my mother and father had to find someone they could trust and rely on, because then they would be compadres. That was first. This is not a baptism *padrino*, because then the *padrino* would also be responsible for helping in all ways to raise the children. But it is the same as a blood relationship. It's a familial relationship.

Spencer: Lydia, are there things I should be doing that I don't know, and have I been a good *padrino*?

Lydia: Spencer has been a good *padrino*. There is a lot of respect between *padrino* and goddaughter.

Charmayne: I can see that this is so, the way you talk about each other. How do you feel about Spencer and Emi living in Casas Grandes?

Lydia: I am very happy because I felt that when he left this area, he left his roots, in spirit and heart. Some people are very sensitive to art and I think that Spencer is one of those people.

Charmayne: Looking at what has transpired from 1976 to the present, we now see a paved road to Mata Ortiz and other changes. Lydia, are you happy and pleased with the quality of work in Mata Ortiz, and do you have any ideas about the future?

Lydia: There's a lot of opportunity in the village now, and the children have a future they would not have had otherwise. That's the good side of it. The negative side is that I am very concerned about drugs and alcohol in the village. That's a downside of having money.

Spencer: Yes, there is a problem.

Lydia: It is painful to look at it, especially when it touches our own families. It's important to have an activity that involves the whole family and one of the best things that has happened is that the pottery allows that.

Charmayne: How do you feel about the creative process? What does it do for you?

Lydia: I feel that it is a special time when I am creating a pot. I'm involved with it and I feel it is a part of me.

Charmayne: How do you account for the brilliance in the Quezada family? Could it be learning at a young age? Could anyone do it? Or is it in the family genes?

Lydia: Everyone has many talents, sometimes many of which they are not aware.

Spencer: Actually, there is so much talent in the village now that I don't think the Quezada family stands out.

Charmayne: Could you talk about that bit more?

Figure 57. *A visit with Lydia Quezada Celado Talavera, 2005*
Courtesy of the Jon Samuelson Collection

Lydia: It's a matter of discovering what is within each person. something more than just Juan and me. God had a lot to do with it. Juan did all that searching for all that material and so forth, but in reality, it was there before Spencer ever arrived, so things worked out in Divine order.

Charmayne: Do you create in any other medium?

Lydia: I like writing. I have always kept a diary. Often you can't feel free to express yourself to another person, but I feel free to write in a journal. And speaking of expressing herself to other people, it was my mother, Doña Paulita, who completely opened up to Spencer. When Spencer came to see her, her face would change and she would brighten up. This was very special.

Charmayne: Do you have any good stories to tell on Spencer, or anything you would like to add about him?

Lydia: I want Spencer to stay as he is and keep on helping people. Because if Spencer had not persisted and kept after us, we would not have had the better life we have had. There are so many potters in Mata Ortiz who greatly appreciate him.

Charmayne: We are doing his life story because we feel it's an important piece of history and that he has led a rich life otherwise, not just Mata Ortiz.

Lydia: That's good because when you write a story like this it inspires younger people. I congratulate you. Good books are good for children. Spencer is a very special person to the family and to the village of Mata Ortiz.

Appendix IV

A Thoughtful and Unvarnished Interview with Spencer

Charmayne: Spencer, let's talk casually a bit. Give me your thoughts about your life overall, from when you were a young boy up to now and thoughts about life.

Spencer: Unfortunately, as a kid, I had the idea that I didn't like school. I don't know where I got that notion. When we went to Mexico everything there was just so interesting that I took an intense interest in archaeology and anthropology.

But in my early life, I especially hated recess time because I was most often the one the bigger boys picked on. I was a loner, and still am. I collected bird's nests and things like that. My mother provided well for us kids and saw to it that we got a good education, but I don't know if Andover was the best choice for me. Maybe a smaller school would have helped me to develop more self-discipline. I did have a good education and started at the bottom of my class. I was surprised at graduation with an award for the greatest improvement of any boy for the four years I had been there. It was kind of a tough time. But graduating from Andover allowed me to go on to Princeton.

The passing of my grandfather, Popdaddy, was difficult for me. I was really sorry to see him go, but I didn't cry. I was so aware of the rich experience that I had with him.

I felt so much fulfillment and gratitude for that experience that it would be hard to imagine what my life would have been without him. To say that I was very immature up to that point is an understatement. To the extent that I learned to think at all, I learned from my grandfather. I would not have been the same person if he had not been in my life.

Charmayne: Does life have any particular meaning to you?

Spencer: Well, life is an extraordinary mystery. Such as why we should be put here in this time and place with no idea of where we came from. Or where we are heading. It's very fascinating, and I am constantly aware of that. I like to make the fullest use of whatever I can. I would like to leave the world better than when I came into it, if I can. Popdaddy used to say it was the mark of a civilized person to leave the place a little better than you found it. When my brother Crawford would take his family on picnics, they would pick up all the trash in the area. He'd call that paying the rent. So, that was leaving a place a little better than they found it.

Charmayne: Do you have any regrets in life?

Spencer: No, we can't plan our life, anyway. From day to day, we don't know what's coming, or what direction or turns it will take. If you lived your life over again, it would be totally and utterly different than the life you have actually lived. And you would be a different person. Isn't it amazing that sometimes, many times, everything depends on the slightest decisions we make? That's something to realize and be aware of.

Charmayne: Would you have changed anything?

Spencer: It would have helped me as a kid if I had been taught some defensive judo or boxing or something like that so I would not have been such a scaredy cat. Throughout my life, I've been scared of things. Still, it surprises me that I will go out on adventures that other people would never in a million years consider doing. I don't know why. I don't understand this, but even so, there is always a current of fear that runs through my makeup. I don't know what would have made it different, but as a kid, I think if I had been able to defend myself it might have helped. If I were raising a kid like me, I would do that, get them some self-defense.

Charmayne: It's an interesting contrast between your fears and your adventures.

Spencer: Yes. At Andover, for example, I bicycled home to Virginia. It was fun. They were very careful when you left the campus and you had to write down your plans and account for every minute until you were safe at your home. I got an OK from my mother to do this, to let me get on my bicycle and travel home by myself. It took five days, and that was it. Funny, because this went so against the norm for Andover. I just wanted to go down through New York and to Virginia. And I did it. Not for a moment did I have any fear about it. Then I had all those other adventures. So, it does seem odd that I had this current of fear in my makeup, yet could also be adventurous. When we came back from Mexico, I was extremely self-conscious. If I would see a girl coming, I would just want to drop through the pavement. And then there was the

315

stuttering. It's a fear—fear of words and fear of social situations.

Charmayne: How about the ultimate—the fear of death?

Spencer: That's changed from time to time and, of course, it will over the passage of your life. I don't know what to say about that right now. I recognize it's around the corner. Not something I dwell on much.

Charmayne: On the subject of freedom in life, how would you define your freedom?

Spencer: I have been very fortunate in having my grandfather's monetary resources and then later, an inheritance from my mother, which had been passed down from him. I inherited her house. So, all of this has given me some freedom. The interesting period for a decade or so after the pottery project when I was entirely on my own and supported myself with the window cleaning business was a very maturing part of my life. I liked that a lot. It was my only experience during my life of going out and earning my own way and knowing that I was doing it and providing a service to people. It was a very good experience. I was dealing with small business people every day and they thought of me as being on the same level as them. They considered me their equal since I owned my small business as they did. I was able to deal comfortably with people on all levels. My peers were the janitors in buildings where I was cleaning windows, and my peers were also the owners of the businesses. It was a very good part of my life, and I enjoyed doing a good job of cleaning windows. There is a definite skill in using the squeegee, so there is more to that job than meets the eye. I got to be really good at it.

Charmayne: When you say your small business experience was very rewarding, how do you contrast that with the prior decade of the pottery project?

Spencer: In the prior decade I was driven by some power I can't explain. I was driven by the desire to cultivate an environment that would be conducive to the blossoming of this talent I discovered in Mata Ortiz. Then the decade before that one was the healing and lost decade. During that time, it was discovered that I had hypoglycemia starting when I was attending college for my doctoral degree. The symptoms were mental cloudiness and the inability to complete anything at all! This lasted for about ten years. [58]

Charmayne: Is there anything about the healing decade and lost decade that you look at analytically, that changed any outlooks, harbored anything that haunts or energizes you today?

Spencer: Had it not been for hypoglycemia, I would have gone on to get my Doctorate. In that case, I probably would have had a life in academia, which may or may not have been a good thing. Probably would have been a good thing. Who knows?

Charmayne: But you recognize a turning point during that time?

Spencer: Yes, although, of course, every day is a turning point. You don't know what small decisions are going to end up being a major turning point. Just like the morning that I had exhausted what yard sales Deming had to offer and wanted to check out Bob's Swap Shop. That smallest of decisions became a fantastic turning point, very much so.

Charmayne: What does sacrifice mean to you?

Spencer: I don't believe in sacrifice, in the literal sense. I believe in self-interest. I don't think we do anything sacrificially. What is it when you deliberately hurt yourself, masochism? Even that is something you want to do. For example, in the small village of Nacosari, Mexico, south of Agua Prieta, there is a famous incident that is celebrated every year. It was back in the 1920s. There was a train loaded with explosives and stray sparks caught some of the freight on fire. Workers desperately tried to save the train but to no avail. It would have blown up Agua Prieta and would have destroyed the town. Jesús Garcia jumped in the cab, got the train going down the tracks as fast as he could out of town, and by the time it blew up it was well out in the desert. He blew himself up with the train, but he saved the entire town. Sacrifice? He was doing what needed to be done as he saw it. He may have thought there was some chance he would get away from it alive.

So, the same, my mother, in a way, sacrificed herself. After the bitter divorce period, she wanted to make a home for us kids. My brother was just graduating from college and I was close to doing the same. It was too late to make a home for us, we were almost out of the nest, and she should have gone to Santa Fe where she had nice friends and connections.

She could have made a life of her own there and made that an example for us to follow. Instead, she felt she needed to make a home for us back in Virginia, even though the timing was off. I think it was a mistake, but in a sense, you could say it was self-sacrificing for her in the name of her kids.

Sacrifice is not a part of my philosophy at all. If there is something you want to do, such as save the town when the train is about to explode, you throw yourself into it and just do it. That is passion for life, not self-sacrifice.

Charmayne: Brilliantly said, Spencer, so what is the importance of truth and integrity?

Spencer: I have been impressed with how vulnerable, how susceptible, humans are to the behavior of people around them. It is really important to have mentors when you are growing up. An example is my experience in the Mexican public schools. Cheating was a common thing. It was something we kids did to help one another. We were against the grown-ups, you know. There was a conspiracy against the grown-up world for putting us in the public school in the first place. (59)

So, we would always make our papers available to each other. We would keep our arm to one side so our classmate could see our paper. It was what everyone was doing. I did not give it another thought. Did I think it was cheating or dishonest? Everyone was doing it. It couldn't be very bad. It was what one does. Then coming back to high school in Winchester, Virginia, I said to a girl in my class, "I can't see what's on your paper. Would you move your arm?" She said, "Why, Spencer MacCallum!" very loudly and very rudely! I'll never forget that.

However, I read surveys in business schools showing that an enormous percentage of students think it is all right to fudge numbers in accounting, if it will serve the purpose of the company. That's indefensible. These people are lacking mentors, people who would point out this is not the way we do things. It is interesting how malleable human character is. Another example of malleability is where the social life becomes so important to the continuity of that culture. Another is how susceptible we are to power—it having discretionary authority over another person or property. It seems if a person is put in such a situation, their character will spoil like fruit under too much heat and moisture. It's just inevitable. There is a famous quote by Lord Acton, "Power tends to corrupt and absolute power corrupts absolutely." [60]

That's so true. That's part of my interest in social organization—as in what can be put into place to avoid this kind of contagion, this rotting of the fruit or character.

Without looking at any particular administration or individual but at the structure of our political organization, I think social pathology describes it best. All politics as it's now structured is the one area where the person must lie effectively in order to be successful in that field. They must. A person who cannot effectively lie should forget about a career in politics, because they have to be able to lie convincingly.

In any other field of human endeavor, a person who lies cannot remain in that profession very long. So, there is a lack of consistency between public or political life and private life, as our society is structured.

Charmayne: Is that a social weakness then?

Spencer: It's a structural problem. An institutional problem. When it's considered to be all right for politicians to lie like this every day, they are not good role models for the youth.

Charmayne: Power is only given by the people, right? The people have to want integrity to the degree that they act upon it and then provide for direction to society.

Spencer: A great conflict of interest is having compulsory public education, so-called. In lighter moments, I

320

call it government indoctrination camps. It does not serve the state to have people who are original and independent in their thinking. It serves the state to have people who will be productive, to pay taxes, and to be more or less docile and obedient. And that's the product we are getting out of our schools. There is a dumbing down. I see a great conflict of interest that has been celebrated as free public education for everyone. But it's a training ground for the obedient citizenry.

Charmayne: Is there a flip side to that?

Spencer: Sure, home schooling is an answer.

Charmayne: But then everyone would have to be motivated to want home schooling. And if they home-school the children, then everyone would have to know their science, calculus, and philosophy.

Spencer: Another option is private schools. But I don't agree with the idea of forcing your neighbor to pay for anything you want, as we do now with school and other taxes. Such as living in New Orleans or any other area where there is a known danger, a known risk of flooding, then forcing other people to bear the costs through federal flood insurance and disaster funds to clean it up.

Charmayne: Money, wealth, power, what do they mean to you?

Spencer: There are three ways of obtaining wealth: inheritance, taking it, and making it. In the ancient world, most likely anyone with wealth was connected with the tax collector. It was taking of wealth. There was not much development of market enterprise in the Old World. The market-to-market process was pretty rudimentary. People for the most part fished or farmed for their own table. In modern times the market process began to take off in the

18th century and it's a dynamic evolving process. This is what is exceptional about social organization, social evolution. It has built on itself and has solved the problem of "stuff" for us.

Do you know why people didn't have closets in colonial houses? They didn't have two suits. It was so laborious to raise the flax or cotton, spin and make the cloth, then sew a suit. It was so laborious that people had very little stuff. Today, "stuff" has become a problem, everything is thrown away. We are drowning in stuff.

But the area that remains unchanged is the area of our public affairs, community services, and all the basic ideas that we need in order to get along. That's something that I see the market process will be instrumental in solving. But it has not gone very far yet and it's not very recognized.

There is more and more recognition now, among economists basically, and they are the people who are the audience for the things I publish. It's an exciting concept to think that the problem of stuff is solved and the whole area of common needs is becoming solved, maybe in the not-too-distant future. So, the kind of authority that people exercise over themselves, and their property will be consistent throughout society. There will be integrity throughout society.

As it is now, society is divided into two classes, rulers and ruled. The head of state is the commander-in-chief of the armed forces, and this person exercises a different kind of authority than you and I do by walking down the street every day. We have done more fieldwork about primitive society in the last half-century and have understood more of the dynamics of primitive social organization.

The rule is that there is a ceremonial head who exercises the same kind of authority as the lowest person in the village. I know that runs against the popular idea, but that is something discovered as erroneous from fieldwork in the 20th century. Primitive society was healthy in a way that ours is not. It had integrity to it although it might have been lacking in science and technology. Now we have this extraordinary explosion of science and technology, but we are grossly deficient in integrity.

Charmayne: How do you differentiate, in a primitive society, between civilized or uncivilized?

Spencer: I wouldn't use the term civilized at all, because of the killing that humans commit, even in so-called civilized societies. Look at the governments world over which kill their own citizens by millions, and not even in a time of war.

But there are divisions made in anthropology between state and stateless societies. There is a pretty clear distinction, and it's an interesting question as to how to account for the pristine emergence of the state. How did a state arise where there had been none previously?

Where a state has been created, pressure is exerted against a nonstate society to establish a standing military for defensive purposes. A standing military is what evolves into a state.

Then, the loyalties of the soldiers will often be more toward those who pay them, their commanders, than to their kinsmen. That is a rather esoteric area of study, but it fascinates me.

Charmayne: What about the Mongolians and other great warrior societies in Asia, and what about the Americas? If you think about the great societies in Meso America and in Mexico, war was often the fastest path for youth to achieve a life goal.

Spencer: Yes, they were states.

Charmayne: The Mongolians didn't have an opportunity to gain bounty through a natural exercise of power as small tribes had been doing—as they gained momentum, they ultimately became a state, but they became states because they borrowed this idea?

Spencer: In kinship societies, the cooperating group is defined by the extent of the tracing of kinship ties. They cooperate within the group and within society. Anything outside of the group is potential enmity or danger. Yes, there was fighting and conflict, but the people who came from stateless societies, and people who gained honor within the society were seldom military types where they could gain recognition for their military exploits.

But take the Cherokee, for example. The summer season was the fighting season. At the beginning of summer, the warrior group would form under the leadership of someone who was particularly suited to that kind of warrior behavior. But as soon as the group formed it had to move outside of the settlement. It could not be tolerated within the settlement because the rules of behavior in the settlement were different. It was not the same discipline that you would find on the warpath. At that point various kinds of symbolism came into play to reinforce this distinction between the warrior and settlement groups. During the war season, the white flag over the council house was replaced by the red flag.

Then they went on the warpath and at the end of the summer came back to the settlement. Those who had survived were not invited back into the settlement for a month, a moon, or two moons. There was a period, what you might call detoxifying, to train them again for a normal life back in the village.

Historically, we find that the Cherokee names recorded as great leaders for a while were the military types who would go out and deal with the authorities in Charleston. But as time went by, their names dropped from the record.

They were not the ones who became the beloved men of the elder council. Those men were the men who had a particular ability to listen to the opinions of other people, completely opposite of the military-type personality. So, on the world scene the military might be remembered, but within the group the military men did not get the greatest and highest honor from their people.

What has happened today in our society is that the cooperating group has become enormously larger, and now through the market process, it has become global. We have problems because we have not learned how to develop something like a kinship system for global relations. Normally, the kinship system is limited to a few thousand people. So today things are, to a certain extent, chaotic. This is how gangs get into power, because of a lack of alternative ways of handling our common affairs.

These gangs become highly sophisticated in their mission, and also justification for their existence. Unfortunately, we just absorb this into our way of thinking that's okay. The fallacy is in thinking that it's always been that way, and it's that way, today, so it must work somehow.

Charmayne: Have spiritual organizations played the same kind of role as gang administration, stepping in and filling that void when there is a lack of a kinship system?

Spencer: I agree with you. It's a wonder some of the religious institutions have lasted so long. Popdaddy used to say that people practice Christianity six days a week and on Sundays, they practice oriental mysticism. For six days a week, they serve one another in the way they like to be served through the market process. That's close to the message of Christ. But I raised the question once, how has the church lasted so long when they don't understand the product they are selling? The product the church has been selling is "inspiration," a product in and of itself. People come out of the church service and somehow, they are walking higher on their feet than when they went in. This is inspiration. If they understood better what their product was, they could sell a whole lot more of it. Popdaddy thought that most people in religion think they are in the salvation business. But I think that perceived salvage is a pretty poor business.

Charmayne: Solitude—you talk about being a loner, about solitude, being with yourself, and about loneliness.

Spencer: Loneliness and aloneness are very different things.

Charmayne: People may not necessarily separate the two. If you are afraid of loneliness, you might also be afraid of solitude.

Spencer: I think of solitude as being our natural place to be. That is where we reach into ourselves and discover things. But when we discover things, we then want to go out and show others what we found. And then when you have done that, you come back into your solitude, your place, your aloneness. It all works together. You go out and see other people and look at or listen to what they find. That interaction inspires you.

Then you go back into your aloneness to digest, and to think, and to come out with new things. It works both ways, both are essential. I don't know if you can say one is more important than another, but the aloneness seems to be in a way more fundamental.

Think about the process of a child growing up. At first, he clings to his mama. Soon he ventures out a little bit, but then he comes back to mama. Next, he ventures farther out as he grows, and becomes more and more independent. And eventually, instead of returning to mama, he comes back into his own self.

Charmayne: If you bring a partner into your life while maintaining solitude, what happens then?

Spencer: Yes, that all has to be worked out. I'm sure no two solutions are alike, either for a man or for a woman.

Charmayne: Fidelity and Infidelity. What thoughts might you have?

Spencer: Frankly, the whole issue is how to respect your relationship, your partner. And that might be different in every case.

Charmayne: How about happy or sad. Are you a happy person?

Spencer: I'm basically happy, and sometimes in between. I am seldom bored; I don't think I have experienced boredom since I was small. I think that happiness is relevant to not being bored.

Charmayne: For me, it is difficult to understand someone who is bored.

Spencer: I have to reach way back in memory to find boredom in my life.

Charmayne: What about humor?

Spencer: I really enjoy understated humor. I can get it better. I like the British understated sense of humor. Slapstick leaves me cold. In Mexico, slapstick is popular but I don't care for it. Ethnic humor is more sophisticated, but I'm very sorry that "political correctness" has made us lose that connection. I enjoy humor that conveys an insight into human weakness.

Charmayne: It seems that on TV there is often a mixing of violence and humor, which is very unappealing.

Spencer: I don't watch much TV. There's too much else to do!

Appendix V

Recap of Conversations with
Mata Ortiz and Casas Grandes Artists

In conversations with other members of Juan's family, with many potters of Mata Ortiz, and with conversations with Manuel and Maria Olivas, the same sentiments were expressed over and over again. All were surprised when Spencer became involved in helping them, and all were extremely grateful. As with Juan and Lydia, they all realized that if not for Spencer, their lives would have been radically different than what they have lived.

Some of them might still have been able to make a living with the pottery. Juan was sculpting and doing some pottery and might have found a way to continue to produce commercial-quality pottery. Manuel Olivas was also making pottery and seemed to be well on his way to at least making a modest living from it.

There have been as many as 400-600 potters at once in the area, such that it is not feasible to include them all in this biography, but more information can be found on many of them in the stunning photography book: *The Many Faces of Mata Ortiz.* [61]

But it is certain that they would only have enjoyed the wealth of tourism as a result of Spencer promoting this pottery all over the world.

Spencer's involvement has single-handedly created an economic impact that may not be like any other in the history of the art world.

Of significance is that all these great artists called themselves Spencer's friends, and it is with sincerity and respect that they did so. His life and influence have been no little thing to them. It is not overtly stated, but there is a certain feeling that this man was included in the daily prayers of the family.

With the entire village thinking you were a godsend, the love they had for him might account for the glowing personality and charming manner that Spencer always had.

Notes

All Internet References Were Accessed In 2022-2023

CHAPTER ONE

(1) Argyllshire, Scotland Genealogy. Family Search, https://www.familysearch.org/en/wiki/Argyllshire, Scotland Genealogy

(2) Visit Scotland. Visit Scotland, https://www.visitscotland.com/info/see-do/kilmartin-glen-p247711

(3) MAC. Britannica, https://www.britannica.com/topic/Mac-surname-prefix

(4) MacCallum History. House of Names, https://www.houseofnames.com/maccallum-family-crest

(5) *Warren and Wetmore*. New York Architecture, https://nyc-architecture.com/ARCH/ARCH-WarrenWetmore.htm

(6) Waldek, Stefanie. *Inside The Secret Life of New York's Grand Central Terminal*. Architectural Digest, August 14, 2018.
https://www.architecturaldigest.com/story/grand-central-terminal-history; *The Top 10 Secrets of 230 Park Avenue, The Helmsley Building in NYC*. Untapped New York, https://untappedcities.com/2016/06/01/the-top-10-secrets-of-230-park-avenue-the-helmsley-building-in-nyc/5/

(7) MacCallum, Ian C. *The Famous Louvain Library Inscription*. Part 1. Page 70. Journal of the American Institute of Architects, October 1948. https://usmodernist.org/AJ/AJ-1948-10.pdf

(8) MacCallum, Ian C. *The Famous Louvain Library Inscription*. Part 2. Page 202. Journal of the American Institute of Architects, November 1948. https://usmodernist.org/AJ/AJ-1948-11.pdf

(9) *Chronogram*. New World Encyclopedia. https://www.newworldencyclopedia.org/entry/Chronogram

CHAPTER TWO

(10) Morton, Stephanie, *39 Chevy Packed With Memories*. The Vidette News. August 4, 2016. https://www.thevidette.com/news/39-chevy-packed-with-memories/

(11) Ramdani, Fatwa, Dr. *History of Remote Sensing, Aerial Photography – Part 2, Period WWII – 1960*. Fatwaramdani, October 21, 2008, https://fatwaramdani.wordpress.com/2008/10/21/history-of-remote-sensing-aerial-photography-part-2-period-world-war-ii-1960/

(12) Schugurensky, Daniel. *Selected Moments of the 20th Century*. History of Education. Last updated November 21, 2006, http://schugurensky.faculty.asu.edu/moments/1940 mexicocitycollege.html

(13) Pedro Armillas. Wikipedia. https://en.wikipedia.org/wiki/Pedro_Armillas

(14) Lake Chapala. Wikipedia. https://en.wikipedia.org/wiki/Lake_Chapala

(15) Saenz, Vargas. Worldcat Identities. http://worldcat.org/identities/lccn-n98000536/

CHAPTER THREE

(16) Cazalet, Sylvain. *Female Medical College & Homeopathic Medical College of Pennsylvania.* Homeoint History of Pennsylvania.
http://www.homeoint.org/cazalet/histo/pennsylvfem.htm

(17) Gorman, Kathleen. *Civil War Pensions.* Essential Civil War Curriculum.
https://www.essentialcivilwarcurriculum.com/civil-war-pensions.html

(18) Wolf Trap National Park for the Performing Arts. National Park Service. https://www.nps.gov/wotr/index.htm

(19) Franzen, Don. *Reason, Free Minds and Free Markets.* Reason. December 1974.
https://reason.com/1974/12/01/citadel-market-and-altar/

(20) *Coaling Stations.* Global Security.
https://www.globalsecurity.org/military/facility/coaling-station.htm

(21) Simon Lake. Wikipedia. https://en.wikipedia.org/wiki/Simon_Lake

22) American Propeller and Manufacturing Co, Paragon. National Air and Space Museum, Smithsonian Museum.
https://airandspace.si.edu/collection-objects/american-propeller-mfg-co-paragon-propeller-fixed-pitch-four-blade-wood/nasm_A19690098000

(23) About page. Institute of Historical Survey Foundation.
http://www.ihsf.org/AboutIHSF.html

(24) Baby Kaiser Doll. Google Arts and Culture.
https://artsandculture.google.com/asset/baby-doll-kaiser-baby-kammer-reinhardt/BgH9Hvc4nCdckw?hl=en

CHAPTER FOUR

(25) Sheldon Jackson Museum. Alaska State Museums.
https://museums.alaska.gov/sheldon_jackson/

(26) Erna Gunther. Wikipedia.
https://en.wikipedia.org/wiki/Erna_Gunther

(27) Treaty of Pontotoc, 1832. The Chickasaw.
https://sites.google.com/site/thechickasaw/treaty-of-pontat

(28) Sequoyah. Wikipedia. https://en.wikipedia.org/wiki/Sequoyah

(29) Minster, Christopher. *The Bogotazo: Columbia's Legendary Riot of 1948.*
Thoughtco. July 24, 2019.
https://www.thoughtco.com/the-bogotazo-april-9-1948-2136619

(30) Constable, Daniel. *In Photos: The 19,000 FT Climb Up Misti Volcano.*
Slight North. Updated
November 26, 2022. https://slightnorth.com/surviving-misti-volcano-a-photo-diary/

CHAPTER FIVE

(31) Lowi, Alvin, Jr., Gadsden Times. January 13, 2022.
https://www.gadsdentimes.com/obituaries/pgad0132156

(32) Wilford, John Noble. *Telescope Is To Open New Window On Most Violent Events In Cosmos.* New York Times. April 2, 1991.
https://www.nytimes.com/1991/04/02/science/telescope-is-to-open-new-window-on-most-violent-events-in-cosmos.html

CHAPTER SIX

(33) Unicorn of the Sea: Narwhal Facts. World Wildlife Fund,
https://www.worldwildlife.org/stories/unicorn-of-the-sea-narwhal-facts

(34) Hillinger, Charles.
https://www.islapedia.com/index.php?title=HILLINGER,_Charles

CHAPTER SEVEN

(35) Object Monday: Ramos Polychrome Jar. Maxwell Museum, July 26, 2020
https://maxwellmuseum.unm.edu/news-events/news/object-monday-ramos-polychrome-jar-0

(36) Juan Quezada, The Legend of Mata Ortiz. American Museum of Ceramic Art,
https://www.amoca.org/past-exhibitions/juanquezada/

(37) Felipe Angeles (1868 – 1919). The Mexican Revolution 1910,
https://themexicanrevolution1910.weebly.com/felipe-angeles.html

(38) Edward Solomon Miller. DVRBS,
http://www.dvrbs.com/people/camdenpeople-EdwardSMiller.htm

CHAPTER EIGHT

(39) Charles Di Peso. Wikipedia,
https://en.wikipedia.org/wiki/Charles_C._Di_Peso

(40) Paquime. Museum of Northern Cultures, https://inahchihuahua-gob
mx.translate.goog/sections.pl?id=52&_x_tr_sch=http&_x_tr_sl=es&_x_tr
_tl=en&_x_tr_hl=en&_x_tr_pto=sc

(41) Bobby Furst. Bobby Furst, https://www.bobbyfurst.com/

CHAPTER NINE

(42) https://www.santafenewmexican.com/pasatiempo/art/native-arts-
pottery/article_acf1565e-f6c3-11eb-bda8-cb6c0b36c9f9.html

(43) Museum of Us, San Diego, CA, https://museumofus.org/

(44) Arizona State Museum, https://statemuseum.arizona.edu/online-
exhibit/nampeyo-showcase

CHAPTER TEN

(45) *The Many Faces of Mata Ortiz.* Amazon,
https://www.amazon.com/Many-Faces-Mata-Ortiz/dp/1887896082

(46) Idyllwild Arts, Idyllwild Arts: https://idyllwildarts.org/summer/

CHAPTER ELEVEN

(47) Valles, Diego; Marroquin, Nicole; Nickel, Richard. History and Story of Mata Ortiz Ceramics: Why Oral Tradition Matters (Part 1). August 1, 2021. Studio Potter, https://studiopotter.org/history-and-story-mata-ortiz-ceramics-why-oral-tradition-matters-part-i

(48) Meier, Kelly S., Dr., Mexican Catholic Wedding Traditions. Classroom, https://classroom.synonym.com/mexican-catholic-wedding-traditions-6404.html

CHAPTER TWELVE

(49) Princeton Friends Meeting. http://www.princetonfriendsmeeting.org/

(50) Michael Van Notten. Wikipedia, https://en.wikipedia.org/wiki/Michael_van_Notten

(51) The Law of the Somalis. Amazon, https://www.amazon.com/Law-Somalis-Foundation-Economic-Develop-ment/dp/156902250X/ref=sr_1_1?crid=2BFOFC6XS20S1&keywords=the+law+of+the+somalis&qid=1666894427&qu=eyJxc2MiOiIwLjAwIiwicXNhI-joiMC4wMCIsInFzcCI6IjAuMDAifQ%3D%3D&sprefix=the+law+of+the+somali%2Caps%2C253&sr=8-1

CHAPTER THIRTEEN

(52) The Miracle of Mata Ortiz. Rio Nuevo Publishers, https://rionuevo.com/product/miracle-of-mata-ortiz-juan-quezada-the-potters/

(53) Tokyo Fuji Art Museum, https://www.fujibi.or.jp/en/index/

(54) About Us. Banff Park Lodge, https://www.banffparklodge.com/about-us/

(55) National Science and Arts Awards. Veracruz University, Mexico, https://www.uv.mx/investigacion/convocatorias/premio-nacional-de-ciencias-y-artes-70-anos/

CHAPTER FOURTEEN

(56) Quinceañera Wikipedia, https://en.wikipedia.org/wiki/Quincea%C3%B1era

APPENDIX III

(57) Lydia Quezada Talavera. Tanner Chaney Gallery, https://www.tannerchaney.com/info/artist/quezada

APPENDIX IV

(58) Hypoglycemia. Mayo Clinic, https://www.mayoclinic.org/diseases-conditions/hypoglycemia/symptoms-causes/syc-20373685#:~:text=Hypoglycemia%20is%20a%20condition%20in,who%20don't%20have%20diabetes.

(59) Students Cheating in Mexico. Semantics Scholar, https://www.semanticscholar.org/paper/Attitudes-and-Causes-of-Cheating-among-Mexican-An-Gayt%C3%A1n-Quintanilla Dom%C3%ADnguez/a4c51d05a3cd630e7cbf918132bf42e4c409c4b8

(60) Lord Acton, Acton Research, https://www.acton.org/research/lord-acton-quote-archive

APPENDIX V

(61) *The Many Faces of Mata Ortiz*. Amazon, https://www.amazon.com/Many-Faces-Mata-Ortiz/dp/1887896082

Books By
CHARMAYNE SAMUELSON

SPENCER MacCALLUM: Memories - Mystique - Mata Ortiz. An outstanding authorized biography of the anthropologist who discovered Juan Quezada and Mata Ortiz pottery.

MYSTERY OF THE LOST KINGDOM OF GOLD: Where There's No Time or Space. A thrilling romance with a unique twist on time travel, and a breathtaking treasure hunt, murder mystery, and tale of ancient Kingdoms of Gold.

THE NO. 1 SELF-HELP TECHNIQUE IN THE UNIVERSE. In easy steps, this simplified guide can help you change your mind and change your world to experience a more fulfilling life.

AWAKENING TO THE GURU. Unique and Inspirational Devotee Stories of Personal Interviews Conducted and Edited by Charmayne Samuelson.

WILD MUSTANGS OF THE ONAQUI MOUNTAINS. A breathtaking coffee-table photography book by Charmayne Samuelson and Jon Samuelson. Blurb.com

"WHAT I LOVE!" SAID RUBEE DOVE" A children's coloring book with a message, co-authored with Cole Martin, Chase Martin.

I REALLY BELIEVE and I KNOW I CAN An amazing coloring book of beautiful flowers with secret messages for people of All Ages, to inspire and instill positive suggestions to live a happier, more productive life.

I AM WHATEVER I NEED – Shaped By Southwest Desert Animals. A unique coloring book of American Southwest animals featuring mandalas within. Descriptions of the animals and inspiring messages of how to express I AM to be the best and brightest. For people of All Ages.

HOW TO DRAW SOUTHWEST DESERT ANIMALS. Beautifully illustrated with step-by-step instructions of how to draw, plus coloring, the most beautiful and unique animals on earth living in the American Southwest. For people of All Ages.

Look for these titles online or ask for them at your favorite bookseller.

About the Author

A Southwest Award-Winning Author and a member of the prestigious academic Phi Theta Kappa Honor Society, Charmayne Samuelson masters multiple genres of biography, fiction, non-fiction, poetry, photography, self-help, and children's books. She delights the reader in the highly anticipated biography *SPENCER MacCALLUM: Memories - Mystique - Mata Ortiz.; MYSTERY OF THE LOST KINGDOM OF GOLD, A Place Where There's No Time Or Space,* a novel with a unique twist on time travel in a romantic adventure and treasure hunt; *THE NO. 1 SELF-HELP TECHNIQUE IN THE UNIVERSE,* an amazing and unique self-help book of self-hypnosis and meditation techniques; *WILD MUSTANGS OF THE ONAQUI MOUNTAINS,* a stunning coffee-table photography book co-authored with her husband, Jon Samuelson; *AWAKENING TO THE GURU,* inspirational stories; *"WHAT I LOVE!"SAID RUBEE DOVE,* a beautifully illustrated children's coloring book, co-authored with her Great Great Nephews, Cole Martin and Chase Martin; *I REALLY BELIEVE and I KNOW I CAN,* an inspiring coloring book for all ages; *I AM WHATEVER I NEED, SHAPED BY SOUTHWEST DESERT ANIMALS,* an amazing coloring book for all ages; *HOW TO DRAW SOUTHWEST DESERT ANIMALS STEP-BY-STEP,* a joyous, educational coloring book for all ages.

Connect:
Wood Duck Publishers
www.woodduckpublishers.com
woodduckpublishers@gmail.com

www.ingramcontent.com/pod-product-compliance
Lightning Source LLC
Chambersburg PA
CBHW060856120626
46553CB00001B/103